The 5C Leader

The 5C Leader

Exceptional Leadership Practices for Extraordinary Times

W. James Weese, Ph.D.

Archway Publishing books may be ordered through booksellers or by contacting:

Archway Publishing
1663 Liberty Drive
Bloomington, IN 47403
www.archwaypublishing.com
1 (888) 242-5904

Because of the dynamic nature of the Internet, any web addresses or links contained in this book may have changed since publication and may no longer be valid. The views expressed in this work are solely those of the author and do not necessarily reflect the views of the publisher, and the publisher hereby disclaims any responsibility for them.

Any people depicted in stock imagery provided by Getty Images are models, and such images are being used for illustrative purposes only. Certain stock imagery © Getty Images.

ISBN: 978-1-4808-6505-1 (sc)
ISBN: 978-1-4808-6506-8 (hc)
ISBN: 978-1-4808-6504-4 (e)

Library of Congress Control Number: 2018909348

Print information available on the last page.

Archway Publishing rev. date: 8/29/2018

To my wife and soul mate, Sherri,

who makes everything possible—and
better—for me and in our family.

To our great kids, Zach and Haylee,

with dreams that they will
experience and deliver exceptional leadership
in all life endeavors.

Contents

Appendices

Preface

For me, the study and practice of leadership has been a little bit like riding a roller coaster. The track is filled with peaks and valleys, uphill climbs where momentum wanes, severe plummets where the speed of my understanding built to exhilarating levels. The curves, corkscrews, and sharp bends continue to foster an exciting, but at times, uncertain journey.

Like the roller coaster on the track, the leadership field captures the attention of a wide-ranging audience. Passersby might stop to watch the roller coaster, often shifting to and fro as they watch the coaster navigate the dips and turns of the track. These observers might want to take a ride themselves, similar to the way leadership enthusiasts get hooked on the art and adventure of leadership.

The path of leadership study can be equally breathtaking and exhilarating. At times it brings on a vast adrenaline rush. It scares and challenges you. Other times you just want to get off. Unlike the coaster ride, the paths of leadership inquiry and leadership practice often present forks in the track, offering new directions, exciting developments, and alternative perspectives. Other times, the path ahead is less clear. One day, leaders and leadership scholars feel like they have the area mastered, only to conduct or read another study that challenges their previous leadership paradigm. However, in the final analysis, most leadership enthusiasts will find their process of discovery to be exciting, filled with the suspense of exploring new territory, navigating the bends of uncertainty, pursuing alternative lines of inquiry, and being whisked away without warning in a new, seemingly uncharted direction. There are peaks of excitement, when the theories and research findings converge. There are deep lows and feelings of uncertainty, when theories or research results contradict one another. Indeed, at times, getting a handle on the topic of leadership seems as fruitless as attempting to catch a runaway roller coaster. However, despite the frustrations and setbacks, my opinion aligns with many others who feel that the area remains a fascinating field of study, worthy of the highest levels of perseverance to research, learn, practice, and write about this seemingly elusive topic.

As someone who has devoted a career in higher education to the study and practice of leadership, I can understand why the area holds such great appeal. Most people have been touched by high-quality leadership, although they might remember the experience as a fleeting moment in time. The electronic media brings us daily exhibits of high-quality leaders from a variety of social movements, business and industrial settings, politics, the armed forces, and the sports world. Our libraries and bookstores are filled with leadership texts, many highlighting a new theory or approach and often romanticizing the topic. The late Warren Bennis offered that writing on leadership has become a growth industry "with writers churning out thousands of articles and hundreds of books on the subject over the last two decades."[1] His claim is indisputable.

How important is leadership? Look no further than the testimony of Peters and Waterman in their time-tested book *In Search of Excellence*.[2] To these authors, leadership is *the* key ingredient of successful companies. Those familiar with their methodology will know that they studied successful companies from a variety of different settings. They initially set out to study the structure, policies, and procedures that set these companies apart. In the end, what they found was that people were aligned and energized because of effective leadership.

More recent books like Jim Collins's *Good to Great*[3] have reinforced the importance of effective leadership (Level 5 Leadership, to be exact) for companies that transformed their performance from good to great. The importance of leadership was highlighted in his follow-up text entitled *Great by Choice*.[4] The late Warren Bennis was equally boisterous in his assertions, stating that leadership matters— and perhaps now more than ever.[5] Like love, leadership is an area in the social sciences that has captured the imagination of poets, scholars, corporate boards, captains of industry, educators, and political analysts. Many leadership scholars have devoted their careers to the study of leadership, and their exhaustive inquiries have produced similar, indisputable results—namely that *leadership makes a difference!*[6]

One might cynically ask why another leadership book is needed. Some suggest that the topic has been studied to death. Others note that if we don't know it by now, perhaps we never will. In some corners, this question would draw thunderous applause. Others believe leadership does not need to be as complex as some contend. I believe this is the case, and this book is designed to help demystify the concept and give scholars and practitioners alike a theoretically based but applied source of information. In the final analysis, leadership is a simple but critical concept that is often misunderstood and ineffectively employed. Others generally expect and deserve more. I hope this book will help address this far-too-common situation, one I believe that high-quality leadership distills into a few commonsense principles that unfortunately don't play out in common practice. There are some universal truths about leadership reflected in the pages of this text. Current and aspiring leaders need to know these truths and habitually employ them. These concepts, later described as the Five Cs of Leadership, are based on my review of the leadership literature, my own research program, my consultations with other leadership scholars, and my consulting work. I've also learned a great deal from practical opportunities as a varsity athlete, team captain, university coach, athletic director, department head, director, dean, vice president, and elected president of a number of boards of directors in my field and community. These experiences have provided me with the ample and valuable opportunities to test and validate leadership theories and substantiate the Five C approach advanced in this book.

This book has been prepared to focus exclusively on the area of executive leadership, and the application of its contents will help all levels of leaders, as well as those aspiring to the role. Examples of leaders from a plethora of industries and settings are profiled to underscore the application of one or all of the Five Cs. While contemporary examples of transformative leaders like Elon Musk, Mark Zuckerberg, and Jeff Bezos are highlighted and highly appropriate, their leadership practices and accomplishments are ongoing. As a result, I have taken a page out of a good biographer's guidebook and focused on leaders whose major accomplishments are complete. They can't change course; their work is done. As a result, you will read about Steve Jobs, Justin Trudeau, Barack Obama, Bill Clinton, and Mary Kay Ash. You will also understand the practices of late leaders like Ray Kroc, Ronald Reagan, and Frank Purdue. I can report on the body of their work, all the time reflecting on their leadership practices relative to the Five C concept.

My research program and lifelong experiences in sport and academic leadership have been the principal drivers for the Five C concept. Both settings are fertile and appropriate environments for studying and understanding executive leadership. The case studies used throughout the text to highlight the Five C leadership model have also been drawn from these sectors.

In chapter 1, "A Leadership Primer," readers are taken on a brief journey through the hundred-year history of theoretical development in the leadership area. Readers will soon understand that the area of leadership has captured the interests of scholars and practitioners alike. I provide a section outlining the significant differences between the processes of leading and managing, along with the writer's perspective that both processes are important to effective operation. Aspiring or practicing executive leaders must understand the key distinctions between these two concepts that are frequently and erroneously used interchangeably. Readers will also be provided with information on the profound impact leadership has in a variety of organizational settings, followed by a section that highlights the acute need for high-quality leadership, in a host of different situations and contexts.

This material, coupled with the "On the Shoulders of Giants" material presented in appendix D and the results of my research program, served as the foundation for my Five Cs of Leadership conceptualization. My research and synthesis of the leadership literature allowed me to conclude that there are some universal, consistently emerging components of leadership that flutter around like butterflies in a number of leadership theories. I have attempted to capture these leadership butterflies and offer them to current and aspiring readers in a valid and intuitive fashion. Metaphorically speaking, this portion of the book is my sorted and integrated rendition of the filled butterfly net. It is packaged in a fashion that has great utility and practicality for current and aspiring leaders in sport, as well as those from business, politics, social service, or any setting where people need to be aligned and inspired to pursue a common goal.

Each of the Five Cs of Leadership is discussed in the subsequent chapters. Each of the Cs represents a leadership practice that consistently—but often independently—appears in the leadership literature. This text is an effort to bring these consistent themes together into a central package of what leaders are, what they do, and how they think. Specifically, the Five Cs of Leadership are as follows:

C1—Credibility

C2—Compelling Vision

C3—Charismatic Communicator

C4—Contagious Enthusiasm

C5—Culture Builder

Although the focus of the text is on the executive level of leadership and on the advice of writers of all genres, many of the examples are drawn from my own experiences, from sports, from my consulting work, or from my academic leadership experiences. I freely realize that other forms of leadership exist. For example, a book focusing on the areas of emergent leadership in sports (i.e., team captains) and how and under what circumstances they emerge to assume the leadership role on sports teams is a fascinating exercise and one that I undertook years ago as part of a master's thesis at the University of Windsor.[7] However, this application goes outside the focus of this text. Another equally compelling and necessary area of leadership inquiry in sports might be the study of coaches (e.g., prescribed leadership). We know that some coaches are outstanding leaders and some are not. Studying these leaders and determining what makes them tick would be a valuable exercise, and such a commentary would be invaluable to current and future coaches. Interested readers are directed to the work of Packianathan Chelladurai, who has made tremendous contributions to the literature bases in this important area. A number of other researchers are focused on gender and leadership, which again is a compelling area of inquiry but one that falls outside the focus of this book. The Five C Leadership concept draws on findings from these other areas, but this text is not focused on emergent or prescribed leadership or gender issues in leadership. This book is concentrated on executive leadership.

Readers are also presented with a diagnostic tool to measure Five C Leadership (see appendixes A, B, and C). Readers can use the instruments to collect data on executive leaders from the leader's perspective (LAQ—Self Form) as well as from the perspective of superiors, direct reports, and other members who have observed and experienced the executive leadership (LAQ—Other form). An interpretive guide is provided to add meaning for the specific LAQ—Self and LAQ—Other scores for each of the five scales.

Current or prospective leaders will find the contents of this book interesting and instructive to their own leadership practices. However, I recognize in advance the challenges of writing to both theorists and practitioners. Others who have attempted to follow this path have been accused of not serving either group. I am willing to accept this risk. For many years, I have suggested that much of what is published has outstanding application to the practicing executive; however, the material is rarely packaged in a format that is accessible and meaning-ful to the practitioner. Much of the research published in the academic journals and selected leadership texts is too obscure and esoteric for the current or aspiring leader to consume and apply. Practitioners often do not come across the material, let alone digest and apply the content. Yet the pages of these journals hold the key to understanding and practicing effective executive leadership. This information is usu-ally prepared for other leadership scholars. I hope this volume runs counter to that unfortunate practice. I believe a book based on empir-ical research and prepared for current and aspiring executives seems both warranted and appropriate. I have attempted to break down the mystery and mystique about leadership for the leadership scholar and the current or aspiring executive leader. I have made a conscious effort to encapsulate the scientific truths about the field of leadership and package them in a format that is easily digestible (although putting these universal truths about leadership into practice is another chal-lenging matter, as Stephen Covey[8] eloquently noted with his mantra that common sense is rarely common practice).

The late Warren Bennis and his colleague Bert Nanus suggested long ago that society is in leadership crisis and that organizations are typically overmanaged but underled. Unfortunately, their words hold true today. Other writers have concluded that the primary reason many American corporations are being overtaken in world markets and in domestic competitions can be directly traced to a void of lead-ership.[9] James Kouzes and Barry Posner have found that the rank-and-file members of groups and organizations are growing increasingly dissatisfied with their respective leaders.[10] Given this malaise in the organizational context, is it any wonder that North American indus-tries are dropping their competitive positions on a global scale? Why should we be surprised when we read about scandals and corruption that plague some of our top universities, industries, governments, or elite levels of sports (e.g., the Olympics, FIFA)? Why are politicians held in such low regard? Are principled and effective leaders a dying breed? Let's hope not.

Being a leader is not easy, but the good ones seem to make effective leadership look easy. They build strong leadership teams comprised of members with complementary skill sets and orientations. They ensure and communicate a clear, clairvoyant vision that the overwhelming majority of members embrace and take ownership for attaining. They lead from an emotional intelligence base that brings the best out in stakeholders. They ensure that a crystal-clear vision and behavior code and progressive edge is baked into an organizational culture that supports and sustains success. Sounds easy—and it could be.

Ronald Reagan is often held up as one of the top presidents in the history of the United States. He never took himself too seriously. He treated people in his charge with dignity and respect. He saw himself as an ordinary person with the privilege of leading an extraordinary country.[11] What a lesson for all of us! The Five C approach to leadership is equally simple but effective in getting leadership, their units/organizations, and the people they lead on this path to sustained excellence.

That said, anyone who has been a leader knows that there are high and low periods. However, effective leaders stay the course, and in doing so serve as a breath of fresh air to their organizations and to the people within them. Unfortunately, effective leadership is not omnipresent, and when it is observable, it is often fleeting. Bert Nanus once suggested that the chances of finding effective leadership might be akin to the realities of setting an Olympic record (and the result often just as temporary).[12] Leadership researchers routinely conclude that people overwhelmingly lack confidence in their leaders. While these data support the spirit of Nanus' claim, it is my contention that effectively leading a group is not as arduous, fleeting, or impossible as he suggested. Blue-ribbon examples of effective leadership abound in a host of different situations from sports, government, business, education, and social movements. To a large degree, effective leadership involves the application of many commonsense principles that must be universally and consistently applied. However, these principles are rarely common practice within our contemporary organizations.

Perhaps a passage from Earl Reum best summarizes the experience of leadership with which readers can identify and seek to live out in their professional and personal lives. Reum's message should resonate in those occupying or seeking a leadership position. He outlines the inherent challenges as well as the expected rewards of effective leadership. Like me, he summons you to lead.

A Wish for Leaders—by Earl Reum

I sincerely wish you have the experience of thinking up a new idea, planning it, organizing it, following it to completion, and then have it be magnificently successful. I also hope that you go through the same process and have something bomb out.

I wish you could know how it feels "to run" with all your heart and lose … horribly!

I wish that you could achieve some great good for mankind, but have nobody know about it except for you.

I wish you could find something so worthwhile that you deem it worthy of investing your life within it.

I hope you become so frustrated and challenged enough to begin to push back the very barriers of your own personal limitations.

I hope you make a stupid mistake and get caught redhanded and are big enough to say those magic words: "I was wrong."

I hope you give so much of yourself that some days you wonder if it's worth all the effort.

I wish for you a magnificent obsession that will give you reason for living and purpose and direction and life.

I wish for you the worst kind of criticism for everything you do, because that makes you fight to achieve beyond what you normally would.

I wish for you the experience of leadership.

It is my genuine hope that the words in this book will have deep-rooted meaning to you as a person interested in understanding more about leadership and being a more effective leader. Hopefully, the words and concepts will spring off the pages as you read about things that you may have observed but not previously articulated or associated with the few inspirational leaders you have encountered who moved you to perform above and beyond your initial expectations. We know that these types are out there. The Five C leader will effectively encourage and inspire others to get on board and invest heart and soul toward the realization of a predetermined goal or objective. It is my hope that you recognize these leaders as you read the material contained in this book and that this material serves you well in developing your own leadership skills and practices so that you too can be an effective Five C leader.

> The greatest danger for most of us is not that our aim is too high and we miss it, but that it is too low and we reach it.
>
> —MICHELANGELO

I wish you well in your journey.

Acknowledgments

Leadership remains one of the most studied yet misunderstood and misguided practices. Leadership scholars, practitioners, and enthusiasts alike have encountered mountainous highs and rock-bottom lows in attempting to understand and apply this seemingly elusive concept. I know that I have faced my share of successes and dark periods. Fortunately, I have been exposed to great leaders, as well as some who were not so great. I learned from both groups. I have also had the good fortune of surrounding myself with strong, supportive, encouraging, and at times challenging friends and colleagues who have questioned me when appropriate, encouraged me in times of need, but always supported me to the end. They have sometimes tolerated my boundless enthusiasm for the study, discussion, and practice of leadership. They have also challenged my assumptions, elevated my expectations for understanding, and supported me where appropriate and in times of need. I have drawn solace, insights, and inspiration from them all.

First and foremost, I extend a deep and sincere debt of gratitude to my wife, Sherri, who has demonstrated a keen interest in my work; proofread countless papers of mine, making them eminently more readable in the process; and provided the requisite support, love, and encouragement that continues to inspire me. Her fingerprints are all over earlier drafts of this book. I'm deeply indebted to her love and support, to say nothing of her exceptional editing.

I'm also deeply appreciative of our two children, Zach and Haylee. They serve as a beacon of pride for Sherri and me, and we know they are going to continue to be great leaders in their personal and professional endeavors.

I'm blessed to have worked at three great universities: the University of Regina, the University of Windsor, and The University of Western Ontario. The last two provided me with abundant opportunities to study, develop, practice, and experience senior leader-level leadership. I've learned so much about leadership, commitment, and collegiality from colleagues at these institutions and in the communities housing them. When I moved into senior leadership roles at Windsor and later at Western, I had the cherished opportunity to practice my Five C Leadership concepts profiled in this book. I am deeply indebted to the students, staff, and faculty for their support and encouragement. They have all confirmed my impressions that leadership is very rewarding. I am also indebted to the leadership teams with whom I worked in these roles. It was a privilege and pleasure to be in your company. These colleagues provided me with abundant personal and professional support and, through their own accomplishments, challenged me to raise the bar of my standard of performance. I'm deeply indebted for their brilliance, insights, and enthusiasm.

This book emerged from my research and experience in the leadership area. Many scholars and practitioners have read my materials and provided honest and open feedback to assist me. The concept for this book was tested in the classroom and in leadership seminars, as well as in an article appearing in the *European Journal for Sport Management* entitled "A Synthesis of Leadership Theory and a Prelude to the Five C Model." Many people took the time to comment favorably on my conceptualization and also encouraged me to repackage the material for a wider audience. I also published a summary of the concept in my dear friend Packianathan Chelladurai's 2014 edition of *Managing Organizations for Sport and Physical Activity*. My decision to prepare this text is largely due to the positive feedback I received from these contributions, as well as the positive comments I have received on the model from participants in my leadership seminars.

The Five C concept resonates with practicing and aspiring leaders who can grasp the concepts and put them to work, immediately and in a sustained manner. They believe that the implementation of the Five Cs makes them heighten their leadership effectiveness and helps them do what all great leaders do—make it look easy. After all, in many ways, effective leadership is common sense.

I will never understate the guidance and support of my dear friend and mentor, Dr. Bob Boucher, who, as my graduate adviser and colleague, ignited my passion for the study and practice of leadership. Bob has been a strong supporter and advocate for me since I first came under his immense influence as an undergraduate student at the University of Windsor. I am profoundly grateful for his leadership, insights, and support. I also acknowledge my colleagues and graduate students who have kept my passion for leadership burning bright. Finally, I would also like to acknowledge the contribution of another mentor and colleague, Dr. Packianathan Chelladurai, who first suggested the brick house metaphor that I now use to illustrate the Five C model, with C1 (Credibility) serving as the solid foundation and C5 (Culture Builder) serving as the enclosure (roof). Compelling Vision (C2), Charismatic Communicator (C3), and Contagious Enthusiasm (C4) represent the rooms in the house. These are essential components of leadership, in my view. Effective leaders develop and embed a desired culture for their group or organization, and this culture helps shape and reinforce desired behaviors and results. This is represented by the roof enclosure (C5—Culture Builder). Finally, leaders need relentless discipline[13] to ensure that each of them and those they lead remain honest and trustworthy, progressive, focused, driven, passionate, and relentless in their pursuit of predetermined goals. Discipline needed to drive the model is represented by the mortar that holds the bricks and the concept together. This metaphor is illustrated in figure 1, and the concept is discussed in detail in the preface of this book.

Five C House Metaphor

 Mortar Holding Bricks Together = Relentless Discipline

<u>Roof/Enclosure</u>
  C5 – Culture Builder

<u>Rooms</u>
  C4 – Contagious Enthusiasm
  C3 – Charismatic
      Communication
  C2 – Compelling Vision

<u>Foundation</u>
  C1- Credibility

Figure 1. The Five C Model

Read on, and lead on!

W. James Weese
2018

Chapter 1

A Leadership Primer

A Reader's Guide

Upon reading this chapter, readers will understand

- the magnetic appeal that the concept of leadership holds for society,
- the vast amount of research that has been conducted in the field,
- the unique and distinct differences between leading and managing,
- the influence that leaders can have on group effectiveness and the satisfaction of group members,
- the need for more effective leadership in the twenty-first century,
- the major thrusts that have emerged in leadership theory development,
- the most recent thinking in the area of leadership, and
- a preview to the Five C model of leadership.

A Leadership Primer

We've all heard about it, probably witnessed it, perhaps experienced it, and perhaps even displayed it. The *it*, of course, is that frequently misinterpreted, often erroneously applied, and generally misunderstood concept of leadership. Some leaders make it look easy. Others who have every opportunity to lead effectively make it appear impossible.

One thing is certain with leadership: like oxygen, people notice it when it is absent.[14]

Our attention remains riveted to the area of leadership, one of the most studied yet least understood social concepts on the planet. The path that researchers have taken is much clearer. Many have grown skeptical of the concept, at times perhaps admitting that the phenomenon exists but at the same time suggesting that we'll never be able to truly figure it out.

One can't discount the accomplishments of great leaders from a variety of different settings and eras. People oriented to the Bible cite the exploits of Jesus, Moses, Abraham, or David in their capacity as leaders. Political enthusiasts might serve up Angela Merkel, Barack Obama, Pierre or Justin Trudeau, Franklin Delano Roosevelt, or Winston Churchill as testimony to the difference that great leaders can make. Sports enthusiasts would hold up Mark McCormack, Pat Summit, Arnold Palmer, Nick Saban, Billie Jean King, or Phil Knight as leaders. Business and industry experts might point to the seemingly unparalleled leadership of Richard Branson, Allan Mullany, Mary Kay Ash, Howard Schultz, Elon Musk, Jeff Bezos, Bill Gates, Walt Disney, or Steve Jobs as the key ingredient to the success of the companies they founded or led. Still others may suggest examples like Bono, Malala Yousafzai, Martin Luther King Jr., Nelson Mandela, or Blake Mycoskie as leaders of social movements and social change. All would be good examples and excellent case studies of leaders who made a difference. "There seems to be an insatiable appetite for stories about the heroic exploits of individuals whose leadership made a dramatic impact, whether as leaders of new organizations that grow into major corporations or as leaders of ailing firms which are brought back from the brink of disaster."[15] While most writers and researchers focus on leaders who influence positive change, some writers have been quick to illustrate that influence cuts both ways.[16] "In bad times, which have been plentiful over the millennial, twisted leaders have been the leading cause of death, more virulent than the plague."[17] In this vein, one can't discount the leadership abilities of Osama Bin Laden, Charles

Manson, or Adolf Hitler, each of whom effectively drew people into his vision, despite its negativity.

People do not need to be politicians, captains of industry, or champions of social change to be considered leaders. They don't need to be media magnates who grace the covers of magazines and newspapers. Leaders exist in all walks of life. Every day and everywhere, people are effectively influencing others through their words and actions. Leaders from every sector are influencing desired change in others by word and deed. As Stewart Friedman noted, leaders must exist in many contexts and settings.[18]

Reflect for a moment on the leaders in your life. Take the time to complete the exercise outlined in table 1. It will undoubtedly confirm that leaders come in all shapes, sizes, contexts, and genders. This reflection exercise will also get you on the path to better understanding the concept of leadership.

Table 1. Leader Identification Challenge

Activity

a. Take a moment and think about someone you consider a leader, and write in this person's name below.

Name: _____

b. List five defining characteristics about this individual's leadership style.

1. _____

2. _____

3. _____

4. _____

5. _____

c. Describe the effect that this person has on your attitude or your performance.

1. _____

2. _____

3. _____

4. _____

d. Having gone through this exercise, confirm why you consider this person a leader.

Leadership has captured the fancy and imagination of researchers and theorists like no other topic in the social sciences. Academics, industry leaders, managers from all levels of organizational life, volunteer leaders, employees, coaches, athletes, and politicians, among others, remain fixated on the term and have struggled throughout time to quantify and understand the concept, with relatively little success. The late Warren Bennis once stated that no topic in the behavioral science field had received so much attention with so little being known—a sentiment held by others as well.[19] That said, many theorists have taken a stab at defining the term.

> Like love, leadership continued to be something everyone knew existed, but nobody could define.[20]

A sampling of a few of the definitions is presented in table 2.

Table 2. Definitions of Leadership

The process by which an agent induces a subordinate to behave in a desired fashion.[21]

The process whereby one person exerts social influence over the members of a group.[22]

The process of influencing major changes in attitudes and assumptions of organizational members and building commitment for the organization's mission and objectives.[23]

A process of social influence whereby a leader steers members of a group toward a goal.[24]

The ability of "individuals to significantly influence the thoughts, behaviors, and/or the feelings of others."[25]

While each definition listed in table 2 is unique and drawn from different times and contexts, there are common elements to all of the definitions:

1. Leadership is a social process.
2. Leaders influence the attitudes and behaviors of others.
3. Leaders focus the efforts of others on predetermined goals and objectives.

Leadership is a *social* process, a conscious activity of initiating change in people or groups of people. Leaders *influence* other individuals or groups to do something they wouldn't have done ordinarily without the manipulation of rewards or punishments.[26]

Effective leaders also ensure that a clear vision of a desired end for the organization or group exists. Colleagues must find this vision desirable, appealing, and compelling, so it only makes sense that their expertise, passion, and insights are mined as the vision is developed. Effective leaders engage colleagues in the formulation of such a vision, and then they use their experience to shape that vision into a compelling and digestible statement that marries the current or emerging strengths of the group or organization with current or emerging needs and opportunities. If engaged, colleagues will assume an ownership for the vision and a commitment for realizing the vision through their actions. The centrality of vision to effective leadership is outlined later in the book.

As noted above, leaders bring about *change*. Without their intervention, a desired end would not be attained. Leaders influence others to act through inspirational mechanisms. They appeal to others' deep-rooted orientations of commitment, quality, fairness, and affiliation with success. Finally, the definitions all encompass the notion of *goal-directed activity*. The leader formulates, most appropriately in conjunction with others from the group, a desired end or focus that the group agrees to work toward attaining. The leader's function is to draw attention to, and add meaning to, the attainment of the desired end.

> A leader is a man [person] who has the ability to get other people to do what they don't want to do, and like it.
>
> —HARRY TRUMAN

Like love, we know that leadership exists, although it is a difficult topic to define, and even more difficult to carry out. Like many concepts in the social sciences (e.g., love, trust, confidence), one might begin to wonder if we'll ever truly understand the concept. However, we have made progress. We know what leadership is, and we know that it makes a difference in a number of areas, including the effectiveness, culture, citizenship behaviors, and engagement levels of people. The best leaders make it look easy.

> Leadership is like oxygen—people often take it for granted until it is gone!
>
> —JIM COLLINS

Contemporary leadership theorists are excited about new thinking in leadership, one that holds intuitive appeal and has withstood empirical critique. The new thinking in leadership deals with the sociocognitive and inspirational components of leadership and draws heavily on the concept on emotional intelligence.[27] Theorists recognize it and have begun researching these aspects. Leaders can be developed. Stakeholders can wish for it and have their wishes come true.

Leadership continues to be an area that will garner considerable amounts of attention in the scholarly and popular press. Presidents and prime ministers who move nations, leaders of social movements who change public opinion and call forth different actions, and coaches who move athletes to perform beyond expected levels will continue to be held in high regard. However, in the interest of balance, it is important to note that some writers suggest that the contributions of leaders are embellished. While they may lead groups or organizations that are successful, these writers suggest that success is due to a number of factors, of which leadership may or may not have played a role. Other writers are more committed to the notion that leadership has everything to do with organizational success. The next section probes this interesting and spirited debate.

> Leaders are often portrayed as heartless number crunchers who are driven by the bottom line, or as humanitarians who wouldn't know a bottom line if it bit them. Skilled leaders … balance their interest in the bottom line with a deep appreciation for people.[28]

The Macro-Level Organizational Leadership: The Leader-Manager Debate Revisited

Much has been written about the nature of managerial work. The writings of Henry Fayol from the early 1900s continue to be embraced and taught in our colleges and universities, although management theories from Mintzberg to Hamel are questioning the relevance of this approach. Why? A manager's job is not as systematic, routine, and reflective as Fayol and his disciples purport. Managers work with people and their complex menu of feelings, moods, emotions, and motivations. However, many have confirmed that there is a clear distinction between the act of managing and leading (although contemporary leadership scholars and this author believe that people often shift in and out of management and leadership activities when responsible for leading a group). That said, what distinguishes a management function from a leadership task? A few have addressed this question, and in doing so, helped advance our understanding of leadership.

Leaders must lead. Managing, while a noble pursuit, is quite distinct from the process of leading. Perhaps the ambiguity surrounding the concept of leadership is partially explained by the popular yet erroneous assumption that leading is synonymous with managing. The terms are often used interchangeably in the literature. However, the late Warren Bennis may have said it best when he noted that:

> Leading does not mean managing; the difference between the two is critical. There are many institutions that are very well managed and very poorly led. They [managers] may excel in the ability to handle all the routine inputs each day, yet they may never ask whether the routine should be preserved at all.[29]

Leadership and management are distinct processes, and recognizing the distinction is a critical step in understanding the concept of leadership. Managing is the process of adhering to the routine tasks; providing the technical, human, and capital resources necessary for employees; and providing rewards to people on the basis of their performance. Management is the fulfillment of a manager's position responsibilities within an organization. Management is position-based. Leadership is influence-based. Leaders focus and inspire people. Managers push. Leaders pull. Managers command and control. Leaders inspire others to think and behave differently.

This debate got underway nearly forty years ago when Abraham Zaleznik's (1977) classic article entitled "Managers and Leaders: Are They Different?" appeared in the *Harvard Business Review*. The letters to the editor that followed this publication confirmed the confusion that existed between and among practitioners and academics. Some accused Zaleznik of making something out of nothing. He held his ground. He noted in defense that functions of management and leadership are fundamentally in opposition and that the practicality of a manager's mind set may be an impediment to success in a leadership role. Managers are presented as deductive problem-solvers, while leaders employ a more inductive approach to solving problems and leading organizations. He suggested that these two groups need different training and education to be successful in their respective roles. Others joined him in the debate.[30] Lists such as the one presented in table 3 began to appear in the literature.

Table 3. Contrasting Management with Leadership[31]

Management	Leadership
does the thing right	does the right thing
tangible	intangible
referee	cheerleader
directs	coaches
what you do	how you do it
pronounces	facilitates
responsible	responsive
has a view on the mission	has vision of mission
views world from inside	views world from outside
chateau leadership	frontline leadership
what you say	how you say it
no gut stake in enterprise	gut stake in enterprise
preserving life	passion for life
driven by constraints	driven by goals
looks for things done wrong	looks for things done right
runs a cost center	runs an effort center
quantitative	qualitative
initiates programs	initiates an ongoing process
develops programs	develops people

concerned with programs	concerned with people
concerned with efficiency	concerned with efficacy
sometimes plays the hero	plays the hero no more

This dichotomy has helped researchers more precisely focus on the aspects of leadership and consequently offer cleaner distinctions to what the concept is all about. This distinction has also helped current and aspiring leaders understand that although one might hold a position that facilitates effective leadership, leading is a verb that requires a different skill set and an orientation quite distinct from the process of managing. However, this author believes that effective leaders often shift in and out of management and leadership though processes and behaviors. Some leadership theorists[32] speak to this in their transactional/transformational leadership concepts, discussed later in this book.

The Impact of Leadership

Despite a rapidly changing world, leadership remains crucially important in institutions ranging from schools to nations.[33]

It has been illustrated that leadership has captured the interest of many people from a variety of different perspectives. The earliest leaders were the chiefs, priests, and kings of clans and tribes. Usually the leadership role was bestowed upon these people because of their birthrights or the fact that they were the biggest, strongest, most intelligent, best dressed, or that they had the ear of a higher authority, perhaps even the gods. From a corporate perspective, many scholars and practitioners are interested in determining the potential impact of macro-level leadership on organizational effectiveness, a factor described by some as the most critical factor in organizational analyses. "Book after book has appeared extolling the virtues of an understanding of leadership, implying that leaders hold the key to organizational effectiveness."[34] Some justifiably note that leadership is an overromanticized concept and that the effectiveness of a group or organization might be due to a number of factors, including timing and luck.

The most consistent measures of leadership effectiveness within the organizational context have been employee satisfaction and employee productivity measures. Some believe that employee satisfaction translates into customer satisfaction and organizational effectiveness. A strong advocate for this paradigm was Fred Smith, the former president and chairman and CEO of Federal Express. He offered that customer satisfaction begins with employee satisfaction. Products and processes help, but the primary quality resources are human resources. And "when people come first, service, quality, and profits will follow."[35]

> Customers will never love a company until the employees love it first.
>
> —SIMON SINEK

Some researchers have uncovered a small but consistent relationship between employee satisfaction and productivity.[36] They noted that the relationship between low employee satisfaction and employee withdrawal (absenteeism and turnover) was more pronounced than the relationship to productivity. Other goal-setting and motivation writers suggested that the lack of association may be due to the managerial safeguards such as employee supervision meetings and production quotas, which may dissuade dissatisfied employees from lowering their outputs within an organization.[37] Others have been more critical. Some questioned the need for employee satisfaction measures.[38] These theorists noted that employee satisfaction is important but unquestionably secondary to the function of most organizations, namely getting the job accomplished. Fortunately, at least from the perspective of leadership enthusiasts, these views have been drowned out by the informed perspectives of other researchers, who have concluded, without qualification or reservation, that leadership directly relates to the satisfaction of colleagues, and this satisfaction positively correlates to member and organizational performance.[39] Today leadership researchers pursue research programs that measure the impact of leader effectiveness on dependent and intermediate variables like organizational culture, organizational climate, member citizenship behaviors, and others, in addition to the tried-and-true measures of members and group satisfaction and performance.

Given that contemporary leadership theory purports that leaders elevate follower confidence that translates into higher follower expectations and performance, many leadership enthusiasts reserve a divine-like standing for the importance of leaders to a group or organization. Some continue to point to leadership as the most critical factor in determining the success of an organization, noting that "the successful organization has one major attribute that sets it apart from unsuccessful organizations: dynamic and effective leadership."[40] Others suggest that leadership provides "the basis for creating organizations that are effective in terms of any criterion of performance or profit."[41] Some note that effective leaders cascade their influence throughout an organization from one unit to another, leading them to conclude that these leaders surround themselves with transformational followers, develop these people this way, or do both.[42] These leaders elevate expectations and performance. They focus and energize colleagues. They empower their colleagues to participate in the process of "transforming and revitalizing" the organization. Effective leaders give colleagues and their units/organizations a sense of purpose and direction.

> Individuals are able to find their own roles both in the organization and in the larger society of which they are a part. This empowers individuals and confers status upon them because they see themselves as part of a worthwhile enterprise. They gain a sense

of importance, as they are transformed from robots blindly following instructions to human beings engaged in a creative and purposeful venture.[43]

In summary, effective leaders (a) lead more productive employees, (b) lead more effective organizations, (c) have higher potential for advancement, (d) have more satisfied staff members, and (e) lead more transformational staff members. Leadership is considered the single most important factor separating effective organizations from their counterparts.[44] In the final analysis: leadership makes a difference!

Transformational leaders are seen as both more effective and more satisfying to work for than ordinary leaders, are promoted more frequently, develop followers to higher levels of individual and group potential, generate better productivity rates, produce more innovative products, receive more patents for work produced by their people, reduce burnout and stress on the job, receive higher levels of volunteer effort from followers, and lead units that perform more effectively under stress.[45]

A leader's impact can often be measured when he or she turns over. Some leadership-succession studies have demonstrated that the quality of executive leadership profoundly impacted the success of the organization. Some have conducted experimental research studies deploying actors trained to be charismatic leaders in laboratory research settings. These researchers found that groups led by highly charismatic leaders (see C3—Charismatic Communication) were more effective than those headed by noncharismatic leaders. In addition to adding to the theoretical base that leaders make a difference, these researchers uncovered a finding that leaders could be trained to be effective.[46] Leaders impact the effectiveness of their organization. Some researchers[47] concluded that leaders impact the culture of an organization (see C5—Culture Builder), which in turn influences organizational success. There are now many claims that the organizational culture can determine the degree of effectiveness of the organization, either through its "strength" or through its "type."[48]

The late Warren Bennis believed that the best leaders energize a group. He noted that leaders give pace and energy to their work and empower the work force, making colleagues feel (a) significant in that they make a difference to the success or failure of the organization, (b) inspired to learn and grow, (c) part of a team or community, and (d) engaged in stimulating work.[49] So what? Is there a call for heightened leadership? The answer is a resounding and unqualified yes.

> What is dangerous is not to evolve.
>
> —JEFF BEZOS

Need for Heightened Leadership

A study of corporate America revealed depressing findings relative to the state of the workforce.

> Fewer than 25 percent of the workforce believed that they were working at full capacity, 75 percent stated that they could be significantly more effective, and almost 60 percent of the sample believed that they "do not work as hard as they used to."[50]

Other researchers who have been doing comparative research noted that United States–based industries were losing ground in areas including innovation, productivity, or excellence, and this decline is attributed to ineffective leadership.[51] Specifically, these researchers stated that companies from Japan, Germany, and the Pacific Rim were assuming leadership roles in their respective industries. Why has there been a decline in North American excellence and presence at the cutting edge of excellence and innovation? The major reasons, according to these researchers, can be traced back to a lack of organizational vision, an uninspired workforce, excessive bureaucracy, and an organizational culture that supports mediocrity—all symptoms of ineffective leadership. What is both interesting and sad is that these authors state that the situation is getting worse, not better, and leaders are required now, more than ever, to focus and empower associates to inject pride and inspire meaning into their work roles. Many have lamented on diminished American competitiveness in world markets and suggested that some business leaders have been forced to adopt an Eastern Hemisphere approach to leadership. Specifically, a dismantling of the traditional pyramid organizational structure in favor of flatter, decentralized structures is evidence of a paradigmatic shift. This adaptation may result in positive outcomes that include: the emergence of "hidden leaders" from within the organization; a more empowered and committed workforce; and heightened contributions from people previously oppressed by the excessively bureaucratic, centralized mechanism of the past. The political arena offers equally depressing examples of the lack of confidence in political leaders. However, leaders can change situations. Leadership-succession studies have produced consistent and convincing evidence that leaders can bring about significant and sustainable success.[52] Other studies have yielded inconsistent findings, pointing to a vast number of extraneous factors influencing the productivity measure as the principal reason for the inconsistency.

So, in the final analysis, does effective, credible leadership make a difference to the effectiveness of the unit, group, or organization being led? This is an oft-debated question that researchers, leadership enthusiasts and naysayers, practitioners, and employees have staged for a long time. They will undoubtedly continue to engage in this debate, but this author and the top researchers in the field note that effective leadership is one of the key variables in a complex equation that defines success. For example, the abilities and motivational levels of followers is a frequently overlooked variable. "Without his armies, after all, Napoleon was just a man with grandiose ambitions."[53] Others[54] suggest that organizational effectiveness is due to a number of factors, many of which fall outside a macro-level leader's realm of influence. "Once all the other factors influencing organizational effectiveness are accounted for, it is likely that leadership will have little bearing on organizational performance."[55] Still others offer a cautionary note to the mix, suggesting that leadership enthusiasts be careful to not to overstate assertions and avoid overstating "the importance of leadership on organizational effectiveness, particularly when one bears in mind the many other factors which are likely to impinge on it."[56]

Perhaps there are factors impacting a leader's ability to lead effectively. It is obvious that leaders often feel overburdened with task requirements (which, if honestly appraised, would fall under the classification of management work as outlined in the Macro-Level Leadership section of this book). Effective leadership takes time, and unfortunately people in leadership positions are often overly consumed with the management functions, at the expense of doing what they are mandated to do—*lead*. They become too focused on the day-to-day activities, at the expense of paying attention to the overall direction of the organization or unit. They involve themselves in too many activities, and in many cases, "they end up with a kind of battle fatigue, overworked, acting as police and/or ombudsman and, what's worse, seriously undermining the legitimacy and effectiveness of the other executives reporting to them."[57]

What is the solution? Leaders must understand the role and the demands of leadership. They must surround themselves with talented people and empower and align them in pursuit of opportunities expressed in a vision for the group or organization. They must see themselves as partners and participants in the leadership process. The best leaders are selfless and invest their time in the development of others. Leaders need to invest in people and inspire them to lead. They must seek to develop a community of leaders who are aligned and inspired to make the vision of the organization or unit a reality. This process takes time—a reality that few organizational leaders appear willing to accept and be committed to through the setting of their priorities and the management of their time.

Unrealistic expectations may also be a factor in understanding why some people downplay the importance of leadership in realizing positive organizational outcomes. Perhaps the grandiose perceptions, if not claims, that leadership is the cure-all have created a situation whereby no concept, leadership included, could live up to the heightened billing that it has received in the past and continues to receive by some writers. Once a leadership theorist disassociates with the heroic, pedestal-positioned models of leaders and leadership and begins to view the concept as more of a servant and advocate, he or she will gain more accurate insights into how leadership really works and the effect it can have on both the satisfaction levels of employees and the performance of the group or organization. This approach to leadership is more consistent with contemporary paradigms and with the trust in organizational design to a team-based mode of operation that effective leaders of the day deploy.

> The great leaders in art, science, and literature lift their companions and their client groups to new levels of beauty, craftsmanship, appreciation, understanding, and skill. The qualities of leaders in all fields are the same; leaders are the ones who set the highest examples. They open the way to greater light and knowledge. They break the mold. Leaders are inspiring because they are inspired, caught up in a higher purpose.[58]

Approaches to the Study of Leadership

While theorists have struggled in their attempts to define leadership and quantify its impact on organizational outcomes, the path to theoretical development has been much clearer and can be documented in six distinct phases (see table 4). Each stage of development furthered the understanding of the area and served as the foundation for subsequent leadership theoretical initiatives.

Table 4. Pathway of Leadership Theory Development

Period	Approach	Corresponding Theme
early 1900s to the late 1940s—with a rebirth since the early 1990s	trait (great man approach)	leaders are born—universal traits a prerequisite to lead
late 1930s to early 1960s	behavioral/style approach	effectiveness determined by the behavior of the leader
late 1960s to mid-1990s	situational/contingency approach	effective leaders match their leadership style with the demands of the situation
late 1990s to present day	relational approach	effective leaders ensure positive relations with members that facilitate desired outcomes
since the mid-1980s	cognitive approach	leaders need vision, charisma, credibility, compassion, and advanced communication skills to transform people and groups
current thinking	team approach	leaders create leadership teams comprised of colleagues with comparable values and complementary skill sets; leaders adapt a servant approach to leadership, inspiring the hearts and minds of followers by deploying emotional intelligence

A Prelude to the Five Cs of Leadership

This leadership primer, in concert with the materials presented in appendix D ("On the Shoulders of Giants") captures more than 120 years of leadership research, although the concept has captured society's attention for centuries. Readers can appreciate the long and onerous struggle that leadership theorists have had in their pursuit of a clear understanding of what leadership is and how it can be effectively employed in groups or in organizational settings. It is a complex and fascinating phenomenon. One would think that centuries of reflection and research would provide ample time to figure out this specific area. However, the cynics are numerous and hold many questions about the direction that leadership researchers and theorists have taken in their quest for a level of understanding in the area. However, this primer does not align with the naysayers. There is something to leadership. Effective leadership does make a difference. Many theorists agree and support their claims with a long line of studies that consistently substantiate the claim. While our understanding of the area has improved in recent years with the developments in the cognitive areas of leadership, there is still much to learn. There will still be research studies that produce contrary findings. Research methods will need to be refined and new paradigms introduced if we are to continue on the path of discovery and heightened understanding and application of the leadership area. As well, we will suffer bumps and bruises along the path of discovery. In the end, we may not have all the answers, but in the words of a former graduate adviser of mine who comforted me in a time of despair, "We will not have all the answers, but we will certainly have better questions."

My synthesis of the leadership literature, coupled with my own research projects (and those of my graduate students), leads me to believe that there are some universal truths about leadership and effective leaders from any sector. These truths are not complex, can be learned and refined, and are available to leaders or potential leaders of every stripe. Specifically, I believe that leadership can be dissolved into five Cs that encompass some acquired traits, consistent behaviors, and respect for the situational context. The concept also draws heavily on the group dynamics and relationship-building literature bases and especially supports current thinking in the team approach to leadership.

> A leader is best when people barely know he exists, not so good when people obey and acclaim him, worst when they despise him. But of a good leader, who talks little, when his work is done, his aim fulfilled, they will say, "We did this ourselves."
>
> —LAO-TSE

My Five Cs of Leadership are:

C1—Credibility: a leader perceived by followers as being trustworthy, knowledgeable, honest, caring, competent, and consistent

C2—Compelling Vision: a leader with the ability to focus the attention of followers on a desired end and inspire them to adopt the vision as their own

C3—Charismatic Communicator: a leader with the ability to effectively communicate with followers in a fashion that is perceived as both uplifting and inspiring

C4—Contagious Enthusiasm: a leader who excites and inspires others to go above and beyond the call of duty through their own words and actions and by creating challenges for people

C5—Culture Builder: a leader who can interpret the dominant beliefs and values of followers and modify

them in a fashion that is consistent with the aims of the
organization

Each of the Five Cs is presented in the following section, along
with a discussion of the merits of each item. An instrument that
measures Five C Leadership from both self-reflection (LAQ—self) and
from the perspective of others (LAQ—Other) is presented in appendix
A and B respectively. An interpretive guide to the research/diagnostic
instrument is provided in appendix C.

Chapter 2

The Five Cs of Leadership

C1—Credibility

A Reader's Guide

Upon reading this chapter, readers will understand

- the centrality of credibility to leadership,
- the collapse of credibility in the eyes of followers,
- the need for leaders to be continually concerned with their credibility rating in the eyes of those they lead, and
- how leaders can heighten their credibility rating.

C1—Credibility

If you don't stand for something, you will fall for anything.

—ANONYMOUS

What do some leaders have that allows them to influence others effectively? What characteristics excite the best people to join his or her leadership team? What contributes to the perception of being an authentic leader with experience and insights to be trusted and respected? In a word, *credibility,* and it is the most basic, yet arguably the most critical and overlooked component of leadership. Because of its importance and centrality, "Credibility" serves as the first of the Five Cs of Leadership. Unfortunately, this area breaks down far too frequently. Leaders have their credibility measured on a daily basis.

Sadly, few measure up, and as discussed later, people are unwilling to fully divest their hearts and minds into an individual they cannot trust. This situation is particularly acute in political leadership, where scandal after scandal has eroded the confidence and faith people have in their leaders.

> Instead of giving a politician the keys to the city, it might be a better idea to change the locks.
> —DOUG LARSON

Leaders must recognize that the essential role credibility plays in developing a trusting relationship with others is the first step to leading them.[59] As noted in the primer, the current thrust in leadership is the creation and deployment of leadership teams. Credible leaders can attract high-quality talent to join them as a member of their team. The people know they will get straight goods from this leader and that they can learn and grow from their experiences with the leader. It is the only way they can attract high-quality people to their leadership teams. Consequently, the area of credibility and its link to leadership is the foundational component of the Five C model.

> I start with the premise that the function of leaders is to produce more leaders—not more followers.
> —RALPH NADER

Credibility and Leadership

Credibility in the context of the Five C model involves two critical components—being honest and trustworthy as well as having the experience and insights to be viewed as a credible source of information. The parts are fundamental to leadership and, as noted later, being able to attract the best co-leaders to form part of a leadership team. Yes, leaders are different. They come in all shapes, sizes, races, and genders.

However, they have credibility in the eyes of those they influence. Let's start with the first component—character.

"Every great leader puts ethics first—before profits, before sales, even before staying in business."[60] It is not lost on me that many leadership researchers are uncovering the undeniable fact that character matters. My University of Western Ontario friend and colleague Gerard Seijts[61] and his associates have been effective in driving home the point that ethics and a strong character are essential to effective, sustainable leadership. I agree. Being credible is paramount to being a leader. My interactions with leaders and followers in industry, sports teams, and volunteer groups confirm this simple but often overlooked assertion. Participants in leadership workshops I have delivered often confided in me that they were hesitant to advance ideas to increase effectiveness or efficiency to senior managers, regardless of how meritorious, because "they'd only take credit for the idea and garner the rewards." Others shared stories of leaders who engaged people and groups. They shared examples that demonstrated that these leaders genuinely cared about them, respected their efforts and ideas, and brought out the best in people. These leaders could be trusted. They were described as outstanding people who would always help out when needed, supported their people when warranted, and "were never the first in the trough line" when rewards were being disbursed. Effective leaders are perceived by those under their charge as people with credible characters who could be counted on for assistance, support, and selflessness.

> The goal of many aspiring leaders is to get people to think higher of them. The goal of exceptional leaders if to get people to think highly of themselves.
> —ANONYMOUS

What is credibility, and how can it be developed? Simply stated, it is something that our parents and grandparents may have drilled into us at an early age; something we learn about and value as we go through life. In his 2015 book *The Road to Character,* David Brooks suggested that this approach to life is critical for sustainable success in a host of settings. He encourages people to reflect on their attitudes and behaviors and consciously pursue the "eulogy virtues" (e.g., kindness, bravery, honesty, faithfulness) versus the "résumé virtues" (e.g., wealth, fame, status) that unfortunately preoccupy most of our time and attention. Brooks's advice works well for those assuming or planning to assume leadership roles.

> Good leaders are made through a life dedicated to constant learning about their careers, their relationships, and the kind of leader that they want to become.
> —DAVID BROOKS

Being a credible, honest, trustworthy individual holds the key to developing and maintaining effective relationships with others and being in a position to influence others effectively. One can decide to be more credible through conscientious effort, although previous experiences and noncredible reputations will take a long time to overcome. It can and must be done if one aspires to a leadership role. Leaders must earn the trust and confidence of their constituents on a daily basis. It arrives on foot but departs in a rocket ship. People demand in from their leaders. If they don't perceive it to be present they will not devote their unconditional energy, time, and talent to the cause.[62] Credibility is about being perceived as believable, honest, trusting of others, and being counted on to maintain an agreed-upon stance, even in, or especially in, the face of resistance. These trustworthy components govern effective human interactions and if implemented lead to stability and survival of a group or enterprise. Conversely, disregard for these elements significantly contributes to the disintegration and destruction of a group or enterprise.

> Being president has not changed who he is—it has revealed who he is.
> —MICHELLE OBAMA, SPEAKING ABOUT HER HUSBAND, PRESIDENT BARACK OBAMA

Leaders accumulate credit points with followers in these areas. At any point in time, followers have an opinion on the credibility of leaders on the basis of their credibility rating. Because of the cynical view many hold for leaders and the concept of leadership, the credibility credit that leaders need is built slowly. Following through on stated intentions, dealing with people in an honest and forthright fashion, and living one's life in an honorable way are virtual givens. As leaders behave in this manner, their credibility credit balance inches forward. However, single incidents that counter a credible pattern exponentially reduce a leader's credibility quotient.

A leader's character and approach to leadership is communicated to others through his or her words and actions. Some of the most effective leaders are master storytellers. Some researchers suggest that storytelling is the most effective way to outline and emphasize priorities and vision. However, a leader's behavior and decision-making must also be aligned with the stories. Actions do speak louder than words. "Those who don't have this alignment are soon labeled hypocrites and not leaders, and hypocrisy quickly and significantly mutes the effectiveness of the stories and the leader."[63]

In the final analysis, credibility takes a lifetime to establish and a moment to destroy. Change happens at the pace of trust and is impossible without it. As the former governor of the Bank of Canada, Mark Carney, loves to say, "Trust arrives on foot but departs in a Ferrari." Perhaps this helps explain how leadership effectiveness can also be so fleeting.

> Yes, in all my research, the greatest leaders looked inward and were able to tell a good story with authenticity and passion.
>
> —DEEPAK CHOPRA

Credibility "fosters favorable work attitudes; greater pride in the organization, stronger spirit of cooperation and teamwork, more feelings of ownership and personal responsibility, and better alignment with personal and organizational values."[64] Scholars have determined that ethics matters. Organizations that are ethically sound outperform those that are not, on a number of important outcome measures including productivity, profitability, innovation, quality, customer retention, and employee loyalty.[65] The leader sets the tone, and based on the convincing evidence presented in C5— Culture Builder, the words and actions of the leader help create and embed a desired culture for the unit or organization. As a result, a leader can embed an ethical culture through his or her words, actions, and decisions, especially during critical incidents. Followers see what is valued. They often model the behaviors of their leaders. The organization is often a reflection of the leader and his or her characteristics and values. A great example that still gets passed down at Martin Marietta involves the CEO and chairman at the time and underscores the company's commitment to ethics. At one point, they were in competition for a large government project. One day before the bid was to be filed, they received a copy of their competitor's bid, presumably from a disgruntled employee. Officials at Martin Marietta promptly turned the information over to the corporate lawyer, informed the government and the competitor of the situation, and *did not* change their bid price. Although they eventually lost the bid, this anecdote has been played over many times by employees and customers seeking the services of Martin Marietta. The story helps reinforce the desired image for the company—that an ethical compromise has no price.

I have had similar situations in my leadership roles. On one occasion, a data stick with the health records of a few people was misplaced or lost. It didn't involve many people and, in all likelihood, would never have resurfaced. We could have buried the issue. We didn't. I recall a quote from the late Robert Kennedy that read "If you have a problem, shine a light on it." We put the high beams on this problem. We gathered members together to attempt to determine what went wrong and devise an operating practice to ensure that this didn't happen again. We wrote a letter to all who may have been affected, explained and apologized for the situation, offering a direct phone number should they have follow-up questions. We advised the government's privacy agency of the situation and our response. We also set up a hotline for members of the public to call if they had questions, and we advised the media. Our reaction communicated our approach to ethics and transparency, and this story continues to get played out in the unit long after it happened. It continues to reinforce our commitment to ethical leadership that we wish to spread throughout the entire organization. We considered this situation a critical incident from which we could learn, improve practice, and reinforce a commitment to ethical leadership practices. We continue to believe that the long-term payoffs of this honest deed will be returned in increased ethical behavior and customer/employee loyalty—and it has been. Recent research advances in the organizational commitment area support our experience—that genuine apologies, sincere ownership of the mistake, and a thoughtful go-forward plan raises commitment from both internal and external audiences.[66]

How can someone access his or her personal credibility? Leaders can periodically reflect on the following questions[67] as a starting point to get an indication of their credibility quotient:

1. Is my behavior predictable or erratic?

2. Do I communicate clearly or carelessly?

3. Do I treat promises seriously or lightly?

4. Am I forthright or dishonest?

Answers to these fundamental questions will provide some insights into a leader's (and by extension) the organization's credibility.

It is critical to note that the credibility is in the eye of the follower. It is the followers' perspective that counts. They must see their leader as being credible, trustworthy, and loyal to the group. Open and honest discussions with followers centered around these four questions might provide the most enriching, valuable information relative to a leader's perceived credibility. An honest, trustworthy approach to all aspects of leadership is required. Followers see through leaders who are not genuine. "If there is not deep integrity and fundamental character strength, true motives will eventually surface and the human relationships will fail."[68] Leaders must authentically exemplify the highest of values. Their words and actions must match. They must "walk their talk." They must continually engage in DWYSYWD practices—that is, they do what you say you will do. They follow through every time. They don't say one thing and do another. Their position doesn't change as a condition of who they are talking to or to appease others.

> Be yourself; everyone else is already taken.
> —OSCAR WILDE

This very point is continually driven home in the political realm, where leaders, perhaps in a desperate quest to get or stay elected, make promises that are subsequently broken. This feeds the high degree of cynicism that so many hold for politicians. Other politicians flip-flop on decisions and are seen as weak and inconsistent in the eyes of followers. Trust that is so critical to leadership is broken.

A trustworthy reputation is not built overnight. It takes a considerable amount of consistent, ongoing behavior to establish and maintain a trustworthy persona. It resonates from consistent actions, underscoring the opinions that people hold for a person they believe is honest, trustworthy, and loyal. Unfortunately, and perhaps unfairly, a single lapse in judgment can ruin a career's worth of consistent, trustworthy leadership behavior.

The Credibility Collapse

> We are all made from crooked timber.
> —DAVID BROOKS

The importance of credibility to leadership is not a new notion. However, in times of heightened leadership scandals, fraudulent actions, obscene financial compensation paid to ineffective corporate leaders while the rank and file are asked to take wage cuts or lose their positions, the concept of credibility has secured a more prominent link to leadership.

A growing sense of cynicism for leaders and the concept of leadership is evident in survey after survey, uncovering a growing dissatisfaction with the quality of leadership people receive. A *New York Times* / CBS News opinion poll uncovered that 71 percent of people agreed that politicians say one thing and do another once they are in office.[69] However ...

> People still want and need leadership. They just want leaders who hold an ethic of service and are genuinely respectful of the intelligence and contributions of their constituents. They want leaders who will put principles ahead of politics and other people ahead of self-interests.[70]

In addition, the heroic leadership models of the past may have clouded an understanding of what true, effective leadership is all about. Effective leaders of the day are not the Vince Lombardi or Henry Ford types as portrayed in the heroic leadership models of the Great Man leadership theories of yesteryear. Portrayals of contemporary leaders are not akin to orchestra conductors or puppeteers who directly control the actions and activities of those in their charge. This model is outdated—it served whatever usefulness it had in its time and has been replaced by a more engaging leadership model that is based on inspiration and empowerment. To lead in this fashion, contemporary leaders must possess and actively demonstrate a credible character, the major component of the successful emergence and effectiveness of a leader. People are unwilling to invest their energy, enthusiasm, and efforts in someone they can't respect or trust.

As noted, this universal truth is not a new idea, merely one that has gained prominence in recent times, largely due to the scandals and fraudulent activities like those noted above. Nearly a century ago, researchers[71] began to document the importance of personality strength to leadership emergence and success. They concluded that people with open, pleasant, and refined personalities were in a better position to inspire, and consequently influence, others to do something they wouldn't normally do without the manipulation of rewards or punishments. True leaders were those individuals with admirable personalities and characters. Since these people were admired and respected, others were more likely to invest their time, interest, and energy in these leaders. These leaders appeared to have the qualities others lacked.

Although the first of the Five Cs is the easiest to comprehend, it is without question the most difficult to carry out on a sustainable basis. People place leaders under a microscope and hold them to a higher standard of behavior. Many are generally cynical of leaders and subconsciously look to bring them down. Think about the blood-sport campaigns of political leaders. Political strategists and accompanying campaigns are usually focused on destroying the credibility of leaders (can't be trusted or not ready—or both) and consequently the low level of trust the general public generally holds for potential leaders. Even when leaders assume roles, people watch them like hawks, just waiting to pounce on them for a perceived or actual indiscretion, with the accompanying "I knew it" comment. Couple this mind-set with the realities of social media and other forms of electronic communication, and it is easy to see why people are often dissuaded from seeking leadership roles. Another approach would be to understand the fundamental importance of credibility to leadership and heed the helpful counsel of writers[72] who remind us to be truthful, trustworthy, consistent, and current—or stay out of leadership roles. Know that being a leader in this day and age takes special people who understand and appreciate the pivotal role credibility plays in leadership. Current and aspiring leaders must be willing to subject themselves to this level of analysis and emerge from the process every day unscathed. They will be respected for following through on their intentions, as well as their honesty and trustworthiness. Although this might sound somewhat simplistic, these leaders will have to maintain this credible behavior on a daily basis in all their activities—and it won't be easy.

> Some politicians lie—even when it isn't necessary—just to keep in shape.
>
> —MORDECAI RICHLER

Credibility Is the Foundation of Leadership

Researchers[73] have long noted that it is the fuel that ignites and sustains relationships with people who can come together and be further inspired to pursue a common purpose. The foundation of this relationship is based on credibility. It is established and measured on a day-to-day basis. Being in the limelight, leaders are always under the watchful microscope of followers, particularly those who cynically believe that anyone and everyone eventually breaks. As such, they look for minor deviations of credible leader behavior, and they are quick to denounce leaders who appear to suffer from credibility regressions. Similar to one's reputation, it takes a lifetime to develop credibility and a moment to destroy it and consequently, the ability to genuinely influence others. People can have the most meritorious vision, possess charisma in spades, even have the ability to challenge and inspire others, but without credibility, followers will not put their faith and their hearts and minds into the hands of another person as a leader.

Since credibility is so difficult to establish and maintain in the eyes of followers, leaders who are credible are often seen as holding special qualities that set them apart from their contemporaries. Some see these people as charismatic. Research into what qualities inspire people to "willingly follow" (a.k.a. leadership) have consistently uncovered that honesty is the number-one thing people expect and need from their leaders. Effective leaders provide evidence of these qualities through their own values, their personal example, their enthusiasm, and their confidence in themselves and others. They are effective because they are viewed as credible. People will put their faith in them only if they are viewed as being credible.

> In organizations in which mutual trust does not exist, people are cautious, less open, less satisfied, less influential, more distant, and more inclined to leave at the first available opportunity.[74]

Honesty is a prerequisite for leadership. People also need to perceive their leaders as being a credible source of information. They expect leaders to understand their field, be aware of environmental cues and opportunities, and clairvoyant regarding future trends. In a sense, leaders must have experience and an eye toward the future.

> When values aren't clear, decisions are easy.
> —ROY DISNEY

People are not expecting earth-shattering visions, Einstein-like intelligence, or John Wayne–like charisma. They merely and desperately want their leaders to be honest and know what they are talking about. Of note, this finding has been consistent over time, as evidenced by the results from research dating back to the early 1980s and across multiple countries. Everyone wants to believe in their leaders. They want to have faith and confidence in them as people. They want to believe that their word can be trusted, that they have the knowledge and skill to lead, and that they are personally excited and enthusiastic about the direction in which the group is headed. Credibility is clearly the foundation of leadership.

Leaders of the day must develop a relationship with their staff members if they hope to inspire and influence them to attain preestablished personal and organizational outcomes. Credibility is the foundation of this relationship. Leaders have to initiate such action. They must get to know their staff members, highlight their value and belief systems, and behave in a fashion consistent with these stated values and beliefs. Leading denotes action. Leaders must take the initiative in developing trusting relationships with their constituents. If people don't trust the leader, they will not fully invest their hearts, minds, and muscles in the vision or plan for the organization. The more onerous and challenging the vision or plan, the more trust is required from followers for the leader. Engaging in exciting, meaningful environments with credible leaders who "make people feel alive, valued, turned on, enthusiastic, and significant"[75] is what truly engages and inspires people to perform beyond what was initially thought possible.

Effective leadership takes time. Leaders must find time to plan, communicate, build relationships, monitor progress, and focus on the future. There are only so many hours in a day, and leaders need a life outside of their leadership role. Many leaders get pulled into a management mind-set that railroads their schedule and takes them away from leadership. They simply don't make time for the leadership role. Their time is gobbled up by the day-to-day details of management, at the expense of future planning, relationship building, and leading. Contemporary leaders build and deploy strong leadership teams that reflect the highest levels of trust. Leaders must surround themselves with people they respect and trust. They need to build a team of strong and committed coleaders who bring shared values and complementary ideas and perspectives to the leadership table. Therefore, taking additional time to watch over people is not an option, and if it were, it would merely serve to stifle enthusiasm and creativity.

Finally, turnover is a costly problem facing many organizations. Securing highly qualified staff members, empowering and inspiring them to grow and meaningfully contribute to the success of the organization or enterprise is one of the essential tasks of a leader. The cost of attracting and orienting new people of high quality is immense and could be minimized if effective leaders develop a community of leaders from within an organization—a situation where people enjoy and are inspired by the work experience. Their work has meaning. They have no intentions of leaving, even if the financial gain is greater. As evidenced by the above, there are no reasonable alternatives to credibility if one wants to truly lead an organization.

> Train (sic Develop) people well enough that they can leave. Treat them well enough so they don't want to.
> —SIR RICHARD BRANSON

Leaders must be perceived as trustworthy. They are viewed as being consistent with their words and actions. They are clear about their value system. They are open to change if compelling and convincing evidence warrants such change, but these leaders don't flip positions to suit the situation or to make some people feel more comfortable. These leaders can be counted on. Once formed, they state their positions on issues in a clear and consistent manner. People appreciate their honesty and consistency, even if they hold a different opinion.

Fortunately, the mode of behavior of these leaders can cascade throughout the unit or organization. Some researchers have determined that followers often identify with, and in many cases, emulate leaders who are perceived as being trustworthy and credible.[76] The ethical actions of leaders have a positive influence on the culture of the organization,[77] which is arguably the most important role that a leader plays (see C5—Culture Builder). Credible leaders help create a positive work environment and foster a community of leaders, focused on and committed to the clearly articulated and widely adopted aims and objectives of the enterprise.

> Perpetual optimism is a force multiplier.
> —COLIN POWELL

How Current and Prospective Leaders Can Heighten Their Credibility

Act the way that you'd like to be, and soon
you will be the way that you act.
— LEONARD COHEN

Developing credibility requires no special training. No university course or professional workshop can teach one to be more credible if the person is not totally committed to being more credible. For most people, the teachers of this important concept of leadership were their parents and grandparents. Yes, you start working on this critical leadership skill before the age of five; however, you never stop working on this pivotal aspect of human interaction in general and in leadership specifically. Listed below are the 11 activities that help leaders heighten their credibility in the eyes of followers. Each of the activities is supported with related anecdotes and theories from other leadership scholars, as well as supplemented with my own research and experience.

1. Be accessible. Effective leaders make themselves accessible, not to such a degree that the leader does the task for employees but in a supportive and encouraging fashion. Followers need to know that leaders will be available to support them. They also need to know that their leader has compassion for them as a person and that they will make themselves available to discuss a situation or offer a word of encouragement. This has been my modus operandi in higher education leadership positions. Be seen, be available, and as noted in the next point, at times, be quiet.

Leaders need to be accessible and visible, particularly given the fact that staff members in many industries work evenings and weekends. It is important for leaders to pop in occasionally in the off hours to see how people are doing. It highlights the fact that credible leaders wouldn't ask others to do something they wouldn't also do. This practice aligns with the latest developments in the servant leadership area (see part A and in particular, the theoretical developments in leadership) wherein leaders demonstrate with their words and actions that they are genuinely interested in the health, well-being, and perspectives of others. Members notice and will appreciate the practice—immensely.

The best leaders are visible. They see people doing good things and praise them for their contribution. This is an important practice of effective leaders. Again, following the accessibility theme, effective leaders do not clamor in their offices. They actively lead their organization by being visible and supportive. Effective university presidents have lunch once per week in the student cafeterias. The best CEOs often sit for lunch with the rank-and-file members of an organization. They are engaged. They are perceived to be caring and approachable. All leaders can and must be visible, engaged, and accessible—and in so doing, they will be seen as being more credible.

2. Be an effective listener—everywhere. Lou Holtz, former college football coach and a popular speaker at leadership seminars, frequently comments on the importance of listening. He's often noted that "People were given two ears and one mouth and consequently should listen twice as much as they talk." Steven Covey noted in his highly acclaimed 1990 book *The Seven Habits of Highly Effective People* that one should "seek first to understand rather than to be understood." He noted that effective people are outstanding listeners. They actively listen to what people are telling them, and in so doing, gain additional perspective on issues. He accurately asserted that most people are formulating a reply when they should be attempting to understand the communicator.

Credible leaders listen well and listen everywhere. Active listening keeps leaders on the cutting edge of what is truly going on in their organization and within their industry. Furthermore, the genuine feeling that one is being listened to is psychologically uplifting. Effective listeners gain insights. They can gather divergent opinions, fresh ideas, and cutting-edge developments by engaging in one of communication's easiest tasks—listening.

> Learn to listen. Opportunity sometimes knocks very quietly.
>
> —UNKNOWN

3. Know your constituents. People want to know that they are appreciated and cared for as a person, not simply a cog in an organizational wheel. Credible leaders get to know as many people in the organization as possible on an individual basis. They see them outside the work environment. They strike up conversations with these people about mutual areas of interest. They try to uncover the value set that their followers hold, what motivates them, and what makes them tick.

It is human nature to appreciate someone taking an interest in them. When leaders do it, their credibility as a warm, caring leader escalates immeasurably. I have made it my practice to send birthday cards to all members in my organization. I also hold a number of professional and social events that involve members and their families. My wife and I host social events for members in our home. We've even looked after the children of some colleagues so they could have a well-deserved night out. These are simple things, but they help members know that their leader is genuinely interested in them as people and that I want to get to know their families. It shows them that their leader cares about them (again, a key tenet in the servant leadership area). I have also made it a practice to spend a good portion of my working day walking the halls of my building and talking with support staff. Yes, it is a challenge given geography and time constraints, but I consider it a strategic priority. It is an important leadership practice and one that I hold as a priority. My experience has been that this makes a difference. Other leadership practices include holding celebrations of success to acknowledge exceptional accomplishments, holding social events for members to encourage member understandings, and heightening communications through a biweekly electronic newsletter known as my electronic communications update that I regularly send out to all stakeholders.

> Too often we underestimate the power of a touch, a smile, a kind word, a listening ear, an honest compliment, or the smallest act of kindness which has the potential to turn a life around.
>
> —LEO BUSCAGLIA

One of the first things Michael Eisner did upon assuming the CEO position for the Disney Corporation was establish a process for actively listening to staff members. In addition to being keenly interested in their ideas and ideals, he wanted to get to know people and show them that he cared for their perspectives. Dennis Hightower, president of Disney Consumer Products in Europe and the Middle East, used to share a story that early in Eisner's tenure, he invited six of the most creative Disney people to his house for a Sunday morning breakfast brainstorming session. Out of this session alone emerged two new Disney television animations. Get people together, showing that you care about them.

4. Appreciate diversity.

> Difference of opinion leads to inquiry, and inquiry to truth. So ask questions and seek answers.
>
> —THOMAS JEFFERSON

Whenever groups of people come together to pursue a similar objective, different personalities, paradigms, and cultural upbringing enter the mix. This reality can be used to the group's advantage if the leader and other members of the group or organization learn to appreciate and capitalize upon diversity.[78] Leaders can't go to the same people all the time or surround themselves with people like them (or people they like). Leaders must also heed Susan Cain's advice and mine the group for introverted individuals who may not automatically be viewed as "leadership material." As she clearly indicated, they can make incredible contributions if given the opportunity. A destructive force known as "groupthink" (a social phenomenon whereby one dominant individual or someone with heightened authority offers an opinion that others adopt, usually without resistance, even if they hold a contrary opinion) can occur if leaders and organizations do not appreciate and embrace diversity of opinion. Appreciating diversity must start at the top of an organization, with the executive leader. It must also cascade through an organization to all hierarchical levels. New perspectives and fresh ideas, if not stifled, are good for organizations that often fall into a repeating pattern of "same as last year" leadership. Leaders must step outside of their comfort zones and encourage others to do the same. Leaders must engage and encourage full participation on decisions and actively invite others to share and explain their perspectives.

5. Stay in touch. Credible leaders actively keep in touch with their constituents. Effective leaders of large organizations are often forced to devise unique methods to stay in touch with their constituents (e.g., lunch meetings, company newsletters, general meetings). Some leaders use social media platforms to keep people informed and communication pathways open. Others hold town hall meetings, lunch-and-learn sessions, or simply make an effort to keep people apprised of things that they need to know. It is the leader's responsibility to share information and engage members. They need to find a platform—or better yet a number of platforms and formats that work for them. As technology develops, there will be new methods of reaching out that we don't know today. Imagine leaders in the 1950s thinking that they could instantaneously reach stakeholders through social media platforms like Twitter or LinkedIn. Who knows what the future will bring with respect to technology? The practice of active engagement and regular communication will always be in fashion—regardless of the communication platform options available to current and future leaders.

> A society grows great when old men plant trees whose shade they know they will never sit in.
> —GREEK PARABLE

6. Consider others' perspectives. Credible leaders attempt to gain the perspective of constituents by spending time in their role. These leaders are more credible in the eyes of their followers because of their "been there" background. Other leaders have gained credibility by getting to know their followers, spending time with them on their tasks, and gaining on-the-spot insights into the inner workings of the followers' responsibilities. By spending time with followers, these credible leaders gain new insights and perspectives as well as securing a more enriched assessment of follower wants, needs, and desires.

> People want to know how much you care before they care how much you know.
> —THEODORE ROOSEVELT

Examples of this type of leadership practice range from leaders working the floor with members (e.g., Southwest Airlines' CEO Herb Kelleher helping flight attendants ice glasses prior to takeoff; former Maple Leaf Sports & Entertainment president and CEO Richard Peddie stopping to pick up garbage while walking in the concourse of the Air Canada Centre). As a dean, I always felt that it was critically important to assume a teaching role, stay active in research, and sign my name *Professor and Dean*. I wanted my professors to know that I understood their roles and was willing to carry my share of similar work. I also wanted them to identify with me as a colleague. On many occasions, after watching them put in long days of committed service, I would give staff members an extended lunch break or an early departure from the office while I sat at the reception desk and fielded calls and greeted visitors. On one occasion, I provided tickets to a concert that they would love (which also had a shopping and dinner component), so I looked after the decanal suite in their absence. Believe me, I got this time and much more back from this highly competent and highly motivated workforce.

Leaders who help with the heavy lifting communicate through their actions that they will not ask others to do things they wouldn't do themselves. This sends a strong and compelling message.

7. Hold regular meetings. People like to be informed. They also appreciate being involved in decisions that affect them. Credible leaders recognize this reality and hold regular meetings (formal and informal) with their key constituents to share information and brief each other on issues. I met with key staff members informally on a daily basis and formally on a regular basis. When I met individually with members, I asked them to submit discussion/agenda items in advance so we could all be prepared and as efficient as possible. These meetings proved to be imminently valuable to heightening communications in the faculty, as well as building a culture of trust, mutual respect, and shared leadership.

In addition to sharing information, these meetings help minimize daily interruptions. When staff members know that they will meet each week, they tend to save items for the next meeting. Meetings must be productive. They need to start on time, be focused on items under discussion, and have an action and accountability plan to ensure words translate into action. They should engage staff members, making them feel like a significant component to the success of the enterprise.

A few times a year, we would hold one- or two-item-agenda meetings to allow us to delve deeper into larger issues or strategic thinking. These meetings have also proven to be a helpful method of mining ideas and facilitating heightened engagement.

Leaders need to gauge the need for meetings prior to holding them. Tight agendas circulated in advance will allow members to prepare. If insufficient agenda items warrant the cancellation of a meeting, leaders would be well advised to do so. Holding unnecessary meetings is a time waster and will build negative feelings toward meetings and likely the leader holding them.

8. Be the first to ante up. Since leadership is about relationships founded on credibility, leaders need to nurture trusting relationships with those they lead. Credible leaders take the initiative by showing their faith in others first. These followers might be surprised initially; however, with time, they'll come to appreciate the faith bestowed upon them and reciprocate trust back to the leader. Naturally, the credibility of the leader's character remains at issue and impacts the degree to which people bestow their trust.

Members often mimic the behaviors of their leader. Think about the type of organization you want. Do you want to project a professional image? If so, you must present one yourself. Do you want a committed workforce where people go above and beyond the call of duty? If so, model this yourself. Do you want an organization where ideas are welcomed and members respect each other? If so, listen carefully and be the first to demonstrate respect to others. Your words and actions speak volumes about your values and beliefs. Be the first to show members the desired modus operandi.

9. Know what bugs people. Getting to know people on an individual basis has many payoffs, as outlined above. You will know what motivates and irritates people. Recognition for accomplishment, support, and credit for member success, and interest in them as people are just a few of the things that members will appreciate. There may be other ideas. Get to know people and what motivates them. Conversely, public reprimands, providing insufficient credit to others for their ideas and contributions, being unclear to members regarding expectations, and being perceived as unfair or condescending are just a few of the irritants to members. Find out what motivates or irritates people by getting and staying close to them. Let them get to know and trust you. If this happens, you will soon know what works and what doesn't work in your setting and with certain people. It is critical for you as the leader to find the *hot* and *cold* buttons of all of your members.

10. **Practice small wins.** One can't win a Nobel Prize every day. However, in every walk of life, minor successes do occur and need to be publicly celebrated. Attaining smaller goals helps build credibility for the leader, the organization, and the members within the organization. Small successes can heighten motivation and confirm faith in the leader and the direction for the future. Leaders should publicly recognize and, where appropriate, celebrate small successes, being sure to give the glory and directing the attention to the many people who made the small success possible. I've preached this in my leadership roles. At the University of Windsor, I would invite members to our conference room, and they would show up without any knowledge as to why they were being summoned. Upon arrival, they would find a cake and coffee waiting for them. A short presentation on the importance of acknowledging success would follow, along with a brief presentation on the recent success of our members (i.e., the securing of a research grant, the news of a major national or international award, etc.). Naturally, the surprise was gone for future events, but they continued nonetheless, with overwhelming support and appreciation. At my current university, we hold social and professional events

to acknowledge and celebrate distinguished contributions to the teaching, research, and service roles. In my decanal role, we created awards where they didn't exist, to highlight what was truly important to us. As noted in C5—Culture Builder—what gets reinforced by leaders gets baked into the culture of an organization. A leader's most important role is shaping and embedding a desired culture for an organization or group as it encourages and supports behavior.

11. Be human. Be humble. Admit when you make mistakes. Own them and publicly disclose the mistake. Set the tone for others. Encourage others on your team to shine a light on their shortcomings as well and to ask for help when they need it.

> Humility isn't thinking less of yourself, but thinking of yourself less.
>
> —RICK WARREN

Summary

Researchers have long determined that "leaders must be trusted and seen as having personal integrity. Without the achievement of these attributes, leaders cannot command loyalty." Furthermore, "without loyalty and commitment, people will put out only that which is necessary. Such trust and personal integrity can be created by behaving consistently and honestly and by demonstrating personal commitment to the organization and the vision."[79] Examples of such action abound from a variety of settings. Mary Robinson, the former president of Ireland, wanted to highlight to her people that she was always there for them. To symbolize this philosophy, she kept a burning candle visibly displayed in her window each evening. This represented her reaching out to people and communicated a message that "I am here. You can count on me; I'll be with you." Some leaders subject themselves to a "national newspaper smell test" prior to engaging in an action or making a decision. Ask yourself how you would feel if this decision or incident appeared on the front page of the *New York Times*. Could you defend it? Could it be embarrassing or career threatening? Principled leaders like those chronicled in David Brooks's *The Road to Character* don't have to worry about these kinds of things because they always act in an honorable and principled manner. They have nothing to worry about. They live their personal and professional lives honestly and expect the same of others on their leadership team. Lee Iacocca's willingness to reduce his annual salary to one dollar per year as the chairman of the Chrysler Corporation during the height of an auto crisis visibly and symbolically highlighted his commitment. He sent a message that personal sacrifice and heightened commitment were necessary if the company was to escape bankruptcy and jobs and pensions were to be saved. The symbolism of his actions spoke volumes to the many Chrysler workers and potential customers.

Effective leaders ask followers to invest their efforts as well as their hearts to attain the goals and objectives of the organization. The greater the commitment required to attain a goal or the more onerous the effort requirement, the greater the need for a genuine display of caring, consistent, trustworthy leadership.

In the end, it is clear that leadership is about developing mutually trusting relationships founded and operated on the basis of credibility. It is fundamental to effective leadership. Goran Carstedt, the late CEO of the IKEA furniture company, noted the importance of employees having direct involvement in the day-to-day activities of the company. The company engages in some symbolic activities that reinforce this operational mind-set such as the "anti-bureaucratic week." People move positions in an attempt to gain different perspectives. During this week, "every manager works on the front lines, and the company tries to eliminate any structures, systems, or barriers that impede the free flow of information."[80]

Leaders must be concerned about maximizing the perception of their credibility in the eyes of their constituents if they have any visions for organizational accomplishment beyond ordinary levels. "No leader can afford to forget that personal and organizational leadership are closely intertwined. Nor can any leader afford to lose sight of the mission and shared vision—the constitution of the organization."[81] The second component of Covey's warning is presented in the next section.

> Great companies are indeed a reflection of their leaders.[82]

C2—Compelling Vision

A Reader's Guide

Upon reading this chapter, readers will understand

- the importance of vision to leadership,
- how effective leaders are characterized as visionaries,
- where visions come from and how they are utilized,
- the three essentials components of a leader's vision,
- how leaders can disburse a vision throughout a group or organization, and
- how leaders can transform visions into actions.

C2—Compelling Vision

> The worst thing in life is a person who has sight but no vision.
>
> —HELEN KELLER

Certainly, one of the most prevalent themes, if not the most prevalent theme, in the current writing about leadership is the concept of vision. While credibility is an essential ingredient to gaining the faith and trust of people and cementing a relationship, people don't become leaders until they can focus another individual or a group of people on a desired end or vision for the future. Other writers concur on the importance of vision to the concept of leadership. Some theorists[83] believe that vision is so central that they title their theory "Visionary Leadership," while other theorists using transformational leadership suggest that vision is one of the most important aspects of their theory. "Vision is an important, if not essential, component of the leadership of organizations and often of divisions within an organization. It gives direction, helps people know where they fit in, and can enhance the motivation and sense of empowerment of members of an organization."[84] I believe that a compelling vision is critical. The key distinction is that a compelling vision implies it is a vision that captures the interest of followers and inspires them to make the vision a reality.

> It is easy to recognize an organization led by an in-
> dividual without a vision. You find a confusing blur
> of intentions, people moving here and there, doing
> this and that, all seeming to have purpose but adding
> up to—what? When a futures-creative leader offers
> a convincing vision of the future, it is as if one has
> been looking at a fuzzy image through a camera lens,
> twisted the lens, and suddenly all comes into focus.[85]

Vision

> In the long run, people only hit what they aim at.
> Therefore, they had better aim at something high.
> —HENRY DAVID THOREAU

Effective leaders require the conceptual ability to visualize a "big picture" for the organization over a particularly lengthy time frame. Vision—the ability to create and shape and effectively communicate a clear direction for a group, unit, or organization—is the central theme of all contemporary leadership theorists and writers. Some have referred to vision as being the essence of leadership.[86] Robert Katz[87] noted long ago that managers require three sets of skills to be effective. First of all, they need technical skills, especially at the low- to middle-management areas. They need to understand the industry.

Secondly, they need human skills, given the fact that they will be dealing with people. Finally, and most importantly for senior managers, they need conceptual skills. They must understand the dynamics of the organization, how everything comes together, where the industry is headed, and where there are threats and opportunities. It is suggested that leaders need these types of skills as well. They need technical skills to give them credibility in the eyes of those they lead. They especially need human skills to understand and inspire people (i.e., emotional intelligence), and conceptual skills to help create and shape a vision. I further argue that leaders need a deeper skill set in the areas of human and conceptual skills.

Leaders must ensure that there is a compelling vision in place that helps focus activity and guide human and fiscal decision-making. That is not to say that leaders have to be the sole source of clairvoyant thought. Hardly! Many times, leaders listen actively to the thoughts and perspectives of those they lead, as well as to other stakeholders, and then use their experience to shape the vision into a brief and inspiring sound bite that they and others can effectively and consistently communicate. These leaders must keep themselves and those they lead focused on the vision and its attainment. They need to ensure that the vision stays in clear focus, and accomplishments that help advance the vision must be publicly acknowledged and appropriately celebrated. This practice will help ensure that the unit or organization stays focused.[88]

> Whenever anything is being accomplished, it is being done, I have learned, by a monomaniac with a mission.
> —PETER DRUCKER

The words, decisions, and behaviors of leaders can help embed the vision into the culture of the organization and, as noted in C5— Culture Builder, the culture of the organization influences the commitment levels and subsequent activities of followers. The vision, once determined (and hopefully from a participative process) becomes something most if not all stakeholders know and can recite with conviction and clarity.

A few years ago, I was appointed the dean of the faculty of health sciences, a large, interdisciplinary academic unit comprised of a number of professional and interdisciplinary schools. It was a relatively new faculty, seeking an identity, a profile, and a place at the table of one of Canada's top universities.

Early in my tenure as dean, and after installing an outstanding leadership group (remember Collins'[89] sage advice: *who,* then *what*), we embarked on a strategic planning/vision-setting exercise. We implemented a number of activities that garnered stakeholder input. Surveys, focus-group sessions, taskforce committees, and more were established to ensure people had the opportunity to express their views and opinions. The leadership group synthesized this information and deployed its experience to develop a vision statement that continues to serve the faculty well, years after it was conceived. I believe it will serve the faculty for years to come. Our vision was clear, aligned with institutional priorities, succinct and memorable, and inclusive so that all stakeholders could see themselves in the vision and could do things to make it a reality. We sought to

- be research leaders of national/international prominence;
- attract, inspire, and retain the best and brightest students, staff, and faculty;
- be leaders in our professions, on our campus, and in our communities; and
- be a great place to work, study, learn, and grow.

Leaders have a fiduciary responsibility to focus and inspire people through their words and actions. Leaders develop those they lead. They inspire and excite them to possibilities and in so doing facilitate quantum changes in their performance, as well as the performance of their teams and the organization. The top-level leader is often responsible for setting policies and procedures for the organization and planning for the organization over the long term. Often referred to as the executive leader, this individual requires the conceptual skills to see the big picture, know that challenges and opportunities that lie ahead, and ensure that the unit/organization is focused and prepared to act accordingly. The leader must ensure that a clear and compelling vision is in place that will guide the unit or organization in the short and long terms.

> High-performing organizations know where they are going. Their leaders set clear purpose and direction so that everyone has a vivid understanding of where the enterprise is heading and what they must do to get there.[90]

Researchers have confirmed what practitioners have long known—that effective, visionary leadership is critical to success. Ensuring a clear and coherent vision is paramount to this success. These leaders need to be visionary, especially when compared to the frontline supervisor. They need to be responsible for creating a vision for the organization and implanting an organizational culture that facilitates the organization operating in a satisfying and productive fashion.

In spite of this reality, many people occupying roles calling for leadership don't do this. They get overly consumed with the busy work. They manage more than they lead. No one questions their work ethic—but it is fair to question how they are using their time.

Many effective leaders build time into their schedules to reflect. They study performance data. They measure the impact of decisions on preestablished goals. They are clear about what the unit or organization is attempting to accomplish. As an academic leader, I used my Friday afternoons for this reflection. No one was scheduled into this time block. It was white space in my planner, devoted to one of my most important roles: reflection and planning. Otherwise, this critical action would get squeezed out. Meetings and other activities would overtake. The urgent would trump the important. Don't succumb to this habit. True leaders are conceptual thinkers. They keep their eye on the prize. They ensure a clear and coherent vision and they regularly reflect on performance against this vision.

> Vision animates, inspirits, and transforms purpose into action.[91]

Leaders from a variety of settings have demonstrated the power of vision to leadership. Readers will be able to identify a number of these leaders. I like to refer to someone from my field of study, the late Mark McCormack, who not only held a vision for a company he founded—the International Management Group (IMG)—but also had a vision about an industry: sports marketing. He refined, if not created, the sports-marketing industry as we know it today.

The marketing *of* sports and the marketing *through* sports is now a focal point for Fortune 500 companies, sports organizations, sports-management scholars, and casual observers of sports or business. This was not always the case. Mark McCormack was described by many as the most powerful man in sports. He created and transformed the field of sports marketing to what it is today. He founded IMG in 1960, and his company laid the groundwork for the more than seven hundred other sports marketing firms that exist today.

McCormack had a vision for sports marketing. Legend has it that the IMG story and in a broader scope the professionalization of sports marketing, began with a handshake agreement between the young Cleveland lawyer McCormack and his first client, the late Arnold Palmer. McCormack knew that television coverage of sports, and in particular golf, was starting to boom. He also knew that Palmer would be embraced by the American public for his charismatic personality and aggressive approach to the game of golf. His clairvoyance was also evident in his second prediction, that sports was about to become more international. Worldwide audiences would be interested in international events. Air travel would make athlete appearances at international events easier. His vision became a reality. In spite of this humble beginning, IMG has grown to a state where it now employs thousands of people in offices across the planet. McCormack continued to be the leader and driving force at IMG and within the sports marketing/event-managing areas until his untimely death in 2003.

McCormack's vision for his company was based on two principles. First of all, he believed that a sleeping giant existed within sports, namely the business side of sports. He accurately suggested that this area of sports was not being tapped to its full potential. He believed that athletes and sports marketing/event-management agents could coexist in a mutually beneficial relationship. Secondly, he believed that athletes should channel their energies into their strengths, that is, what they do on the golf course, ski hill, or tennis court, and leave the business side of the game to people who have the proper background and sufficient time to do the job correctly. He quickly gained credibility for his vision through his work with Palmer. He convinced Palmer that his strengths rested in playing the game, and the business components could be handled by someone prepared in the legal and entrepreneurial areas. He knew Palmer was going to be outstanding on the pro circuit, that his dynamic personality would be embraced by both corporations and the American populace alike, and that if his plan worked, Palmer would be a figurehead for his emerging IMG company. Palmer's golf game flourished, and with it, the demands on his time increased. McCormack provided legal and business advice to assist Palmer and build his credibility with the golfer. McCormack extended Palmer's visibility through entrepreneurial activities. He secured lucrative exhibitions for Palmer. He arranged corporate outings. He landed lucrative endorsement contracts for Palmer. His success with Arnold Palmer, and Palmer's satisfaction with the arrangement, soon brought two more golfers into McCormack's IMG stable. South African sensation Gary Player and a rookie by the name of Jack Nicklaus combined with Arnold Palmer to become Mark McCormack's "Big 3." He later diversified his sports marketing clients into other sports, signing skier Jean-Claude Killy and tennis player Rod Laver, two leaders in their respected games who, like Palmer, were athletes with engaging, charismatic personalities who would be dependable ambassadors for their respective sports, for corporations, and for IMG.

Recognizing the untapped potential in sports representation and professional career management, McCormack pressed on. He created a demand for his clients. He put them in the spotlight. He looked after the tedious details of travel and negotiations, much to the delight of his clients. He served as their chief negotiator and advocate. Over the years, IMG strengthened its reputation in the sports marketing and event-management areas by representing high-profile athletes of that era, people like Wayne Gretzky, Joe Montana, and Nancy Lopez and managing world-class sporting events like Wimbledon, the Skins Game, and the British Open. "McCormack foresaw the future and, in the best traditions of American industrialists, prepared to meet it. McCormack not only built a company, he built an entire industry."[92] International Management Group continues to be the largest and most successful sports management/marketing company in the world. McCormack's vision and fortitude allowed him to see and take advantage of an opportunity and expand it beyond anyone's imagination. Creating an industry where one never before existed is no small accomplishment, yet McCormack succeeded. His vision has become a reality and has led to professionalization of the field of sports marketing as we now know it.

More recent examples of a leader's compelling vision can be garnered from the example of leaders like Blake Mycoskie, who had a vision that tapped into people's desire to help others less fortunate. Mycoskie founded TOMS shoes (short for Tomorrow) and its two-for-one policy (purchase of one pair of shoes ensures that a second pair is produced and donated to a person in need from Argentina). The company has since expanded into other products based on the same two-for-one policy (e.g., eyeglasses). Some visions are for new products like those of Elon Musk, who acted on a vision for cars operating on renewable batteries (Tesla Automobiles) and space travel for ordinary citizens (SpaceX). Other leaders bring process-visions to the forefront, such as Allan Mulally's teamwork and synergy vision that worked so well at Boeing and later at the Ford Motor Company. Herb Kelleher's vision for making the workplace fun and exciting has been a popular case study in business schools throughout the world because his leadership focus worked in keeping Southwest Airlines at the top of the competitive airline industry. All of these leaders had vision and brought the vision to life in their leadership practices.

It is clear to me that effective leadership is synonymous with a leader's ability to develop and impart a powerful and well-communicated vision. The best leaders ensure that there is a clear and clairvoyant vision for their unit or organization. They have the ability to clearly communicate this vision to members of the organization compellingly—in a fashion where members adopt a sense of ownership and commitment to making it a reality. Strong leaders create and interpret meaning to followers through the vision. These individuals provide a sense of clarity to followers through the vision, drawing attention to the key components of what needs to be accomplished and at a prescribed degree of excellence. In most cases, leaders present an image that the status quo is unacceptable. Some turn to the exceptional advice offered by change expert John Kotter,[93] who outlines an eight-stage process to creating change in his seminal *Leading Change* text. Kotter's eight steps are as follows:

1. Establishing a sense of urgency

2. Creating the guiding coalition

3. Developing a vison and strategy

4. Communicating the change vision

5. Empowering broad-based action

6. Generating short-term wins

7. Consolidating gains and producing more change

8. Anchoring new approaches in the culture

The very best leaders …

> get people to see "what is," to see reality, to see that they are not contributing to the best of their abilities, and to see that the product is inferior. You must lay out whatever the reality is. Then you have to get them to buy into your vision.[94]

Leaders are change agents—they want to move the group or organization forward. They want to break with tradition. They are not afraid to challenge the status quo. Their visions are shaped by their own life experiences and ambitions; current and future market forces; the status quo and degree of acceptance of the status quo; and the needs, wants, and desires of group members relative to where they want to go.

Some suggest that leaders who might be labeled visionary or transformational think differently. They can (a) determine the long-range (ten-to-twenty-year) vision for what the organization could and should become, (b) understand the key components of the vision, and (c) communicate the vision in such a compelling fashion that members of the organization support and strive to realize this end.[95]

Examples of visionary leaders are plentiful. For example, Bill Gore, founder and leader of Gore-Tex, founded his company on a vision that small, enlightened workforces encourage teamwork and heightened levels of empowerment. Gore insisted on four values that governed decision-making and operations at Gore-Tex:[96] (a) fairness—and a dedication to maintaining it; (b) commitment—so that people can be counted on and can count on others; (c) freedom—to stretch the limits of one's capabilities and to expect this behavior for others in the company; and (d) water line—as a basis for the autonomy that people in the company have to make decisions. (If it doesn't go below the water line and sink the ship, make the decision.) Gore's vision of his company to produce innovative and required outerwear was founded on his belief that creativity and empowerment are the keys to organizational success and survival. He believed in the potential of employees ("associates," in his words) and the need to encourage and reward their efforts, creativity, innovation, and enthusiasm. Compensation at Gore-Tex is determined by a committee of associates. People are empowered to be creative and feel a sense of ownership in the company. Gore's vision of what his company could and eventually did become is testimony to the merits of his vision and has resulted in thirty-one consecutive years of growth, prosperity, and profits.

> Every great dream begins with a dreamer. Always remember, you have within you the strength, the patience, and the passion to reach for the stars to change the world.
>
> —HARRIET TUBMAN

Ray Kroc's vision of a quick, affordable, and consistent hamburger would fill a niche for people on the move and translated to his establishment of the McDonald's restaurant chain. No one can argue with the success of this vision, one that continues to be celebrated, posted, and embraced in modern-day McDonald's restaurants. Other examples that readers may know are:

Steve Jobs (Apple): a computer for the rest of us

Ursula Burns (Xerox): know customer needs/challenges and innovate

Walt Disney (Disney Corporation): make people happy

Diane Wojcicki (YouTube): a profitable company and an attractive alternative to television/other social media platforms

Herb Kelleher (Southwest Air): make flying an enjoyable experience for all

Richard Peddie (Maple Leaf Sports & Entertainment): win

Origin of the Vision

Some leadership writers have created confusion with respect to the origin of the vision. Some imply that the vision is the leader's sole creation—extending the illusion that if people do not have clairvoyance, if not grandiose visions, then they can't assume the leadership role. Others suggest that a vision derived from the input of all staff members is the "true" organizational vision. I firmly believe that this is usually the case. Great leaders are active listeners. They know their industry. They keep up on trends. They mine the ideas, perspectives, and aspirations of colleagues and, using their experience, help shape the vision into an exciting, inspiring, and memorable phrase. An organic, collectively produced vision is often the most accepted focus for the organization. Leaders need to tap the ideas of colleagues and integrate them into a vision that can be persuasively communicated to multiple stakeholders. Naturally, the leader needs to have some idea as to the current and anticipated future state of his or her organization, although this vision needs to consider the wants, needs, and desires of the entire organizational membership.

> In the end, the leader may be the one who articulates the vision and gives it legitimacy, who expresses the vision in captivating rhetoric that fires the imagination and emotions of followers, who—through the vision— empowers others to make decisions and get things done. But if the organization is to be successful, the image must grow out of the needs of the entire organization and must be "claimed" or "owned" by all of the important actors.[97]

Leaders need to communicate a vision throughout the organization to provide direction, stability, and a common purpose to all members. Furthermore, leaders need to clearly mesh the organizational goals with the goals of subordinates. Allowing for subordinate involvement in the establishment of organizational goals may be helpful in meshing and integrating personal goals within the organizational agenda. Finally, the leader's role in presenting organizational goals and continually reinforcing them appears to be a major component of the current thinking in the area of leadership.

Marshall Sashkin[98] once categorized the process of visioning into four distinct steps, each based on a cognitive action. He labeled the first step "expressing the vision" and suggested that leaders must behave in a manner that reinforces and advances the end result of the vision. These leaders must "walk their talk"—their actions must be consistent with their vision. In doing so, followers see tangible evidence of the importance of the vision and perhaps begin to understand why the vision is important to the overall operation or enterprise. As the reader will see in the third step, the vision must be general enough so that followers can adopt the vision to their specific area of responsibility.

The second visioning step, according to Sashkin, was labeled "explaining the vision." During this stage, leaders take the time to thoroughly explain the vision in a compelling and charismatic way. Followers need to clearly see the overall aim of the vision and the necessary steps to bring it to fruition. Followers need to be convinced that the vision is reflective of the "correct way to go." They need to adopt some sense of ownership, a reality that is considered and integrated in the third visioning step that Sashkin called "extending the vision." It is during this stage that leaders must allow followers to see the application of the vision in activities that fall in the followers' jurisdiction. The vision becomes their frame of reference. Followers are given the liberty to see how the vision can be integrated into their domain. This stage helps transfer ownership of the vision from the province of the leader to the level of the follower. It is at this stage that it becomes important for the overall vision of the leader to be general enough that others can adapt and apply the vision to their respective situation.

The fourth and final visioning stage is referred to as "expanding the vision." It is during this stage that the leader and followers look to a wide variety of situations and circumstances to apply the vision. The leader must draw on his or her conceptual skill at this stage to see the application and integration of the vision into other units within the organization. The vision has to be both positive and inspiring.

Consider the executive leader who appreciates the need for customer service. This person realizes that the way the customer is treated plays a big part in determining whether they will remain a loyal consumer of the organization's product or service in the coming years. All indicators point to the fact that customer service will become a more important factor as we see heightened domestic and global competition. Consumers will undoubtedly be more discriminating when it comes to parting with their hard-earned dollars. In "explaining the vision," the leader behaves in a fashion that clearly illustrates his or her orientation toward the customer and heightened service to this group. Later, once the leader has engaged in a number of "critical incidents" that are observed and passed down to other organizational members, the leader initiates the second step in the visioning process, called "explaining the vision." At this stage the leader outlines, in a charismatic and compelling fashion, the need for all members of the organization to be oriented toward the customer, as well as how this might be attained. Followers clearly see the relevance and appreciate the need for engaging and adopting this vision, and as a result, the third step, "extending the vision," is carried out. At this point, the leader and followers begin to pinpoint specific areas within the organization where the customer-orientation vision can be extended. Followers assume a sense of ownership for the vision, some to the point of believing that it is their idea, and consequently, they're more inclined to make it a reality. Finally, the leader expands the vision by exploring new areas and circumstances where the vision might be integrated. The leader attempts to integrate the entire organization to the vision. The leader monitors the impact of the implemented vision and measures its effect on the other units within the organization. The vision might be fine-tuned at this point to be adaptable and transferrable to other units within the organization.

Sashkin believed that most people can carry out the four visioning steps on a short-term basis (e.g., day, week, month); however, the true visionary leader has the ability to see deeper into the future. This rare type of leader has the ability to conceptualize a vision for a ten- to twenty-year time frame. This may help to explain why true visionary or transformational leaders are described by some as being as rare, and often as temporary, as an Olympic record.[99]

Three Components of a Vision

Sashkin believed that a vision for an organization generally involves one or more of the following three elements: change, goals, or people.[100] These three areas provide leaders with the latitude to develop clear and transferrable visions that can be integrated within virtually any unit of an organization and at a variety of hierarchical levels. He bases this assertion on both theoretical and pragmatic findings. Talcott Parsons noted long ago that successful, sustainable organizations stay focused in four visionary areas: (a) managing change, (b) attaining goals, (c) customer orientation, and (d) coordinating teamwork.[101] Sashkin concurred and wrote eloquently on this perspective. He also incorporated the work of others[102] who studied successful organizations and concluded that highly effective organizations (a) engage in entrepreneurial orientations, (b) keenly focus on the customer, and (c) genuinely care about and value their people. Let's turn our attention to the specific areas of change, goals, and people.

Focus on Change

Vision is the art of seeing things invisible.
—JONATHAN SWIFT

To illustrate a CEO envisioning in the area of change, Sashkin[103] cited the examples of three successful industry leaders, Ray Kroc

(McDonald's), Frank Purdue (Purdue Chicken), and Jan Carlzon (Scandinavian Airline Systems—SAS). Each of these successful CEOs created visions that had a change orientation and serve as the hallmark for their respective organizations. Current examples might include Tim Cook at Apple, Jeff Bezos at Amazon, Elon Musk of SpaceX, or Nick Saban at the University of Alabama. All four of these innovators have clear visions that drive their unit's strategy and facilitate sustainable levels of success far above their competitors. History has provided us with innovative leaders who changed their industries. Let's take a look at some of these game-changers.

The late Ray Kroc transformed McDonald's restaurants on the belief that customers wanted an affordable, fast, consistent product. His focus on the area of consistency has become legendary. It was his belief that the McDonald's product and experience should be consistent, regardless of the location of the restaurants—be it in Moscow or Montreal. As a result, it is the "absence of change" that distinguished Kroc's vision. This vision trickled down to each vice president, through to each regional supervisor, to each restaurant manager, to each shift supervisor, and finally and most importantly, to each employee. The establishment of McDonald's University to educate employees on the importance of quality, cleanliness, and consistency is further testimony to how McDonald's continues to implement Kroc's vision for quality, cleanliness, and consistency.

Frank Purdue did the same for the chicken industry. He had a vision of change for his chicken business. He believed that quality had no limits, and he wanted his organization to be the best in the field. Who doesn't? However, he delivered on his vision of continual improvement and innovation, designed to produce higher-quality chickens to satisfy the consumer. Purdue and his team of leaders focused staff members at every level on this common aim. Purdue's success in the chicken business was unparalleled, in spite of rising competition.

The example of Jan Carlzon from SAS is equally convincing. Carlzon believed that providing passengers with greater reason for being satisfied was the ultimate aim of SAS Airlines, a vision he suggests is common with all players in the airline industry. He had a vision of SAS actually delivering this vision. He believed that customers needed to be satisfied and all employees could and should go out of their way to satisfy consumers. His vision for SAS Airlines involved changing the approach that people brought to their positions to one that was focused on customer satisfaction.

My favorite Canadian prime minister is the late Pierre Elliot Trudeau (father of Canada's current prime minister, Justin Trudeau). Justin seems to share his father's vision for a caring, inclusive country that also makes a difference on the world stage. They also appear to share a charismatic leadership style for communicating the vision to stakeholders, and through their words and actions, inspiring stakeholders to help make the vision a reality.

The history books tell us that Trudeau was elected the fifteenth prime minister of Canada in 1968, largely on the shoulders of his vision of a "just society" for all Canadians. He believed that Canadians could and should be afforded a quality existence, regardless of their geographic roots or economic status. He championed the creation of the nation's Charter of Rights and Freedoms, a document that underscores the social fabric of the country. He was committed to the vision of Canada being a bilingual country with a metric measurement system that supported an international relevance. Finally, he believed that Canada had a role to play in changing the world, certainly not through the military power of its armies, but more accurately, through its example, the culture of its people, and the ideals of the Canadian populace. His notion of a just society, while having its roots in Canada, was a concept that Trudeau held as an agenda for the world. His activities on a world stage, specifically in meetings with the other national leaders, confirmed his commitment to this vision. His vision of language and economic equality as reflected in his "just society" was readily embraced by Canadians, given his meteoric rise and longevity in the Canadian political arena.

His opinions were not universally embraced. He needed to take strong stands on issues that ran counter to his visions—including his

National Energy Program that alienated many Canadians from the oil-rich western provinces. His stand against separatism alienated many from the province of Quebec. On both issues, Trudeau was standing up for a strong, united Canada, where citizens helped one another. No one could ever argue that Trudeau did not hold a clear vision for Canada. His policies and actions never deviated from this vision, even when faced with adversity.

It could be successfully argued that Donna Lopiano has done more for women's visibility and rights in sports than any other individual. Her rejection from male sports teams at a young age manifested itself into a desire not to allow that to happen to other young women. Her athletic career was distinguished and inundated with awards and championships. She participated in twenty-six national championships in four sports: softball, basketball, volleyball, and field hockey. Later she served as the director of intercollegiate athletics for women at the University of Texas at Austin. More recently, Dr. Lopiano has served as executive director of the Women's Sports Foundation, where she has been instrumental in creating more opportunities for female athletes and specifically ensuring that United States–based institutions of higher learning that receive federal funding comply with Title IX legislation. As an advocate of equal opportunity and access for female athletes, she has demonstrated her leadership talents as well as her courage. She made a difference by ensuring that the integrity of the legislation surrounding Title IX was adhered to, and she tackled the pro-male college sports enthusiasts with equal or greater determination and preparation. Her personal mission remains the equal treatment of female athletes and administrators and the advancement of the female sports agenda.

> Courage is the virtue that facilitates all others.
> —GREEK PARABLE

Lopiano was a game-changer. She was the preeminent leader and spokesperson on Title IX legislation and women's sports in the United

States. She is an interesting and captivating speaker who continues to garner high praise for her tireless efforts and philosophical views.

Effective leaders continuously talk in terms of vision. They reinforce the key and critical aspects of the vision in an effort to draw others into the fold. Jack Welch, former CEO of General Electric, wanted a company full of vibrant and creative people who were continually excited by the challenges and opportunities available from the work experience. He would state that "Ten years from now, we want magazines to write about GE as the place where people have the freedom to be creative, a place that brings out the best in everybody. An open, fair place where people have a sense that what they do matters, and where that sense of accomplishment is rewarded in both the pocketbook and the soul."[104]

Dee Hock, chief executive officer of Visa International, believed that the banking industry had lost touch with their customers.[105] Consequently, he developed a vision that allowed Visa cardholders to access their banks through electronic transactions at any time on any day. He believed that people would enjoy this level of customer service and support. Although many struggled with and lacked trust in the concept initially, most people today appreciate and fully utilize this service. Other credit card companies and financial institutions have followed the lead of Visa in an effort to better serve their clients.

The late Steve Jobs's clairvoyance and vision about where personal computing was headed drove innovation at Apple. His vision for unbounded innovation is embedded into the culture of the organization. It is evident in the creative leadership of the current CEO Tim Clark and lives in the DNA of the company.

Now, think about the impact of contemporary leaders. Think about the creative genius of Jeff Bezos. His creative leadership, his understanding of people, and the power of technology have been coupled into the company we know as Amazon. This company disrupted and revolutionized the area of retail marketing—and many brick-and-mortar shopping centers felt the effects. Mark Zuckerberg's clairvoyant vision for what social networking might become resulted in his creation of Facebook. Don't be fooled by his casual dress and informal leadership style. He is a strong and fearless leader committed to personal and professional growth. He challenges members of his leadership team to push the boundaries of innovation. He models personal and professional development. His leadership style is embedded in the culture of Facebook.

Innovation and technological brilliance also form the leadership style of Elon Musk, a leader who has pushed and continues to push the boundaries of innovation with game-changing companies like Tesla, SpaceX, and formerly PayPal. Musk challenges himself and those around him to think differently. Disruptive innovation is at the heart of his leadership style. It works!

Focus on Goals

If you don't know where you are going, any road will do.

—LEWIS CARROLL

Effective CEOs also incorporate goals statements into the vision as a tangible and powerful means of measuring progress and determining if corrective action is required. Bezos, Musk, and Zuckerberg continue to push the limits in their industries, and their stories are not yet complete. It is easier to study the focus and end results of leaders whose body of work is more complete. For example, Kroc's vision of a consistent food product, served in a clean and welcoming environment, was operationalized in the form of goals that will allow stakeholders to gauge performance relative to the goals and vision for the organization. Stakeholders know what is being measured and therefore know what is important. Staff recognition events add further emphasis on what is important. Phil Knight's insistence that Nike employees "experience the emotion of competition, winning, and crushing competitors"[106] remains the prime focus for his maverick and highly successful company. Offering higher-quality (plumper, yellower) chickens remains the goal of employees of Purdue. Having customers report higher levels of satisfaction with all operational aspects remains a goal of Scandinavian Airlines Systems. Being a leader in product innovation around customer wants, needs, and desires remains an ambition of Visa.

This theme is particularly prophetic when it comes to ensuring a vision for a group or organization. People need a sense of direction. They need to know that they are not spinning their wheels and that they are making progress toward the attainment of their personal or group goals.

On an individual level, the waste of energy and unrealized potential is limited to a personal level. However, the effect is multiplied when the collective energy and efforts of members of a group or organization are not focused or channeled. This is the area where effective leaders pay handsome dividends. "A strong sense of purpose, a passion, a conviction, a sense of wanting to do something important to make a difference—that is what makes every true leader."[107]

Focus on People

The final piece of the vision puzzle focuses on people. Sashkin noted that both the customers and staff members are essential components of an organization, and as such, need to be integrated into the vision of the organization. Without satisfied customers, the organization will undoubtedly become a fading memory. Staff members must be focused on the needs, wants, and desires of customers and attempt to do all they can to build a reputation for satisfying this important group.

The people who create and/or deliver the products or services are the staff members. If they do not feel valued or if they feel that their role in the operation is so trivial that they can shirk their responsibilities, the product or service (or its delivery) will not be at the optimal level. This important group of people must be made aware of, engage in, and adopt a sense of ownership for the vision of the organization. In order for the vision to be widely shared, all executives and staff members need to be aware of the vision. If the vision is to be implemented with success, the majority (if not all) of the executives and employees need to adopt a sense of ownership for the vision. They need to see how and where it applies to them and the carrying out of their activities. They need to genuinely believe in the vision and be committed to acting on the vision through their contributions to the organization. A lack of awareness or a lack of acceptance of the vision will unquestionably impact customer satisfaction and, if not corrected, ultimately lead to the demise of the organization. Leaders must therefore ensure that their vision is oriented toward people—both to the customer and to their staff members.

How Visions Translate to Action

Visions remain a theoretical, intangible creation of the leader unless they are transferred to value statements, integrated into the culture (see C5—Culture Builder) of the organization, charismatically communicated to all members of the organization (see C3—Charismatic Communicator section), and committed to paper. These values must be widely shared and embraced by the majority (if not all) members of an organization if they are going to be effectively translated into routine activities. The words and actions of leaders, as well as the opportunity for allowing followers to help shape these stated values, will go a long way to determining the degree that these values are adopted, integrated into daily activities, and maintained over time.

Some have suggested that North American companies have been reluctant in the past to engage in this activity, in comparison to many Japanese companies that have historically given more credence to the importance of the exercise.[108] Visions must be transferred from the intangible to the tangible. They must take the form of organizational values or philosophy. They need to be created, widely discussed, and eventually committed to paper in the form of a vision statement.

Vision statements must be clear, directional, and broad enough to encompass all organizational members—from the highest-ranking CEO to the lowest person in the organizational hierarchy. Perhaps the best example of such a vision statement comes from the Disney Corporation and their mission statement "to make people happy." All employees at Disney know this philosophy and can see its application in their personal work and in the way they interact with customers. It certainly works for that successful company. It is baked into the comprehensive orientation programs for new employees and reinforced in the culture of the organization.[109]

Vision statements provide clarity, uniformity, and meaning to personal and organizational activities. They are interested in uncovering the existing values and beliefs of people who make up the organization. The collective beliefs and attitudes shape the culture of the organization (see C5—Culture Builder section), and this culture helps define and shape the behavior of people in the organization.

Once the organizational values are clearly stated and widely shared, organizational leaders must then turn their attention to the implementation of action steps that align with the stated values. For example, the addition of a customer service unit may be required if the organizational values highlight customer satisfaction as one of its primary values. This may cost money; however, it is a *critical incident* for the leader, and it transpires at a time when the leader can clearly demonstrate to organizational members how committed he or she is to the stated values of the organization. If the values are well conceived and consistent with the attainment of the organizational objectives, the long-term payoff will be worth the initial investment.

One of my mentors, Richard Peddie, the former president and CEO of Maple Leaf Sports & Entertainment, was highly successful in the industry. He stayed current in his industry *and* in the leadership literature. He remains a voracious reader and, of late, writer in the leadership area. His most recent leadership text underscores the centrality of vision to his leadership practices—and the commensurate impact on his organization. He continually talked about "vision and values," and he proudly and truthfully noted that the short, inspirational vision statement could be recited by employees throughout the organization. He stated as well that the vision statement provided direction to the organization, guided decision-making, and was a source of inspiration for stakeholders in good times and bad. I couldn't agree more.

Peddie believed strongly that the vision has to cascade deep into the unit or organization. He shared this with my graduate students each year during class visits to his organization. He also wrote about this eloquently in his latest book.[110] The vision statement for Maple Leaf Sports & Entertainment didn't waver during his fourteen-year tenure as the president and CEO of the company. Visions can't fluctuate in response to fads or anticipated trends. No, a vision and values statement must be the bedrock of the unit or organization and something that is embraced and reinforced on a regular basis.

> Vision without action is just a hallucination.
> —THOMAS EDISON

Summary

Having a compelling vision that stakeholders help shape, recognize, adopt, and commit to realizing is an essential component of Five C Leadership and consistent with most of the contemporary leadership theories. Credibility (C1) is a precursor to being a leader. However, one does not become a leader until a vision is introduced to focus and align members of a group or organization to a goal. The spirit of this concept is inherent in most definitions of leadership (i.e., influence others toward the attainment of a predetermined goal or objective). A compelling vision focuses members of a group or organization and helps communicate to them that their efforts are required and will not be wasted toward the attainment of the vision. It provides a tangible target to rally others around.

This chapter provided readers with the information relative to the importance of a compelling vision to the leadership process, as well as helpful advice on developing a vision. Examples of people like Ray Kroc, Mark Zuckerberg, Jeff Bezos, Elon Musk, Frank Purdue, and Steve Jobs were offered as leaders who created and transformed their industries. The three components of a vision were also discussed, as was the need to involve people in the development and transmission of the vision to secure a greater sense of ownership for those charged with making it a reality. The following chapters of the book highlight other areas that will help leaders become more effective in communicating a vision to followers and inspiring them to make the attainment of the vision a reality on a long-term basis.

> Obstacles are things a person sees when he takes his eyes off his goal.
>
> —E. JOSEPH COSSMAN

C3—Charismatic Communicator

A Reader's Guide

Upon reading this chapter, readers will understand

- the concept of charisma and its linkage to leadership,
- examples of charismatic leaders,
- the components of charisma,
- how charisma is reflected in a leader's verbal and nonverbal communications,
- the powerful link between emotional intelligence and leadership, and
- how leaders can heighten their charismatic attributes.

C3—Charismatic Communicator

In the companies where I have studied leadership, I have seen remarkable differences in the levels of creativity, motivation, commitment, and even personal zeal that the subordinates of charismatic leaders bring to their work.[111]

It is clear to leadership scholars of the day that the trait theories of leadership were prematurely discounted. The methodological shortcomings and narrow conceptualizations held by leadership theorists of the 1930s and '40s led to the discounting of the trait theory of leadership and prompted researchers to consider first the leadership behavior components, followed by a focus on the situational elements of leadership. Stogdill's later studies (1948—1974) confirmed his initial contention that specific traits were important to the leadership process.[112] However, it was too late for many leadership theorists who pursued other avenues, namely the behavioral and situational aspects of leaders. Proverbially speaking, perhaps the baby was thrown out with the bathwater.

Long ago, leadership scholars noted that leaders had a special ability to captivate their groups. In recent days, leadership scholars[113] suggest that these leaders were charismatic, or more specifically, charismatic communicators. However, keep in mind that leadership scholars[114] in the 1940s were stating that a leader's words and actions inspired followers.

Prolific scholar Howard Gardner has made a number of exceptional contributions to the social science areas (e.g., multiple intelligences), including an entry into the leadership area (his *Leading Minds: The Anatomy of Leadership* book). Leadership guru Warren Bennis offered high praise for Gardner's text by noting in the *Harvard Business Review* (1996) that Gardner's book is more than just another addition to an already-crowded market, but more accurately, Gardner's book will go down as a classic contribution to the field. Gardner has brought an interesting background to the leadership field. He has pioneered a research program that produced landmark findings in the areas of creativity and multiple intelligences. He entered the fray of leadership with a fresh paradigm as to what makes leaders effective. Needless to say, his earlier work in the creativity and intelligence areas influenced his thinking in the leadership area and provided a fresh perspective to a heavily analyzed area of study.

Gardner suggests that leaders must play the leadership part. They must think, act, and talk like leaders. It is what followers expect from leaders. It helps people extend their credibility as leaders. Harvard professor and leadership expert Amy Cuddy agrees. Cuddy writes and speaks extensively on the importance of body language and how leaders can heighten their impact by adopting some of her practices (spreading their arms, making themselves larger, taking up more space).[115]

Gardner noted that leaders can build on this credibility and advance their leadership capacity to lead. Another of the central themes that Gardner extols is the importance of leaders capturing the attention of their followers, especially through the use of storytelling. He suggested that effective leaders—from Martin Luther King Jr. to Mahatma Gandhi—verbally, behaviorally, or symbolically moved followers by sharing stories that had an underlying purpose to influence. He offered that "perhaps the key to leadership, as well as to the garnering of a following, is the effective communication of a story."[116] Effectively turning stories into learning opportunities requires a charismatic appeal to capture the attention of people and provide them with the opportunity to learn. Heightened charismatic and communication skills are essential elements to the task of sharing a story and presenting a learning opportunity.

> The first step to being a leader is to start thinking, acting, and talking like one.
>
> —AMY GALLO

Think of leaders and their exceptional communication skills, and former leaders of countries often come to mind. Consider the example of Winston Churchill's incomparable command of the language. Be mindful of Pierre Elliot Trudeau's ability to turn a phrase to drive home a point. Ponder the storytelling examples of Ronald Reagan, whose words and actions charismatically captured the attention of followers and reinforced his perspectives and priorities. More recent examples come in the form of Barack Obama and before him Bill Clinton, whose legendary speeches underscored their personal gifts as skilled orators. Their voluminous command of the language, their effective use of pauses, voice, inflections, and hand gestures are all noteworthy. They make eye contact with people. They make effective use of pauses in their delivery. They are captivating, charismatic orators and skilled communicators. When speaking to large groups, they move around the room with their eyes, and at times their bodies engage people in the process who are left thinking that they were talking to them on a personal level. They are so captivating that they can be speaking to thousands of people and many would state after that they could hear a pin drop during the speech. They have a gift for communication and speak the language of leadership. They are prime examples of C3 leaders who are charismatic communicators.

> The heart of leadership is making other people better.
> —TIM KIGHT

A plethora of leadership writers[117] suggested that these individuals have charisma. They noted that these effective leaders have a predisposition for influencing others (i.e., charisma). They cite leaders from a multitude of fields like Ronald Reagan, Lee Iacocca, Mary Kay Ash, Barack Obama, Bill Clinton, Martin Luther King Jr., and Justin Trudeau as examples of charismatic communicators. They also list people like Lyndon Johnson, Jimmy Carter, John Major, and George Bush (Senior and Junior) as examples of people whose lack of charisma impacted their effectiveness and popularity in their leadership roles.

Leadership transitions often provide the best examples of the importance of charisma to leadership. History books provide us crystal-clear examples of charismatic leaders and their impact, compared to leaders who lacked in this critical area. For example, the charismatic appeal that John F. Kennedy had in comparison to his successor, Lyndon B. Johnson, is a blue-ribbon indicator of the advantage that a charismatic person holds over someone who is not charismatic in a leadership role. Kennedy has a demigod leadership reputation to this day—many years after his death. Conversely, Johnson had the image of a country bumpkin who filled the office of the president of the United States. He did not have the image of a charismatic leader. Some researchers have noted that " Lyndon B. Johnson emphasized his 'just plain folks' background and ability, yet managed to propose and succeed with more administrative and legislative actions than John F. Kennedy" and that Kennedy was "generally perceived as a highly gifted person, and one with whom the American public formed a strong, deep, emotional attachment."[118] Both had good ideas. Objectively analyzing the situation, Johnson may have been the better president. However, Kennedy's charismatic appeal and specifically his ability to effectively communicate his ideas in a charismatic fashion set him apart and afforded him this lofty perception.

An equally compelling case study on the importance of charisma to leadership comes in the example of former United States president Ronald Reagan. Reagan was very charismatic. His acting background served him well in politics. In spite of his famous laissez-faire leadership style, Reagan had a very high popularity rating. The late speaker of the house Tip O'Neill often referred to Reagan as the least-informed president that he'd ever encountered. Any tangible measure of his effectiveness as a leader of a country was low. For example, environmental problems were escalating; social problems like increased poverty, crime, and illegal drug use were well out of control. The deficit was climbing to an unprecedented figure, and the country's education programs were experiencing high dropout rates, producing graduates of limited capacities and skills, to say nothing of the high proportion of the population who might be accurately labeled illiterate. Certainly the country was in worse shape after his tenure than it was prior to his taking office in 1980. However, when he vacated the office of the president of the United States in 1988, he left with one of history's highest popularity ratings.

The late, charismatic Pierre Elliot Trudeau left the prime minister's office in 1984 after a sixteen-year reign. Many Canadians believe that he remains the greatest prime minister in the history of Canada, largely due to his vision and his ability to articulate it charismatically. He took unpopular positions on matters of national interest, but his magnetic personality, coupled with his vast command of the language and heightened oratory skills, assisted him in advancing his positions. These critical incidents helped elevate him as a natural leader in the eyes of many. Obviously, charisma makes a difference!

While it is one thing to be a charismatic individual, it is quite another to be a charismatic leader. The other aspects of leadership (such as vision) have to be part of the package. However, charisma cannot be considered a vital component of the leadership concept unless it is also packaged with a predetermined goal or vision for the organization, subunit, or group of individuals. Lee Iacocca's reign at Chrysler serves as an effective example of an individual coupling charisma with a vision. He personified the underdog, taking over a company in financial and spiritual ruins, and transforming it into a viable and successful enterprise. On the day he assumed leadership for the company, it reported its greatest quarterly loss.[119] It was a company steeped in tradition and overcrowded with bureaucracy. Thirty-three of thirty-five vice presidents were removed when Iacocca determined that the company could be leaner and more responsive to change by eliminating unnecessary administrative networks. He downsized the organization to the level required to make it cost efficient, letting people and peripheral businesses owned by Chrysler go in the process. In five years, he transformed Chrysler from a hopeless, disjointed, overly bureaucratic nightmare to a profitable leader in the industry, generating the largest profit in company history of $925 million.[120] He broke traditions. He refused to accept the time-honored practices of the corporation. He provided fresh, charismatically communicated ideals that members of the Chrysler community accepted and felt challenged to obtain. He also engaged in other symbolic acts that heightened his charismatic appeal.

> He dropped his salary to one dollar, obtained massive government-backed loans, introduced money-back guarantees on cars, brought union representation onto the board, appeared in advertisements featuring Chrysler products. All were highly unconventional actions for the automobile industry, yet ultimately they were effective tactics for revitalizing Chrysler.[121]

His "if you can find a better car—buy it," and "we borrow money the old-fashioned way—we pay it back" statements helped solidify his charismatic style and unfailing belief in his vision for Chrysler and the people who would work to make it a reality. Most everyone got caught up in the movement and vision to resurrect Chrysler from near extinction and elevate it to a position of leadership within the automotive industry.

Charisma is important to the field of leadership and specifically, being a charismatic communicator has a major role in leadership, and as such is presented as one of the Five Cs of Leadership.

What Is Charisma?

The term "charisma" was derived from the Greek translation of *gift*. Charisma refers to the special personal attributes that people perceive in another individual and govern the social relationship that develops between the two people. According to the acclaimed writings of Max Weber (1886–1920), the German sociologist credited with labeling and advancing the concept of charisma, these highly esteemed individuals are perceived to be gifted with divine-like qualities that result in a magnetic attraction between people. Weber believed that these individuals portray heightened levels of confidence, offer a clear idea and a path toward a better future for followers, and provide people, particularly those seeking innovative or better solutions or focus, a sense of purpose and fulfillment. Every leadership writer of the day owes an intellectual debt of gratitude to Weber for his work on charisma.[122] His concept of charisma is in the DNA of contemporary leadership theories and support elements like focus, inspiration, respect, and risk-taking. Some researchers have noted that a charismatic leader has the capacity to heighten feelings of confidence, affiliation, determination, and identification within followers—all precursors to the leadership process.[123]

Your time on earth is limited, so don't waste it living someone else's life.

Don't let the noise of others' opinions drown out your inner voice.

Follow your heart and your intuition.
—STEVE JOBS'S MESSAGE TO THE GRADUATES
AT THE 2005 CONVOCATION CEREMONY
AT STANFORD UNIVERSITY

A considerable number of contemporary leadership writers include "charisma" as a major component of their leadership theories. Most writers comment on these leaders possessing: (a) high esteem and self-confidence, (b) a dominant personality, (c) a keen sense of purpose, and (d) the ability to clearly articulate the goals and necessary action steps in a manner that followers are psychologically prepared to adopt as their own. Some researchers have noted that charisma is "the most general and important component of his conceptualization of transformational leadership, and because it is a piece of the puzzle, he rendered the label charismatic leader incomplete."[124] Don't be misled. Charismatic leaders are not limited to world leaders or captains of industry. Some occupying these roles are charismatic, and some are not. In fact, charismatic leaders can be found in many types of organizations and differing situations. They are found at all hierarchical levels.

Charismatic leaders often emerge in a time of crisis (e.g., Rudy Giuliani and his leadership in the aftermath of the 9/11 tragedy in New York City; Barack Obama's economic recovery in response to the financial crisis in 2009; Justin Trudeau's vision for a more compassionate Canada that welcomed refugees in time of turmoil in their home countries). In these difficult times, effective leaders project an alternative way forward, and clear rationale for why this approach is the right one, and a plan for making it a reality. Followers experiencing psychological distress due to these circumstances are often more susceptible to the charismatic leader who appears to have answers for a better tomorrow. The gift-like qualities and magnetic personalities of these charismatic leaders tend to be highlighted in these times, compounding the degree of influence they are able to hold over other people. The youthful, vibrant, charismatic attributes of John F. Kennedy live on, many years after his assassination. His legend will continue to live on, being passed down from one generation to the next.

Charismatic leaders often emerge in response to crises that help pave the way for their message of a better, more just tomorrow. Followers get caught up in the rush of support for the leader and the vision, compounding the charismatic qualities attributed to the leader. These leaders are "seen as prospective saviors, who by their magical endowments, will fulfill the unmet emotional needs of their completely trusting, overly dependent, and submissive followers."[125] Other examples include Martin Luther King's nonviolent protests of the oppression and discrimination facing black Americans in the early and mid-1960s. His vision, consistent with the approach of Thoreau and Gandhi, was effective. He effectively convinced politicians and the overwhelming majority of citizens that change was required. The principles of fairness and equity must be embraced. He emerged at a critical point in time when sufficient numbers in society felt it to be important to lift the oppression facing the black population. He drew others to his views through his charismatic and symbolic actions. For example, in response to the violence he faced in an effort to register voters in Selma, Alabama, he organized and led a five-day march to Montgomery, Alabama. This walk highlighted the degree of conviction that he and his followers had for equal-rights legislation and the degree of hardship that they would endure in the quest for securing justice and equality for all.

In a similar vein, but specifically to focus attention on the living conditions of many black citizens, King moved his headquarters to an apartment in a Chicago slum. This move also attracted attention from the various media sources and highlighted his efforts for racial equality. King's charismatic rating escalated as a result of both symbolic actions.

Charismatic leaders engage their followers in a number of ways. Researchers[126] have suggested that certain leadership behaviors reinforce the charismatic qualities in a leader and help reinforce the bond that followers have for leaders. Specifically, they noted that the following five aspects (futuristic vision, willingness to take calculated risks, supportive, confident, and open to other possibilities) help to embed a charismatic quality for leaders:

1. **Futuristic Vision**—Often in the form of a novel idea or direction that breaks with tradition and highlights the need for followers to be committed to making it happen. Followers view the current situation as stagnant, nonprogressive, and insufferable, and seek a brighter, more prosperous future that is inspirationally presented to them by the leader in the form of a vision.[127] Consequently, these people often emerge in times of crisis. Followers hold considerable confidence that the leader and the vision will improve the followers' current situation. Readers are encouraged to review the content and examples of visionary leaders in the C2—Compelling Vision chapter.

2. **Willingness to Take Calculated Risks**—The type that puts the leader in some jeopardy, yet the leader is willing to assume this level of risk. Leaders need to take risks by putting their vision in public view. While it takes courage to do this, taking a stand on issues may inspire followers to align with the plan and produce the desired outcomes. Some suggested that "the benefits gained from taking risks inherent in opening oneself to others appear to be a greater degree of personal empowerment, an important requisite for empowering others."[128] Leaders are willing to break free of the status quo and assume challenging goals for the group. They know what people in the organization can and want to assume and they are willing to put their necks on the line for them. They extend

the credit for successful attainment of the goal to the people who are responsible for the attainment, and they will assume blame if things do not work out. They take responsibility for the group's success and are not ego driven to assume all the credit when it is doled out at the end of the day. Some have suggested that the charismatic leader, specifically those from the business realm, must be

> part prophet, part hero. He or she has a "vision" which alters the audience's expectations about risk. The deeds of the leader turn parts of the audience into followers who accept that only through obedience can a new vision be realized.[129]

These leaders have the charismatic qualities to alter and excite their followers to a far-reaching task and challenge and commit them to making it a reality.

> The only thing that limits our realization of tomorrow will be our doubts of today
> —FRANKLIN DELANO ROOSEVELT

3. Supportive—Genuine concern for the well-being of followers. These people perceive this quality and believe that leaders have their best interests at heart. However, it is not to say that these leaders are easy on their people. Leaders could increase their charismatic standing by holding challenging performance expectations for followers. "Ideally, the dependency and affection between top leaders and their followers binds them in a transforming relationship."[130] Leaders who genuinely care for those they lead are plentiful, but perhaps the best examples are leaders like Herb Kelleher (Southwest Airlines) and Allan Mulally (Boeing and Ford). They went out of their way to demonstrate their concern for people. In spite of the fact that they led large organizations and had all of the commensurate pressures and demands on their time, these leaders, and others like them, routinely did all they could to demonstrate a genuine caring for their people.

Leaders genuinely care about their members. It helps built a powerful level of trust and commitment among followers. This concept has been effectively captured in the emotional intelligence and leadership area noted in the next section of this chapter.

4.   Confident—These leaders project a confident image. They are committed to making the vision a reality and exude such confidence that followers genuinely believe that the leader can orchestrate the successful attainment of the vision. Smaller successes along the way help embed the charismatic attributions that people hold for the leader and instill greater levels of confidence in the leader and the vision. Leaders help embed a charismatic presence by setting a personal example consistent with the vision and the behaviors required to make it a reality (e.g., high energy, honesty, commitment, trust). In addition, a leader appears to be more charismatic in the eyes of followers when they genuinely express the highest degrees of confidence in followers and their abilities to make the vision a reality.

> Whether you think you can or think you can't—you are right.
> —HENRY FORD

5.   Open to Other Possibilities—Leaders don't necessarily do things by the book. As noted earlier, they "do the right thing— not do things right." They sometimes break with conventional wisdom. They often float a new idea or perspective that others embrace and commit to making a reality. They excite followers and thus further enrich their charismatic presence by focusing on long-range challenges rather than the day-to-day problems confronting an organization or group. In fact, once leaders begin to operate in a bureaucratic fashion (i.e., hold up policy manuals to interpret situations, continually refer to past methods as the only way forward, or are resistant to new ideas), their charismatic appeal wanes considerably.

> Management is efficiency in climbing the ladder of success; leadership determines whether the ladder is leaning against the right wall.
>
> —STEPHEN R. COVEY

Perhaps one of the best examples of a nonconformist organizational leader is the late Sam Walton, founder of Wal-Mart. His reputation as an unconventional and charismatic CEO was legendary. His chain of department stores was founded on the theme of heightened product quality and superb customer service. He believed that being smaller and less bureaucratic was critical to stimulating innovation and overcoming inertia. His chain of stores regularly outperformed many competitors because of this philosophy.

Walton believed in the personal touch to business, and his approach is reflected in each employee of the corporation. Personal service, commitment to the customer, and a friendly atmosphere typify each of his stores.[131] Walton prided himself in personally visiting each store once per year, a tremendous feat given the number of stores and their geographic disparity. Rather than sitting behind his desk pushing paper, Walton insisted on being in the stores, telling staff members that he cared for them, and reinforcing their role in maintaining and furthering his commitment to customer service.

> Wal-Mart, under Sam Walton's direction, had only four layers of employment, from the chairman's office to the cashier. Sears had twelve layers. A new product idea would come to the attention of Wal-Mart, and they could get it out in thirty days. Sears would probably still be forming a committee.[132]

Weber noted that charismatic leaders must continually offer evidence of their charismatic qualities. These people are perceived to be special and as such must offer novel ways to bring about change and demonstrate their extraordinary abilities and characteristics (have vision, will take risks, support others, have confidence in others, aren't overly bureaucratic). Slipping in the areas outlined above destroys the charismatic attributes that followers bestow upon leaders. Like credibility, it takes a considerable amount of time to gain a charismatic reputation and a single behavior or incident to alter follower perception.

Recently, researchers have been writing on the topic of emotional intelligence and leadership. This concept has tremendous implications for effective leadership, and in many ways, may help to explain how leaders built trust and commitment as well as heighten their charismatic standing with those they lead.

Emotional Intelligence and Leadership

The best leaders understand the role that emotions play in the leadership process.[133] Some suggest that emotional intelligence separates great leaders from their counterparts.[134] They set the mood for members of their team. Consistent with the theoretical principles of servant leadership, they know that leaders have the best interests of those they lead in the forefront. They have genuine interest in their members. They seek members' opinions. They get to know their members (and their families). They build powerful relationships that are foundational to authentic leadership. They are considered emotionally intelligent leaders. This type of leader appears to let go of power, appears vulnerable at times, and focuses largely on the emotional needs of their members. This approach to leadership may appear to be counterintuitive to those who hold an outdated perspective that leaders must be strong-willed, driven individuals who command and control their followers. Emotionally intelligent leaders ask and inspire followers, rather than direct them. They are self-confident, committed leaders who are sensitive to their own emotional needs as well as those of their members. They understand the role that emotions play in relationship building and leadership. They work hard to build strong, trusting relationships with stakeholders. They awaken and arouse curiosities. They heighten their levels of commitment. They channel the energies of followers to collective achievements. Leaders operating from this base know that "emotions are powerful drivers of their people's moods, and ultimately, performance."[135] Leaders must be aware of their emotions and recognize the impact of their words and actions on others. They must be able to maintain their composure and listen empathetically to the needs, wants, and desires of their followers. They must be clear and honest in all their interactions. This is hard work, but the benefits are worth the investment.

I recall a number of situations in my career where I had the opportunity to truly demonstrate my care for members of my group and build my emotional intelligence standing. These stories get passed on—and my ability to lead gets increased at every turn. I recall one situation where a new mother on my staff was concerned about her son who had contracted a severe case of the measles. This was her first child, and I caught her crying at her desk during one of my walk-around tours. She confided in me that she could only think of her child and his condition at this time. I agreed and gave her the balance of the day off to care for him. She has mentioned her appreciation of this gesture to me countless times. She became one of the most committed employees in the unit. She routinely and quickly volunteers to help out after hours and frequently went above and beyond the call of duty to make our organization stronger. Her commitment was infectious. In doing the right thing, we energized an employee (and workforce), and her commitment (and that of her colleagues) soared.

I recently stumbled on a letter that Joe Biden, the former vice president of the United States, circulated to his staff. Biden has endured significant personal loss in his life. He lost his wife and two children in an automobile accident and more recently lost a son to cancer.

These losses help provide some context to his instructions to his staff. Biden personifies an emotional intelligent leader. I can't imagine the commitment and energy that his staff members bring to their roles, knowing their leader cares so much about them.

MEMORANDUM TO STAFF OF THE VICE PRESDIENT
FROM: VICE PRESIDENT BIDEN

RE: FAMILY OBLIGATIONS

DATE: NOVEMBER 7, 2014

To My Wonderful Staff,

I would like to take a moment to make something clear to everyone. I do not expect nor do I want any of you to miss or sacrifice important family obligations for work. Family obligations include but are not limited to family birthdays, anniversaries, weddings, any religious ceremony such as the first communions and bar mitzvahs, graduations, and times of need such as an illness or a loss in the family. This is very important to me. In fact, I will go as far as to say that if I find out that you are working with me while missing important family responsibilities that it will disappoint me greatly. This has been an unwritten rule since my days in the Senate.

Thank you for the hard work.

Sincerely,

Joe

Charisma can be initially attributed to individuals on the basis of their title, office, or celebrity status (e.g., sports figure, movie star). These attributions afford these people a higher starting point; however, followers will soon begin to make assessments of their charismatic qualities on the basis of what they personally see, hear, and experience.

Leaders can do things to heighten their charismatic standing in the eyes of those they lead. (See the "Heightening Charismatic Attributes" section of this chapter.) Leaders can build their charismatic standing, and followers bond with a charismatic leader.[136] Members of a group or organization bond to charismatic individuals on the basis of their special attributes. Because of perceived traits and behaviors, these charismatic individuals are in an advantageous position to lead others. Followers generally have intense feelings for the C3 leader.[137] In the final analysis, charisma refers to the "leader's ability to articulate a captivating vision, to inspire and encourage higher-order effort on the part of followers, and to instill respect, faith, loyalty, and trust in the leader."[138]

Charisma and Communication

Charisma is a difficult concept to pinpoint. However, there have been some similarities in the writings of scholars on both the charisma and leadership areas. For the most part, charisma is reflected in leaders' communication habits—their words, actions, or interpretations of their actions. Some have suggested that "charismatic leaders are likely to display high levels of emotional expressiveness, self-confidence, self-determination, and freedom from internal conflicts."[139] The stirring speeches of noted charismatic leaders like Martin Luther King Jr. and John F. Kennedy are prime examples. Many believe that their emotion and delivery were as effective as their actual words. Listeners continue to be moved by taped renditions of their passionate addresses.

Others[140] have suggested that charismatic leaders have advanced levels of self-confidence. They have strong convictions for what they want to accomplish, along with a plan for making the vision a reality. Charismatic leaders have a strong need to influence others—to be in control. This need manifests itself as leaders are given an opportunity to influence others, attain minor successes, and consequently, greater numbers of people are drawn by the leader's rapidly growing charismatic appeal.

Charisma is a difficult concept to grasp. It is a perceptual phenomenon that others attribute to an individual. A review of the charismatic literature uncovered a list of seven components that appear in many of the writings on charisma. These elements appear below along with a discussion of the factor as it relates to charismatic leadership.

1. Power of Persuasion—Charismatic leaders have tremendous capacities to persuade people. They used their personalities and communication talents to convince others that their approach is the way to go. "Charismatic leaders are differentiated by dominance, self-confidence, a deep need to influence, and a strong conviction in the moral rightness of their beliefs."[141]

In many cases, these leaders persuade others through involvement. They actively challenge their followers to get involved in the organization and the decisions required to make it effective. Their solutions and suggestions are encouraged and expected. One can make the analogy to a poker game, where each person has a chance to name the game when they deal. Without exception, the dealer takes the cards and enthusiastically explains the intricate details of the game. Once that particular hand is completed and the deal moves to the next person, the previous dealer loses enthusiasm for the game until the deal returns to his or her hands. At this point, the person is reborn, recharged, and excited once again about the game. The message is simple—people like to be involved, as it is emotionally uplifting and psychologically stimulating. Effective leaders "understand that unless they communicate and share information with their constituents, few will take much interest in what is going on."[142] This isn't an earth-shattering announcement—really just common sense.

2. Hypnotic Eyes—Some may believe that charismatic leaders have hypnotic eyes.[143] They cite examples like Jim Jones and the

People's Temple in Guyana; Charles Manson and his followers; David Koresh of the Branch Davidian cult of Waco, Texas; or the late Fidel Castro.

3. Unlimited Energy/Commitment—Another characteristic of charismatic leaders according to many leadership writers is their unfailing commitment and energy, often reflected in their work ethic. Stakeholders respect and admire leaders who are committed to their ideals and stick to their convictions. They are consistent and will not flip-flop on issues. They are solid, reflective, and can be counted on to uphold stated values and maintain their perspectives, even in the face of adversity.

4. Captivating Orators—As noted earlier, charismatic leaders are outstanding orators. They are articulate, reflective, confident, and compassionate speakers. Significant change can transpire when a charismatic leader also has a compelling vision. This blend sets the foundation for change. An analysis of the speeches delivered by Barack Obama or Justin Trudeau highlights the elevated oratory abilities of charismatic leaders, as do the powerful addresses by John F. Kennedy and Martin Luther King Jr. These leaders appeal to the emotions of people. They energize their audiences. They stay on message and communicate with clarity and passion. They can bring tears to the eyes of audience members because of their emotional attachment to the words and ideals expressed in their speeches.

That said, one doesn't need to be a world leader to be a skilled orator or a charismatic communicator. Be an active listener so you understand the hopes and dreams of stakeholders. Dream while you are awake. Reflect on the stated values of the group or organization (and if not previously identified, engage people in an activity to do so). Be a great storyteller who stays on message. Weave the values and vision into your stories and speeches—be them in the lunchroom, in meetings, or in addresses to the larger group. Share some of your personal experiences. Humor can also help capture and maintain the interest of members.

Martin Luther King's "I Have a Dream" speech, delivered on August 28, 1963, during a civil rights march in Washington, will go down in history as one of the most moving addresses of all time. This speech was effective because of King's uncanny ability to deliver it with passion and emotion. He also utilized alliteration, symbolism, and metaphors with great effect. He talked of his dream—a dream well worth pursuing where "people of all colors and religious origins would ring the bell of freedom that would be heard throughout the land." As well, he asked people to "join hands and stand united for fairness and equity for all." His delivery was punctuated with such flair and flamboyance that people were captivated by every word. He inserted pauses and vocal inflections for dramatic effect. His speech remains the gold standard for leaders intent on galvanizing support and influencing change.

Theorists[144] have held up charismatic leaders from industry like Donald Burr (airline industry), Stephen Jobs (computers), Lee Iacocca (automotive), and Mary Kay Ash (cosmetics) as examples of charismatic leaders who have made a difference in their respective fields. They are all noted for their ability to inspire a large workforce to go above and beyond the call of duty for the good of the organizations.

Political leaders from Bill Clinton and Barack Obama to Justin Trudeau subtly but consciously (and effectively) use a technique called "refusing invited applause" to heighten their charismatic appeal with their followers. A video analysis of their speeches clearly confirms how "refused invited applause" can be used for great effect. Both speakers would attempt to speak over the applause of the crowd. If the crowd was reacting favorably to a point the speaker made, the speaker would begin the next section, only to stop two or three words into the section. This manipulation technique communicated a perception in the minds of followers that these leaders had many important things to say and they couldn't squeeze everything into their speeches. There appeared to be applause for everything they stated. Applause seemed to connect like chain lightning. Waiting for the applause to subside would break the momentum and lose the effect of the message. These leaders would toss in the occasional "thank you" comment to let the audience know that they appreciated the support. However, by the same token, the leader would consciously appear flustered by not being able to communicate the next point. He or she might attempt to speak over the roar and applause of the audience (before it subsided) for effect. These leaders and other leaders using these techniques are "stirring speakers (who) make abundant use of carefully constructed rhetoric to get their message across."[145] Their oratory techniques helped embed a charismatic quality for these leaders in the minds and emotions of their followers. These leaders carry an "elevated eloquence" and use strong action verbs, reiteration, vocal inflections, alliteration, and designed pauses to help communicate and embed their message.[146] People know what these leaders stand for and capture their message thanks to the leader's heightened communication skills. They frequently and effectively use metaphors and symbols to create and reinforce meaning in the messages delivered to followers. The use of symbols and metaphors helps draw attention to the key elements of a leader's message and helps reinforce the leader's charismatic standing.[147] People are drawn to this clear, interesting orator and the confident message for a better future.

Current and aspiring leaders can heighten their communication skills and subsequently develop an important component of charismatic leadership. Being confident in the speaker's role is the first step. People can learn through experiences if they analyze their strengths and weaknesses, attack speeches from their strength areas, and continue to work on their weaknesses. Many people are nervous in front of a crowd. Some surveys suggest that people fear public speaking more than they do death! Many speakers are nervous prior to speaking to a group. They use this nervous energy to their advantage. They convince themselves that everyone gets nervous (and most do), and nervousness is a signal of being excited and enthused about one's content. Some comedians suggest that if they are not nervous, they do not want to go in front of an audience because they won't be as sharp as times when they felt the nervous signals prior to delivering their act.

Avoid the common habit of speech hesitations—the "ums" and "ahs" that detract from a speaker's message and charismatic appeal (not to be confused with the effective refused invited applause techniques outlined above). These speech hesitations often suggest uncertainty, causing listeners to be distracted and disengaged, regardless of the merits of the speech.

Vocal inflections are extremely helpful in communicating a powerful message and heightening one's charismatic appeal. Voice tones should emphasize the key components of sentences or sections of a speech and not be left for the end of sentences or the end of a speech. Forceful, confident, powerful speaking is an important component of charismatic leadership and something that current or aspiring leaders can develop or refine.

5. Attentive Listener

> Success comes from listening. I've never learned anything by talking.
>
> —FORMER COLLEGE FOOTBALL
> COACH LOU HOLTZ

Be mindful of the fact that a solid command of the language is not the only important communication component of charismatic leaders. Leaders must be willing to actively listen to constituents. Unfortunately, listening is often the forgotten component of communication—and consequently leadership. Charismatic leaders often gravitate to an autocratic style of leadership.[148] They are not as effective in listening to the wants, needs, desires, and perspectives of followers and consequently lose some of their charismatic appeal and standing. As well, this type of behavior has deleterious effects on the motivation and performance levels of followers.

"The best thing that leaders can do and show others
that they respect them and consider them worthwhile
is to reach out, listen, and learn."[149]

Active listening helps leaders gain the perspectives of followers, their dreams, desires, input, and suggestions. Listening can be motivationally uplifting for followers who develop a belief that their leader cares for them, is willing to listen to their ideas, and wants to engage their minds, muscles, and energy. Listening affords leaders with the valuable opportunity to provoke enhanced thinking on situations, arouse follower curiosity, and heighten the involvements, all factors that increase their commitment to the organization and the leader. Additionally, listening helps nurture the relationship between leaders and their constituents, and this relationship is the sole basis of what constitutes leadership. "Leaders demonstrate that they value others when they listen to them, trust them, and are receptive to having others point out their own mistakes and other problems."[150] This is a must for leadership. "No respecting leader would initiate a plan without such information (i.e., feedback from other people affected by the decision) and good leaders learn to ask for it if it is not offered. Effective communications flow in all possible directions at all times."[151]

Noted management consultant Peter Drucker believed strongly that two-way communication was essential for leaders. Heroic leadership perspectives of the past reinforced the erroneous notion that leaders are one-way communicators. Naturally, they need some gifts and talents in delivering their message. However, they need equal amounts of skill and talent in the listening department. While leaders should actively listen on a day-to-day basis, Drucker suggested that leaders also engage in a formal, regular process of sitting with constituents (individually if possible) and listening to their perspectives—questions like the following:

1. What do I have that helps you in your current situation?

2. What could I do to better assist you in your role?

3. What do my people (leaders) do to help you in your current situation?

4. What could my people (leaders) do to help you in your current situation?

5. What do we do that hampers your productivity and/ or makes life more difficult for you?

It is important to note at this time that listening does not mean agreeing. There is a significant difference. Hearing one's perspective and actively seeking to understand his or her insights may or may not shift a leader's perspective. Leaders are provided with an excellent opportunity to enter a process of dialogue at this point. They can openly and honestly invite others to provide their perspective and follow this up with their personal thoughts and perspectives. Effective leaders may also begin the process by presenting their thoughts and perspectives first and inviting others to challenge or "push back" their ideas. This requires a trusting relationship between people who do not feel intimidated challenging a leader's idea. Effective leaders welcome this type of exchange. Ineffective leaders stifle this type of communication, preferring followers who are yes-men or attaboys.

I insisted on this type of leadership with my associate deans and school directors who formed my leadership team. I told them in advance that I was an idea person. Some of these might be brilliant, some might help us advance with some work, and some may be detrimental to our long-term success. I needed them to filter these ideas and tell me when I was running with scissors. I also needed them to bring ideas and perspectives to the table for us to discuss, dissect, and debate. As leader, I needed to establish this culture. Members of my team needed to feel empowered to willingly share and critique. This approach must be in the DNA of a team approach to leadership, which has so many benefits for success and sustainability.[152] When leaders have the opportunity to hear followers' thoughts, they are afforded the perfect opportunity to solidify a trusting, inspiring relationship with those they lead and relay their personal perspective. Followers do not appreciate leaders who lack a perspective or who flip-flop positions to satisfy the individual with whom they are speaking at that particular moment. Moreover, followers appreciate leaders who stick to their convictions if they believe they are correct. Effective leaders of the day have a plan, but they involve followers in the formation of the plan, leave themselves open, and are willing to hear alternative points of view. However, they stick to their guns if they see themselves as being right.

Effective leaders encourage dissent, as it forces people to crystallize their thought processes (including those of the leader) as well as their values, beliefs, and positions. This healthy process can take the place of the leader concluding a statement with "This is how I feel. What do you think?" or "I really need your input on this idea. Are there other alternatives that I am not seeing?"

It is equally important that members of the group recognize the fact that there will be no negative repercussions from challenging the thought processes of the leader. They recognize that their leader is very comfortable with their own persona and genuinely seeks and will consider the input of the group. Leaders who sincerely thank their members for their input, particularly those members offering contradictory opinions, will, over the long haul, lead healthier, more vibrant units comprised of members more committed to both the leader and the organization. They'll appreciate the value that both the organization and the leader have for their perspective. They'll feel empowered to continue offering new and unique approaches that might lead to more options, better options, and potentially better decisions. These leaders do not encourage others to freely and confidently offer their opinion. Their followers frequently fear retribution or consequence for offering conflicting, "against the grain" opinions.

> Credible leaders invite others to elaborate their own perspectives, which are often quite different and incompatible.[153]

Effective leaders appreciate followers who privately tell them that they are "wearing no clothes," metaphorically speaking. Conversely, effective leaders do not appreciate followers who behave like sheep, agreeing with everything that the leader says and adding no new insights or perspectives. These followers lack the confidence, and in many cases, the invitation to be meaningfully involved in an organization, and consequently, their motivation and commitment to the organization or group is generally stifled at a low level.

6. Heightened Self-Confidence—Charismatic leaders carry an aura of self-confidence that is visible and healthy.[154] They project an image to followers of being in control of their situation. They are confident in the aspired vision and in the people charged with making it happen. These leaders communicate a feeling about what the unit or organization needs to attain and what it will take to realize this end. They are focused on the needs and future of their particular organization or group and are confident that they can make a difference. Effective leaders project a high degree of self-efficacy and believe that they can and will make a difference for the organization and the people who comprise the organization or group.

> Confidence is contagious. So is lack of confidence.
> —VINCE LOMBARDI

These leaders are omnipresent. They come in all shapes and sizes. They exist in many facets of everyday life— the town preacher, the leader of a local social-service agency, an organizational leader, a coach, or a parent. In each instance where someone is perceived to be a charismatic leader, followers attribute this charisma to the individual. They adopt this feeling that the leader can and will make a difference. They are willing to put their faith and efforts in the leader to be successful—as a group and as individuals.

In the end, people want to put their faith in a leader. They want a leader who will not waste their time or energy, who will recognize and appreciate their accomplishments, and steer them in the right direction when required. Bill Bradley, a Rhodes Scholar and former New York Knicks basketball player who later served as a United States senator, frequently commented on his sports background and how it prepared him for leadership in other settings.[155] Bradley noted that leaders need to keep score. They need to be held accountable and called to task when their behavior or accomplishments don't measure up—just like he was held accountable by his basketball coaches. He also believed that leaders needed to be on a path of continual improvement. They have to train. They need coaching. They need to work in a synergistic fashion with their teammates.

> "If you're not practicing, someone, somewhere is practicing, and given equal ability, if the two of you ever meet, he will win."[156]

Bradley has since prided himself on being prepared and going the extra mile to prepare himself, regardless of the setting or context. Preparedness is a double-edged sword. If you are prepared, you can go into a situation knowing that you have done all you can to be ready. This assists in projecting a genuine aura of self-confidence. On the other hand, knowing why you are not prepared produces a genuine feeling of not being confident. This will be transmitted in the verbal and nonverbal messages that are transmitted to those with whom you interact and attempt to influence. You might be able to convince another of a course of action on the basis of your authority, but you won't be able to influence and truly lead them unless you are confident and those in your charge genuinely feel you have prepared yourself and them for a specified challenge.

7. Encourage Dissent—As noted above, heightened listening skills are paramount to leadership. Effective leaders show a high degree of interest in what followers have to say. They are emphatic listeners. Followers appreciated the opportunity to voice their perspectives, even if they eventually turn out to be contrary to the selected course of action. Leaders in this day and age must be different.

In the postbureaucratic world, the laurel will go to the leader who encourages healthy dissent and values those followers brave enough to say no. The successful leader will have not the loudest voice but the readiest ear. And his or her real genius may well lie not in personal achievement but in unleashing other people's talent.[157]

Effective leaders encourage healthy dissent. They seek alternative opinions and are willing to discard their personal perspective if the alternative suggestion is more meritorious. Frank Shrontz, former chairman and CEO of Boeing, credited his company's willingness to view alternative opinion and adapt to change as a key to future success and survival. He noted that "the ability to cope with change—in fact to take advantage of change to improve competitive advantage—is central to our successful future."[158] People in today's society who do not encourage others to express their opinions or are intolerant of alternative opinions won't be in a position to lead. Others may go through the motions, but performance above and beyond the call of duty will never occur. People who invest heart and soul in a mission do so because they are inspired by a leader. This is impossible if the person in charge calls all the shots and doesn't stimulate the intellectual and emotional curiosities of those in their charge.

Richard Peddie, the former president and CEO of Maple Leaf Sports & Entertainment, explicitly tells his direct reports that he will always present ideas. He believes that roughly 33 percent of them are good and should be adopted immediately. He tells his leadership team that 33 percent of his ideas have potential and, with some work, should be implemented to attain a desired end. He also states that 33 percent of his ideas will not be good for the company, and he expects his direct reports to recognize them and speak against them.

While it is important to consult with others, effective leaders will make and stick to a course of action when appropriate. Leaders who flip positions can't be trusted. Consequently, others will not invest their precious time, energy, and commitment in these people. "One of the things you hear about the least effective leaders is that they do whatever the last person they spoke to recommended."[159] Effective leaders know where they are going and, more importantly, where their group or organization is headed.

As a longtime academic leader, I felt that it was imperative to surround myself with strong-minded associate deans and school directors / department chairs who were confident sharing their opinions, especially when they countered a position I held. Naturally, we had to agree on values, but it was always important to me that members of my leadership team felt comfortable enough, if not compelled, to share their perspectives on strategy.

I publicly thanked people for challenging my ideas, and I encouraged others to do the same. When I saw examples of constructive disagreement, I publicly acknowledged it and highlighted the fact that this type of honest discussion would help us make better decisions. Naturally, I also felt that it was important to land on a decision and reinforced how important it was for all of us to stand behind it, even if we presented an alternative view that was rejected after a healthy debate. This approach is fundamental to the helpful perspectives that Patrick Lencioni[160] advances in his informative books and lectures.

Charisma and Leadership

Although some aspect of charisma appears in most of the recent leadership theories, writers have varied with respect to the extent that the concept of charisma is integrated in their model. For example, charisma is so central to the theorists[161] that it is reflected in their titles (i.e., charismatic leadership). Other prominent theorists[162] refer to charisma as an important, complementary component of their leadership. Finally, another group of prolific leadership scholars[163] didn't use the term *charisma*, but a deep analysis of their leadership writings spoke to a magnetic appeal of leaders. In the final analysis, charisma does appear to be a component of leadership and is reflected in the verbal and nonverbal communication habits of leaders. This serves as the motivation for making Charismatic Communication the third spoke in the Five C Leadership model.

Some[164] believe that charismatic leaders are more likely to emerge in religious or political arenas where leaders can promise "a better or proper existence." Followers of these leaders believe that the leader has a plan that will make current situations better for them and their future generations. There are strong emotional bonds to both the leader and the vision—thus, people are willing to make these extreme sacrifices. These types of leaders don't get too close to their followers, as part of their mystique may erode. They tend to distance themselves from a personal relationship with their followers so as not to unveil their noncharismatic powers. This is why some suggest that charismatic leaders are more likely to emerge in religious, political, or social movements, or major corporations where large masses of people can come under the influence of a charismatic leader, and less in smaller organizations where more personal interaction might erode one's charismatic attribution. [165]

Contemporary leaders will often work in teams. They are seen to be part of a group, not above a group. Some writers[166] have noted that charismatic leaders often emerge in concert with increased teamwork and member participation once organizational rigidity diminishes over time. Many examples exist where leaders of small groups or organizations exist and people put their faith and trust in the leader and the vision the leader holds. These leaders are engaged. They deploy emotional intelligence and connect with followers. They frequently serve as role models for the followers and consistently reinforce an inspiring vision of what the organization could and should become. They challenge followers by setting high expectation levels and show-ing faith and confidence in followers' abilities to meet these high expectations. Followers of these leaders invest their faith and energy. In many cases, the interaction and participation displayed by these leaders help reinforce their charismatic attributes. There is a sense of togetherness, uniformly focused on the mission or vision of the or-ganization. Followers come to believe that their leader truly cares for them as a person. They know that their leader has their best interests at heart. These leaders build trust and commitment. As a result, they often get performance and commitment beyond initial expectations. Leaders align and excite people. These researchers noted that par-ticipants in their leadership workshops long for quality leadership, usually don't see it in their current situations, and describe their ideal leader as someone with charismatic qualities. The concept of charisma is important to the understanding of leadership, and the topic of cha-risma may have been lost in the initial translations of what makes a transformational leader. Many contemporary writers refer to charismatic qualities in their theories.

Charismatic leaders excite their followers in three ways: (1) developing and extending a common vision for the organization that is operationalized in the form of goals and objectives that followers can appreciate, adopt as their own, and work toward their fulfillment; (2) inspirationally and intellectually challenging followers to adopt the vision and hold them accountable for their measurable contributions to it; and (3) extending a genuine feeling of confidence and personal value to followers, engaging them, inspiring them, and making them feel more important, confident, and powerful. Charismatic leaders excite followers; extract greater levels of commitment, loyalty, and congruence for the organizational mission; and heighten the self-esteem of followers.

The best leaders have the ability to heighten subordinates' motivation by presenting the vision in a compelling fashion, especially in times of crisis. These leaders are effective in illustrating to staff members "the tough things that need to be accomplished and the reasons for them. Elevate their aspirations. Show them a brighter, more successful future for themselves if the organization achieves its vision."[167]

Charisma coupled with heightened communication skills are viewed as requisite leadership skills in contemporary leadership theory. Charismatic leaders can effectively communicate their vision to organizational members in a compelling fashion. "It is safe to conclude that these empirical studies provide support for charismatic leadership theory in a wide range of populations using a variety of methods."[168]

Heightening Charismatic Attributes

Is charisma a product of nature or nurture? Certainly there are some elements of both. Some might have the physical tools (e.g., physical appearance, height, hypnotic eyes, etc.) that would predispose them to be charismatic individuals. However, there are many elements of charisma that are behaviorally based, and aspiring leaders can develop these qualities. One of the top authorities in the field, Alan Bryman, offered five ways potential leaders can heighten their charismatic appeal and potential. Each of the five items is discussed below, with specific application to becoming a charismatic leader.

1. Endure early hardship. While most people are unwilling (for good reason) to subject themselves to hardship, those who have experienced earlier hardships may have learned from the event and risen above the conditions. The experience made them stronger as a result. Furthermore, they may be granted a loftier charismatic attribution than those born with the proverbial silver spoon in their mouths. Mistakes must be viewed as learning opportunities, and people have to take risks if they want to reap the benefits of leadership. French philosopher Jean-Paul Sartre, citing a significant correlation between an early death of a father and subsequent success of a sibling, remarked that the best thing a father can do for a child is to die early. Some researchers[169] have focused on this area and concluded that people who: (a) had parents who held high expectations for them, (b) emerged from a challenging upbringing, (c) have learned to manage conflict, (d) have experienced a leadership role in the past, and (e) possessed a strong desire to maximize their potential through personal and professional development experiences seem to make the most effective leaders. Howard Gardner noted that a number of leaders (60 percent of major British political leaders) lost a parent in childhood, usually their father. These people endure this hardship but mature quickly in the process. They become more self-reliant, which may contribute to the advanced level of self-efficacy that leaders seem to possess.

> "Leaders often exhibit the wounds from their early losses and have a tenacity, almost a ruthlessness, that may prove difficult for others to comprehend."[170]

Clearly, leaders have to learn some lessons along the way, some of which are more painful than others. Some of these lessons are in the form of life experiences, some lessons are through mentoring and formal training programs, and other lessons come in the form of observation. People can learn to be leaders most effectively by experiencing leadership—both good and bad examples of others. I believe that the best principals in our elementary and secondary school systems are people who paid their dues as teachers; who watched effective and ineffective principals lead their schools; who kept current with educational leadership and also with understanding the needs, wants, and desires of current teachers, board members, students, and their parents; and who applied all of these lessons in their own leadership practices. I feel the same about university deans and presidents. People who paid their dues generally have relevant experience, sharp insights from the front lines, and credibility in the eyes of the people they lead.

Some companies develop their staff members and future leaders by ensuring that they have opportunities to grow. For example, the 3M Company prides itself on innovation. New ideas such as the Post-it note are an example of the company encouraging others to dream and take risks. Someone from the company came up with this idea that people now take for granted and use to great effect. A story often shared throughout the IBM Corporation reinforces the view that mistakes should be viewed as people taking chances and learning from mistakes. Legend has it that an IBM employee made a mistake that ultimately cost the company millions of dollars. The employee was called before CEO Thomas Watson with the full intention of being fired. When his meeting was concluded and Watson had not fired him, he inquired as to why. To his surprise and delight, Watson stated that he'd just invested millions in his education, and the last thing he wanted to do was fire him. Watson was certainly not encouraging people to make mistakes; however, he realized that people have to take risks and try things if exceptional results are to occur. He believed that if mistakes were not embraced as learning opportunities, initiative would be stifled, and some of the best ideas would never be presented and consequently followed up. Effective leaders encourage others to try things, to show initiative, to make things happen, and to be creative. Managers remain deeply scripted in the status quo, encouraging people to conform, to follow through, in essence not to be creative or take chances. Performance above and beyond the call of duty rarely transpires out of this form of leadership.

People who have overcome earlier hardships are recognized for their triumphs. John Thompson, the former basketball coach of the University of Georgetown Hoyas, was a perfect example of someone overcoming a challenging situation to be successful later in life. Raised in a poor Washington neighborhood by parents with little education, he struggled in school until a teacher uncovered his vision problems and showed an undying faith in his potential. He learned the value of hard work and commitment, things that he insists upon with his college basketball players. He often refers to a placard that was given to him by another coach that continues to serve as his credo.

Thompson's work habits are legendary. His teams were always extremely well prepared. His players were always in top physical condition. Where necessary, they would outwork any opponent. They were a reflection of their hard-working and committed coach, who learned at an early age the value of having a strong work ethic. He was known to schedule practices at all hours of the night, to reinforce the need for total commitment and hard work. Others respected his high energy level and commitment to hard work. This image, particularly given his humble beginnings, helps embed a charismatic stature for Thompson.

Jesse Jackson often talks of being raised in poverty and rising to be a legitimate contender for the office of the president of the United States. Bill Clinton's charismatic appeal was heightened during his presidential campaign when stories of losing his father at an early age and assuming the father-figure role in the household surfaced. Both individuals are examples of how others appreciate and respect the conditions that these two leaders had to endure and reinforce the initiative and determination that they must have to rise above these circumstances to assume their current roles in society.

> He who loses wealth loses much; he who loses a friend loses more; he who loses courage loses all.
> —CERVANTES

2. Develop the capacity for intense study and heightened literacy. Charismatic leaders are intelligent people who can communicate their knowledge and insights on a variety of topics. They need the knowledge base to be able to intelligently converse on a wide range of topics. These leaders stay current on situations and topics that fall outside their immediate realm of responsibility. Consequently, these leaders are voracious readers—particularly of newspapers. One of Bill Clinton's part-time jobs as a university student was to clip articles for a high-ranking government official. He was required to read six newspapers a day and clip articles that the official should be briefed on. Clinton credits this job with fueling his voracious reading habits and his subsequent knowledge of issues.

Effective leaders stay up to date on issues, and they have reflected on issues. They formulate opinions and share them where appropriate. They also ask others how they feel about issues. They also have the literacy and oratory skills to effectively communicate their opinion to others in a convincing and compelling way. They are passionate readers of other types of materials (fiction and nonfiction). These sources provide additional insights and perspectives into situations and help develop the leader's vocabulary and abilities to tie words together that helps heighten their charismatic appeal. These leaders have had the opportunity to develop and refine their speaking skills. They may have received some formal training (e.g., Toastmasters, Carnegie courses), or they may have learned to be effective speakers through observation, coupled with adequate doses of trial-and-error experience. Regardless of the methods they've used to develop their oratory skills, without question, these leaders have the ability to package and deliver their thoughts and opinions effectively—many times in spine-tingling ways.

3. Develop visioning skills. Leaders with a vision are often afforded a higher charismatic rating by their followers. These leaders who have demonstrated over time that they can bring about success carry a higher charismatic rating. Minor success should be recorded and referred to by leaders and their supporters as a way of heightening support for their leader, as well as their charismatic appeal. This strategy also helps establish the self-efficacy factor in the eyes of potential followers—the idea that these individuals can and will make a difference and that they will be successful in an organization or enterprise once again.

4. Develop negotiation/persuasion skills. Charismatic individuals are active listeners. They show genuine interest and respect for the interests, paradigms, and perspectives of others, particularly those they lead. They challenge people to react to their ideas and widely consult prior to committing their organization or group to action. They invite people to react to their ideas as a way of clarifying their thinking and building group support for their decision. They recognize that the best ideas often emerge from lower levels of a hierarchy, and they inspire people by getting them involved.

People are not accustomed to this style of leadership, which further contributes to the uniqueness of this type of leader. Followers appreciate the interest and confidence that their leader holds for them and consequently often hold great affection for their leader. This also contributes to the leader's charismatic attribution.

5. Develop skill in attracting others to a vision. These leaders recognize the importance of surrounding themselves with others who share their visions for a desired end. Adolf Hitler was notorious for attracting a small group of committed and loyal followers to his ideas in order to reinforce and promote his larger-than-life profile and image. The more people leaders can attract to their vision, the larger appeal they will garner from their followers. People who align with the leader and the vision have a subconscious interest in promoting both the leader and the vision.[171] Even those who do not agree with the leader's vision will have to respect his or her charismatic abilities to captivate such a large group of people to the vision and leadership.

Summary

The literature is clear that those individuals who can capture the attention of others, focus them on a course of action, and inspire them to new heights often carry a magnetic and mystical persona that sets them apart from others. Weber labeled this phenomenon "charisma," and many leadership writers of the day believe that it is a fundamental requirement for leading others. I concur with their assessment.

One has to convince others to invest their faith as well as their hearts, minds, and energy in an effort that they may not have supported or endorsed to the degree necessary to make it a reality. Those who are charismatic and have a vision that makes sense for people and is consistent with where they may now want to go have a distinct advantage. Charismatic leaders from a host of different settings have demonstrated over time the importance of charisma in gaining and maintaining the attention of others and influencing them to do something they would not ordinarily have done without the leader's intervention.

The charismatic attributes were listed as vision, risk, supportiveness, confidence, and being antibureaucratic. Examples of leaders displaying these tendencies, from a host of situations, were presented in this section. Current and aspiring leaders were presented with a list of activities in which they could engage to heighten their charismatic standing in the eyes of their followers. Like leadership, charisma can be learned.

Since charisma is projected to others in verbal (e.g., speeches, discussions) or nonverbal (e.g., actions, physical appearance) communications, the labeling of this C as Charismatic Communicator is appropriate. Current and aspiring leaders who understand the components of charisma, how it can be developed, and how it is manifested in daily communications will be well served in leading others to the attainment of focused performance above and beyond initial expectations.

C4—Contagious Enthusiasm

A Reader's Guide

Upon reading this chapter, readers will understand

- that enthusiasm is often an overlooked but essential element of leadership,
- examples of leaders generating enthusiasm throughout a group or organization,
- the role of passion in leadership,
- how leaders excite and inspire others around challenges and risks, and
- how seemingly impossible things can be accomplished with focused enthusiasm.

C4—Contagious Enthusiasm

> Every great and commanding movement in the annals of the world is the triumph of enthusiasm. Nothing great was ever achieved without it.
>
> —RALPH WALDO EMERSON

Many writers[172] subscribe to Emerson's notion that enthusiasm (a.k.a. passion) is a critical component to getting things accomplished. From a leadership perspective, these same writers suggest that leaders who are enthusiastic can extract the same from those they lead, and in the process, bring about change in their organization or group beyond initial expectations. Enthusiasm, particularly the contagious type that spreads to other members of a group, is closely linked to leadership and consequently is fingered as the fourth C of successful leadership—"Contagious Enthusiasm."

Enthusiastic leaders are passionate about what they are doing and the people engaged with them in the process of attaining a predetermined goal or objective. Their enthusiasm is clearly exhibited, modeled by some, and infectious to many who come into contact with this leader. They project higher levels of energy and commitment to the task at hand. They energize people with their words and actions. They meaningfully involve others in the planning and delivery of actions designed to accomplish predetermined ends. They understand that "when people are meaningfully involved, they willingly commit the best that is in them. Moreover, when people identify their personal goals with the goals of the organization, they release inordinate amounts of energy, creativity, and loyalty."[173]

This scale in the model seems to gather the most debate. Critics point to soft-spoken leaders like Bill Gates, Bill Belichick, or Angela Merkel as examples of leaders who are not overtly enthusiastic. However, writers like Susan Cain[174] support the perspective of this author. These leaders are passionate about their field, about the leadership, and about the people charged with making the predetermined vision a reality. They often get overlooked. The opinions of extroverts are usually offered up early. Cain cautions us to mine the opinions and leadership of introverted individuals. I agree and suggest that passion be the quality that we look for in our leaders.

Take the example of the introverted but passionate Bill Gates. No one can question the passion that Gates brings to technology or his high enthusiasm for innovation as the founder and leader of Microsoft. Computers and telecommunications were his passions. He projects a fun, hobby-like passion to his work and encourages others to carry the same affection and enthusiasm to their assignments. He understands that when people are creatively and enthusiastically involved, great things can and will happen. His playbook has been adopted at Google, Facebook, and other high-technology organizations where a passion for innovation is contagious and omnipresent.

> You have to be burning with an idea, or a problem, or
> a wrong that you want to right. If you're not passionate
> enough from the start, you'll never stick it out.
>
> —STEVE JOBS

The late Mark McCormack, former chief executive officer and founder of the sports marketing firm International Management Group (IMG) brought a similar passion for his work and company. His enthusiasm was often shared by employees who talked about his indefatigable work habits (often arriving at his office desk before four thirty in the morning) and his hands-on management approach as testimony to his enthusiasm for IMG, the field of sports marketing, and the people who make up the organization. People couldn't help but be moved and influenced by his words and actions—all underscoring his passion and commitment.

These leaders recognize leadership for what it is—a verb. It is action-oriented. It is about forming relationships with others and inspiring them to the attainment of an agreed-upon vision or ideal. These leaders "search for their own chances to make things happen; they also instill this attitude in constituents, creating ways that they can take charge of at least their own responsibilities."[175] They appreciate the fact that leadership is an interpersonal process, conducted with, by, and through people. Effective leaders align people. They focus them on tasks and inspire them to higher levels of performance. They awaken the potential in people around new possibilities. Walt Disney recognized this fact and led his organization accordingly. Disney's method was to challenge, provoke, and stimulate his staff. He "hired the best talent available, and by means of his own example, his own drive, enthusiasm, and obsessiveness, he encouraged them to new heights. His enthusiasm was infectious."[176] Conversely, those charged with leading a group of people without exhibiting a passion for the task or people committed to making it a reality have a demoralizing and detrimental effect on a group. They are not inspiring and consequently can't inspire others.

Examples of both types of leaders in a variety of organizational and group settings are abundant.

> A person can succeed at almost anything for which they have unlimited enthusiasm.
>
> —CHARLES M. SCHWAB,
> AMERICAN STEEL MAGNATE

Enthusiasm was a critical component of moving and inspiring people. Researchers have suggested for years that leaders described as charismatic were found to be more enthusiastic than their counterparts.[177] The leaders are perceived to be genuinely excited about what they are doing, as are the people joining them in the pursuit of a predetermined goal. Enthusiasm is a key component of effective leadership. Some researchers have suggested that effective leaders inspire people in such a way that they are more "enthusiastic about their assignments."[178] Bernard Bass noted that a workforce was inspired to higher motivational levels by an inspiring leader, particularly those composed of higher-educated people who typically seek advanced levels of self-actualization from their work experience (and possibly have the opportunities to seek other positions if they do not receive sufficient levels of job enrichment from their current position). Other researchers[179] have confirmed Bass's assertion by uncovering that effective leaders inspire followers. They respect and admire the inspirational qualities of true leaders. True leaders enable and empower their followers and in the process, raise their excitement levels. Furthermore, through the leader's excitement and enthusiasm, followers begin to see work as a fun experience and an exciting venture. Some scholars have drawn the analogy between work and play by suggesting that truly effective groups and organizations fuse work and play.[180] Much like a sports team, these organizations rally to accomplish tasks with a level of excitement and risk evident in the sports environment. Coworkers assume a teammate role, leaders often a coach's position. Inspirational leaders make things fresh and energizing. A renewed and sustained sense of excitement disseminates throughout the group or organization for the leader and the task at hand. Effective leaders display passion and through their words and actions inspire their followers to do the same.

Inspiring and Empowering Others

The first and most important step towards success is the feeling that we can succeed.

—NELSON BOSWELL

Leaders who empower others make people feel significant and important to the cause. They are better prepared to learn from new experiences, more open to different ideas, better team players, and view their affiliation with the group as an exciting experience. People who come under the influence of this type of leader are generally self-confident and highly motivated.[181]

Followers read situations and look for passion and commitment in their leaders. When this happens, leaders will soon find out that passion—or lack thereof—is contagious. It can energize and excite people, and when absent, it can deflate and disempower colleagues. Leaders can soon expect less than total commitment and contributions. While some followers may not physically withdraw from a situation, they will with their hearts and efforts. Performance beyond expectations will not be witnessed. People will go through the motions of carrying out their assigned duties, but not with a full investment of their talents, energy, and loyalty.

Great leaders of the day are active listeners who are keenly attuned to the needs, wants, and desires of their constituents. Relative to their staff members, these leaders "keep their mind open about what people can contribute to an enterprise."[182] They recognize that people will be more excited about an idea or direction if they have had the opportunity to shape the idea or direction. They will be more committed to making things work, because they have an emotional investment in the idea or direction. A community of leaders, enabled and empowered to act, develops from this style of leadership. People within the group or organization are more focused on what is really important for the organization and dedicated to liberating the leadership potential in other members of the workforce.

Some organizational leaders have built-in mechanisms to acknowledge and reward people generating and sustaining high levels of enthusiasm with other members of an organization. For example, employees of the United Kingdom-based Harvester Restaurant can expect to receive a "YIPEE" (You Inspired Pride and Enthusiasm in Everyone) Award for brightening others' days and adding a sense of spirit and teamwork in the organization.[183] Leaders can also build pride and enthusiasm in their members by publicly and privately telling them that they are doing a great job (when warranted).

Empowering/Enabling Leadership Style

If you want people motivated to do a good job, give them a good job to do.
—FREDERICK HERTZBERG

Transformational leaders empower the workforce in ways that often differentiate successful from unsuccessful leaders. They focus on the development of followers to higher-functioning, more productive, more engaging members. They inspire and challenge these people to become leaders in their own right and determine their own course of action within the framework of the vision of the organization or unit. "A consistent theme of this effect is that the followers have a sense of taking charge; they feel empowered to exercise effective leadership with their own followers or colleagues."[184] Followers of these leaders recognize the personal care and attention afforded them and feel a greater sense of commitment and satisfaction toward both the organization and the leader. These leaders entice "individuals to transcend their own everyday routine and to have their horizons stretched beyond the here-and-now. It is this kind of leadership that breeds commitment and loyalty and which allows organizations to be propelled to new levels of activity."[185] Google, Amazon, Facebook, and AT&T have been identified as companies that place a high premium on empowering their workforce. These companies are committed to this process because of their deep-rooted belief that "empowered employees develop a sense of pride and job ownership, which motivates them towards continuous improvement. They continuously seek better, smarter ways to do their work."[186] Given the tastes, opinions, needs, attitudes, and backgrounds of the contemporary workforce, leaders have no other option than to lead using an empowering/enabling style. Researchers through the years have conducted studies in business, industry, education, and government settings that all produced results confirming a high correlation between empowering leaders (classified as "visionary" or "transformational") and elevated levels of employee satisfaction. This type of leader has the ability to …

> inspire followers to high levels of achievement by showing them how their work contributes to worthwhile ends. It is an emotional appeal to some of the most fundamental of human needs—the need to be important, to make a difference, to feel useful, to be part of a successful and worthwhile enterprise.[187]

Although the ability and willingness of the leader to create a vision for the organization is a major component of the new thinking in leadership, effective leaders must also empower their people around the development and implementation of the vision. Strong, passionate leaders form the basis for creating organizations that are extremely effective in terms of any criterion of performance or profit, that contribute to society a vision that benefits members, clients, and the larger public, and that provide an extremely high "quality of work life" for all employees. It is hard to imagine what more one might ask of organizations ... or leaders.[188]

Empowerment

Followers seek inspiration and excitement from their leaders. They also seek opportunities to learn and grow. Leaders who trust their colleagues and empower them to make decisions and complete tasks tap into an important aspect of contemporary leadership theory that was virtually neglected in previous leadership theory. The best leaders develop colleagues, assisting them in becoming more productive, effective, and able to realize their full potential. These leaders identify and eliminate the barriers that impede follower success, and they provide followers with the authority to carry out their responsibilities and make a significant contribution to the organization or group. Some writers have suggested that these leaders "see that people have more creative energy, resourcefulness, and initiative than their jobs presently allow or require. People are crying, 'Believe in me, believe in me.' These leaders awaken the inspirational/enthusiastic giants lying dormant in people."[189]

Contagious Self-Confidence

Other writers have focused on other elements related to contagious enthusiasm. Some[190] have suggested that these leaders serve up a type of leadership that leads to a contagious self-confidence and a trust in their respective leader that is not evident in other types of leadership. Followers of this type of leader are committed to the vision of the group and feel empowered to do all they can to make the attainment of the vision a reality. Self- confidence is an important aspect of this type of leadership. Self-confident leaders positively impact the performance of others. Leaders projecting a high level of self- confidence communicate a perception of self-assurance to members of a group. Members begin to believe that the leader can make a difference in the outcomes of the organization. Conversely, managers who lacked self-confidence continually found fault with others and did not project the confident image required to influence others to invest their time, hearts, and energy in the proposed vision of the leader or organization.

Strategies for Inspiring a Group or Organization

There are many things a leader can do to create heightened levels of enthusiasm throughout a group or organization. Strategies other leaders have used to inspire members of an organization and the organization at large include: (a) involving people in decisions that affect them; (b) taking greater care in introducing, addressing, and rewarding people; (c) not being a magnet for attention; (d) getting to know your people; (e) being enthusiastic; (f) recognizing the different situations that call forth different decisions; and (g) being persistent. Many of these suggestions could best be described as commonsense activities. However, they are not common practice in organizational life. These strategies are discussed below.

1. Involve people in decisions that affect them. Members of an organization are people, complete with egos, feelings, and emotions. They genuinely want to be treated with respect and dignity. Leaders who seek the opinion of others prior to implementing an idea or a direction go a long way toward heightening the enthusiasm of people in an organization. People feel meaningfully involved and valued. Leaders who do this will empower their organizations and the people within them to such a degree that people see value and meaning in their roles and become effective in making a dream a reality. It is natural for people to be more committed to their own ideas and resistant to ideas for which they had no opportunity to provide input, regardless of the merits of either decision.

Once the goals are agreed upon, it is essential that leaders draw attention and provide meaning to followers relative to the agreed-upon goals. Leaders must keep members of the workforce focused and motivated toward making the desired end a reality. Members of organizations often lose sight of their goals and organizational agendas. Peter Drucker's classic management letter concept is one that might be effective for leaders. The process calls for staff members to submit a letter to their leader outlining a proposed plan, anticipated outcomes, resources required, and possible consequences. In addition to heightening the accountability of followers, this process keeps all members of the organization focused on what the organization as a whole, and what individuals within the organization, hope to accomplish. Effective leaders exhibit "confidence in people's ability to perform effectively and meet challenges."[191]

2. Take greater care in the manner in introducing, addressing, and rewarding people. People need to feel important and valued. Simple things like the way in which leaders introduce them go a long way to creating a bond between followers and the leader. Rather than introducing a person as an employee or staff member, referring to the person as an associate or a colleague has the potential to increase one's sense of self-worth and value. W. L. Gore, founder of Gore-Tex, insisted that employees be called associates. This label gave people higher status, value, and sense of pride as members of the organization. Leaders must be careful with their terminology when referring to those in their care and not label them *followers* or *subordinates*. Gore's *associate* or *colleague* terminology is a more appropriate term for those involved in contemporary leadership situations.

Leaders must also be sure to give credit where credit is due. Too frequently, people in authoritative positions take credit for things accomplished by others in an organization. This can have devastating effects on the morale of people in a group or organization. People will be less willing to invest their time and energy for above-average tasks or assignments if they don't perceive the credit coming back to them. Introduce these associates to others as "outstanding contributors." Build them up in the presence of others. Make them feel important to the group or organization. Let them know publicly that you recognize and value their contributions.

Finally, the reward system must recognize the above-average contributions of people in an organization. If people believe that they will receive both tangible and intangible rewards for their efforts, they will be more likely to offer heightened contributions. Conversely, if they believe their efforts aren't formally or informally recognized, it will be easy for them to slip into the mind-set that "nobody notices" and "nobody cares."

3. Don't be a magnet for attention but disburse it to others. Former New York Knicks basketball star and United States senator Bill Bradley often drew analogies from his sports experience to interpret to other areas of life and leadership. Perhaps the most memorable and poignant example of this process occurred in the summer of 1992, when Bradley returned to Madison Square Garden, the home venue of his former basketball team. His purpose this time around was to offer a keynote address to the thousands of delegates in attendance at the Democratic National Convention and to a television audience numbering in the millions. He was there as a senator to promote Bill Clinton as the Democratic candidate for the office of president of the United States. The content of his speech captured one of the many lessons he learned from sports: the importance and power of teamwork. He electrified the live and television audiences that evening with his opening comments when he stated that

for ten years I played basketball for the New York
Knicks in this building. The guys on the team came from
many places—a variety of backgrounds. We respected
each other. We gave up our own personal agendas
so that the team could win. The idea of giving up
something small to gain something big for all of us is
not new, but putting an ancient idea into practice is the
central necessity of our new age. Giving up the desire
for more of everything now is the key to having more
of something better in our future.[192]

Bradley went on to state that Bill Clinton was the type of leader
who could bring the country together to tackle and overcome the
challenges the United States was facing at the time. He described
Clinton as an unselfish leader with a vision for making those he
influenced responsible for contributing to a greater nation. He described a selfless leader who challenged people to be the best they
could be—and someone who would give people the credit they
deserve once the result was realized. Barack Obama and Justin
Trudeau display the same characteristics. This type of leadership
has tremendous potential in any field, from sports to business to
social groups to politics. People have a genuine need to feel important, to feel like a critical player in the process of attaining a
challenging end. They need to see that their efforts contribute and
that they will be credited with making their contribution.

Many of the employees I have met through consulting assignments comment on this point. They suggest that the leaders
frequently seek the limelight and will even take credit for ideas
that are not theirs. These leaders carry themselves in a superior
fashion, and the only time they communicate with those in their
charge is when problems arise. Employees who experience this
type of leader state unequivocally that they withhold effort, creativity, and commitment because this leader will only take the
credit and be first in line when rewards are dispensed. They offer

that loyalty is a two-way street and that they must see it in their leader before they are willing to invest heart and soul in the unit or organization. Conversely, some of these employees have also experienced the true leader, who recognizes that his or her unit is only as effective as the expertise, energy, and creativity levels of its employees. These leaders appreciate the contributions of staff members. They acknowledge the contributions of other people. They extract higher levels of commitment and creativity from these people who feel energized and appreciated by this type of leader. These leaders are part of the group—not above it. At times when mistakes are made, these leaders often help shoulder the blame. Employees comment that these leaders make them feel valuable— and that their interests are critically important to the leader. Consequently, they are proud to be a part of this group and in the company of this leader

Teamwork and camaraderie are paramount. Members often comment that they feel a sense of ownership for both the group and the vision they are pursuing. As a result, they would do almost anything for this leader to ensure the fulfilment of the mission of the organization. These leaders could do no wrong in the eyes of their staff members. Mark Twain offered that true leaders help others and never stop to count the number of times.

> It's amazing how much can get accomplished if no one
> is concerned with who gets the credit.
> —FORMER UNIVERSITY BASKETBALL
> COACH JOHN WOODEN

These types of leaders "do not place themselves at the center, they place others there. They do not seek the attention of people, they give it to others. They do not focus on satisfying their own aims and desires; they look for ways to respond to the needs and interests of their constituents. They are not self-centered; they concentrate on the constituents."[193] It may be as simple as being the last one through the food buffet at a group or organization's social event or as simple as ensuring that other voices are heard prior to yours as the leader.

Personal Development of Followers

Leadership is all about unlocking the potential in others.
— CARLY FIORINA

Effective leaders of the day recognize and implement the spirit of this suggestion. They surround themselves with the best people possible and find a way to unleash and channel their energies. They are keenly focused on the development of their followers and recognize the ultimate payoffs that can be accrued from this investment strategy. Followers of these leaders recognize the genuine concern that their leader holds for them and their personal development. Consequently, they are more willing to make personal sacrifices for the leader and the organization, as well as investing their own heightened levels of commitment to both the leader and the organization. Developing and inspiring followers is particularly important and pays handsome dividends in times of hardship or when followers are asked to make a personal sacrifice for the long-term benefit of the organization or unit.

> CFO: What happens if we spend all this money in leadership development and people leave?
>
> CEO: What happens if we don't and they stay!

Thus, leadership begins with a commitment from the organization and the leader to the follower. If this is done in good faith and followers can vividly see the level of concern that leaders and the organization have for them and their personal development, they will be more likely to make these sacrifices later or offer efforts that extend above and beyond the call of duty for the good of the organization and the unit. They will be more receptive to change, to assuming challenges, and to investing extra effort for the good of the group. "Transformational leadership is an integral part of ensuring a committed workforce focused on co-operation and innovation."[194]

In the final analysis, leaders are only as effective as their ability to surround themselves with highly qualified and committed people whose energies are focused and maximized to the attainment of a predetermined goal or objective. "Leaders should understand that they aren't really leaders until they are influencing the behavior of others."[195] Without followers, one cannot lead. Furthermore, followers who are present but not focused on the accomplishment of a mutually agreed-upon end will not result in an optimal success level for the group.

4. Get to know people. Leaders who inspire from the heart get to know their people. They ask questions and actively listen to what their staff members have to say. They see these people in the community. They get to know their families. They uncover the interest areas of staff members and talk to them about common pursuits. They lead actively, be it in the form of walking around and talking to people on the job, having lunch with them, or visiting with people informally in the community. They show interest in people as people with wants, needs, and desires. They are much more than an employee or a servant to the group or organization. Having and showing respect for all people who come in contact with a group or organization (employees, clients, and competitors) is critical to long-term effectiveness. Respect can be a powerful and critical motivating factor for how employees view the organization and their specific role within it, their willingness to invest heart and soul to the accomplishment of stated objectives, and the way they treat others (coworkers and customers) in their day-to-day activities. Granting and ultimately gaining respect starts with the executive leader.

5. Be enthusiastic. As simple as it sounds, one can't expect others to be enthusiastic about an idea, direction, or vision if the leader is not filled with enthusiasm. Anita Roddick, former managing director of the Body Shop International, credited her success to her energy, enthusiasm, passion, and stamina. She believed that her intensity fuelled her, and helped ignite those around her."[196] Speak enthusiastically with others. Show people with your actions indicating that you are deeply committed to the organization and the people within the group. Be visibly excited about what you are doing. Thank them for the leadership opportunity, and let them know that you will do everything in your power to work with them to attain the agreed-upon goal or vision. Inspire people with a commitment to this common purpose.

> Different leaders engage in energizing in different ways, but some of the most common include demonstration of their personal excitement and energy, combined with leveraging that excitement through direct personal contact with large numbers of people in the organization.[197]

Leaders cast the longest shadow. Their actions speak louder than their words. They may need to be reminded that leading is a verb. It connotes action. Leaders must be enthusiastic and must be *seen* to be enthusiastic.

6. Recognize that unique situations call forth different decisions.

> It is a wise man who said that there is no greater inequality than the equal treatment of unequals.
> —FELIX FRANKFURTER

Inspirational leaders believe that unique circumstances warrant different but equitable decisions. True leaders are not afraid to make the best decision to suit a situation. This implies that these leaders treat people differently. Bernard Bass termed this approach "individual consideration," noting that leaders must assess each situation and make an appropriate judgment after all of the unique aspects of the situation have been considered.[198] This dimension also measures the leader's interest in professionally developing staff members to maximize their personal potential. Leaders should be concerned with the developmental needs of their staff members and ensure that adequate resources are invested in the potential of their people. This level of interest is quickly perceived by members of the group or organization, who see the importance placed on them as members of a group. Furthermore, the bond to both the leader and the organization are solidified through this obtrusive act of personal development and concern.

7. Be persistent. McDonald's founder Ray Kroc was a firm believer in the need for persistence. He believed persistence was the key to being successful. In his opinion, leaders who visibly and consistently demonstrated their persistence were in a better position to heighten the same qualities in those they led. His credo, prominently displayed in most McDonald's restaurants is:

Nothing in the world can take the place of persistence.

Talent will not; nothing is more common than unsuccessful men (or women) with great talent.

Genius will not; unrewarded genius is almost a proverb. Education will not; the world is filled with educated derelicts. Persistence, determination alone are omnipresent.

Howard Schultz brought a similar level of passion and leadership style to Starbucks; the late Sam Walton, the founder of the successful Wal-Mart chain of department stores, offered a similar measure. He suggested that success comes to those committed to being successful. Overcoming obstacles and remaining focused on the task at hand is a philosophy that governed Walton and all employees of the Wal-Mart chain.

In summary, the seven strategies for inspiring others (involve people in decisions that affect them, introduce and treat staff members as colleagues, give credit where it is due, get to know your colleagues personally, be enthusiastic, apply unique decisions to different situations, and be persistent) are all common sense leadership practices. However, they are not common practices. Leaders need to remind themselves of these strategies regularly and ensure that they are integrated into leadership portfolios.

Generate Enthusiasm by Creating Challenges

To achieve all that is possible, we must attempt the impossible.

—UNKNOWN

Highly effective leaders exude contagious confidence in people. Followers enjoyed being associated with these successful leaders and a winning group. The leaders displayed tremendous levels of respect for the people they led. They genuinely sought their opinions. They asked for their perspectives. People associated with these leaders were expected to challenge and push back the leader's ideas without fear of retribution. These leaders awakened the curiosity and sense of self in their followers, who felt more appreciated and consequently more receptive to accepting greater challenges from their leader. They felt empowered, leaders in their own right. "Excellent leaders set group standards, teach them, live (exemplify) them, and inspire others to live them."[199] A community of leaders emerged, all focused on a predetermined goal and process for making it a reality. Many people within a group or organization have the capacity and potential to develop into leaders, and education, training, experience, and opportunity hold the key.

These leaders were acutely concerned about providing opportunities for the professional development of their followers, reinforcing their concern for the person's well-being and personal enrichment. This change in perspective is a welcome and new development in leadership theory. While showing concern for the follower was reflective in the earlier leadership behavior studies of the 1940s, following up this concern with specific resources and opportunities for personal and professional enrichment is a specific alteration reflective in the leadership literature of today. That said, relatively little leadership research has been carried out that focused on maximizing both the productivity of the group and the quality of experience for a workforce. They further noted that one of the biggest challenges for leaders, yet one with the biggest payoffs from a productivity and enrichment perspective, is intrinsically motivating a member or members of a workforce. Inspiring people to be committed and perform beyond expectations by creating challenges, recognizing and rewarding people for challenging current paradigms, and exhibiting a genuine concern for people are certainly a place to start.

> One person with passion is better than forty people merely interested.
>
> —E. M. FORSTER

Effective leaders challenge their followers to go above and beyond the call of duty because followers genuinely like the leader, know that they have some input in the decisions that affect them, and feel intellectually engaged in the activities of the group or organization. They employ the use of "stretch goals" with themselves, their staff members, and their organizations. Leaders feel equally awakened, challenged by the people they are working with, and know that their followers expect high-quality involvement, input, results, and leadership. This has positive implications for the group or organization. Leaders are kept on the edge by a focused, energized workforce—all contributing to a more healthy and vibrant group, unit, or organization.

The notion of challenging followers and elevating their personal expectation levels has received increased treatment in most of the recent leadership literature. Bernard Bass also introduced leadership enthusiasts to his concept of "Intellectual Stimulation." He considered the leader's ability to awaken the intellectual curiosity of followers, particularly those with higher levels of education, as a fundamental portion of this concept of transformational leadership.[200] Warren Bennis wrote about the importance of leaders managing "meaning" by showing followers, often through involvement and challenge, the important issues facing the group or organization.[201] James Kouzes and Barry Posner talked of "Encouraging the Heart" as a way of calling forth greater efforts and commitment from followers by appealing to their sense of pride, involvement, and challenge.[202] Other researchers suggested that effective leaders engage and challenge members of a group or organization to take calculated risks. The pursuit and accomplishments of these challenges energizes people to alter their personal and organizational expectations to higher levels, consequently moving both to higher levels of achievement.

Max De Pree, former chairman of Herman Miller, Inc., referred to this process as the leader developing a community of leaders.[203] He felt that this was the best approach to leading a group or organization. These leaders create a community of empowered and inspired followers who, when aligned, help the unit reach new heights (in addition to maximizing their own potentials). They inspire followers to be active learners, hungry for information and maximizing their personal skill sets. They focus followers on the ambitions of the enterprise and get them thinking about the attainment of results. They encourage followers to offer opinions and perspectives on issues as well as be flexible to change and adaptation. They are the true leaders. They become leaders of other leaders. Effective leaders garnered affectionate feelings from followers, made work exciting and stimulating for them, heightened their expectation levels, and challenged them to focus on purpose and direction rather than process. In summary, these leadership writers suggest that effective leaders encourage and inspire followers to offer more than they originally thought possible or desirable. They energized their workforce to be more personally empowered. They operated on a premise that members of a workforce who were more self-actualized and inspired by the leader and the work experience would be better, more committed performers.

Leaders can energize a group of people in a number of ways. The following six ideas are presented as ways current and aspiring leaders can energize their followers and challenge them to higher levels of performance: (a) be creative, (b) take calculated risks, (c) be cognizant of perceptions of personality, (d) invite others to push back your ideas, (e) hold people accountable, and (f) pursue personal effectiveness. Each of these suggestions is represented below, along with anecdotal and research information to support their presence.

1. Be creative. Creative people energize themselves and others who fall into their sphere of influence. They view situations and perspectives differently. They encourage others to look at things differently. They never get caught up in the "we tried it that way and it didn't work" mentality that plagues many organizations and stifles enthusiasm and fresh ideas—and often holds the key to better solutions for persistent problems. People like to get caught up in the excitement of implementing a creative idea, particularly if they've had roles in contributing to it or they can see the relevance in the idea. They break the "same old thing" mentality and begin to look at issues and challenges in fresh, more creative ways. This has a tremendous impact on the vitality and enthusiasm that pervades an organization. People begin to feel energized, alive, and excited about the prospects of the challenge and overcoming it. Taking calculated risks is tangible evidence of leaders and organizations implementing creative solutions in a creative fashion to overcome an obstacle or attempt to realize a desired end.

Leaders must be creative and extract the same from those they lead. Lord and Hall noted that "leaders create situations that affect the creativity of others, and effective performance may also require that leaders be creative themselves."[204] Giving members problems and the authority to solve them is a key step in ensuring that this scenario plays out. Giving members the problem without the authority to make decisions to fix the situation is a recipe for disaster.

2. Take calculated risks. Effective leaders create challenges for their organizations by assuming calculated risks. They ensure specific measurable and time-bound stretch goals are put in place to focus and challenge members. The entire organization gets behind a respected leader who puts a personal and organizational reputation on the line and engages the minds and talents of followers in collectively overcoming the odds of success. These leaders invest considerable energy in working toward the attainment of these challenges, which rubs off on followers who respect and appreciate the contributions of their respective leader. Followers share in the exertion of effort toward the attainment of the challenge as well as share in the realization of the rewards that follow. These leaders ask followers to assume arduous challenges, and through their actions and behaviors, inspire followers to make them a reality.

> If your dreams don't scare you, they are not big enough.
> —MUHAMMAD ALI

Conversely, not taking risks, being trapped in a status quo mind-set, is not stimulating to people and does not result in extraordinary outcomes. Fear of failing is often the reason why some people and organizations do not take calculated risks. People need to be encouraged to try new things, to show initiative, to let their creative juices flow. "Fear of failure paralyzes us and leads to risk-adverse, conventional organizations. This negative view of risk blinds us to opportunities inherent in intelligent risk-taking."[205] Some of my proudest moments have been when associates have independently and proudly solved situations that have plagued the group I have been leading.

3. Be cognizant of perceptions of personality. Many leaders are now aware of the need for a softer, more empowering style of leadership. However, they are unaware of their tendencies to be overly dominant and controlling in their communication styles and personality. That said, a leader's behavior speaks volumes about his or her values and principles, in most cases so loudly that others can't hear a leader's stated values and principles. Naturally, leaders have to be consistent with what they say and how they behave. Any inconsistencies will be interpreted in the leader's behavior and erode his or her credibility in the eyes of followers.

Leaders must also project an image that welcomes dissenting opinions. They need to make others feel comfortable, sharing their thoughts and perspectives on issues that impact them in the organization. Otherwise, followers will continue to do the things they have always done, with reduced initiative for changing for the better, and less motivation to make the work experience a challenging, successful venture from all perspectives. The enlightened follower, operating at a maximal capacity in a direction that is agreed upon and focused on the goals of the organization, remains an unfulfilled ideal. A leader's words and actions do this, often in unsuspecting, unintentional ways. Naturally, leaders primarily interested in their own agendas, success, and recognition tend to unplug the exemplary followers. Conversely, leaders who empower others, recognize them for their accomplishments, and involve and engage them in the creation and pursuit of a vision for a better future energize and awaken their members and spur them on to greater levels of achievement.

4. Invite others to push back your ideas. Effective leaders don't surround themselves with like-minded people. They recognize the importance of diversity of thought and perspective.

John F. Kennedy and his administration learned the hard way during the Bay of Pigs fiasco what can happen if team members do not challenge ideas and hastily agree on a course of action. Consequently, he handled the Cuban Missile Crisis in another way by securing contrary opinions in advance of decisions. He asked key members of his executive team to play the devil's advocate, to identify shortcomings in the prevailing decisions. This provided a valuable opportunity to study the issue more thoroughly before engaging in a specific action.

Pierre Elliot Trudeau believed in a similar process. As the prime minister of Canada (1968–1982; 1982–1984), he called on his ministers and cabinet members to become more involved. He believed that better decisions resulted from having members actively involved in the process. I lead my faculties the same way. Many times, I changed my opinion on a strategic direction, having heard from members who were closer to the action. I used to tell them if we only do what I want to do, we really don't need a leadership team. They knew the folly of this approach, and so did I.

Effective leaders do this. They engage others in the activities of a group or organization. They invite others to offer their opinions and encourage others to search for and offer suggestions for new ways of doing things. They explore new paradigms, focus on new ways of doing things, not engaging in the status quo unless it is deemed to be the best alternative. They break tradition in their thinking and actions and ask others to do the same. Effective leaders recognize that their thinking is only clearer and more effective when it has to be defendable and subject to alternative opinions. They also avoid groupthink. They support followers thinking for themselves. Increased alternatives are identified by having other alternatives, from the perspective of having more and better alternatives to heightening the motivation of group members who feel a genuine part of a group or organization. Some writers have referred to this leadership style as a "lubricant for individual and organizational change."[206]

Kouzes and Posner concluded that effective leaders benefit from honest and at times heated discussions that can lead to the generation of diverse thinking and new perspectives. New alternatives and ultimately better decisions and more prudent courses of action can result. Leaders who do this "motivate followers to make significant personal sacrifices in the interest of some mission and to perform above and beyond the call of duty."[207] Encourage people to be critical of ideas and mistakes but never of the people advancing or making them.

5. Hold people accountable. Holding people accountable is often seen as a punitive process. However, many leadership writers disagree and assert that followers who know they will be accountable for their actions are positively motivated. Generally speaking, people genuinely want and need the opportunity to display their competence and contributions. Leaders must hold people accountable and be held accountable by others.

Bobby Knight, the retired university basketball coach, offered a similar opinion. When asked how he coaches student athletes who have changed so markedly from past generations, he quickly asserted that kids haven't changed, but adult influences around the kids have changed. He argued that his athletes need structure, regulation, and consequences. Once presented and accepting of these aspects, they function like they always functioned. The scenario breaks down when adult influences (or leaders) do not hold those in their charge accountable for their success and lack of the same. Coach Mike Krzyzewski also runs a very tight ship with his Duke University Blue Devils basketball team. He holds his players to high academic, social, and athletic standards, and his players obviously respond well to this leadership style. He expects them to be leaders—as a member of his team and after they graduate from Duke.

Followers view the process as an opportunity to show their stuff, to be appropriately recognized for their efforts and contributions. They know the process will illuminate their strengths and draw attention to their contributions. Followers' motivation to increase their commitment and contributions to a group or organization will only improve when they accept a challenge to attain a predetermined goal and they know they'll be evaluated and receive feedback on their performance. Accountability is an essential element of effective leadership. People need to be accountable, otherwise they lose their sense of responsibility. Soon they are pointing fingers at others and projecting blame. Conversely, when people are involved in setting standards of conduct and performance, they understand the factors that make the rule important, and they tend to be more accepting of the decisions rendered.

As a former varsity hockey player, I played for a number of coaches who invoked curfew rules. Team members routinely violated these rules. One coach understood this point well. He gathered the players together at the start of the season to engage in group goal setting and to set team rules and discipline if the rules were broken. One of the rules we set was our curfew rule for the season. We also established the disciplinary action if the rule was broken. Members of the team had input. They understood the basis of the decision. In the end, we set a rule that was fair to all involved and established a disciplinary action to be taken if the rule was violated. We didn't need to employ the disciplinary action. That year, we did not break the rule. After all, it was our rule, not the coach's rule. The same situation can be played out in other settings. Involve people in decisions that will affect them, and undoubtedly there will be significantly greater understanding, buy-in, and cooperation. Tell them what the rules are, and you will be in the role of cop, not coach. Naturally, leaders are expected to follow through on the positive and negative consequences of the accountability process. People expect to be recognized for making the contributions they agreed to make to a leader and an organization. Conversely, if inadequate performance and commitment are not dealt with, the leader and organization lose credibility and the outlined benefits of the accountability process are lost.

6. Pursue personal effectiveness. There are strategies that make a current or prospective leader more effective in the role.[208] While these steps may appear simplistic on the surface, rest assured that they are difficult to implement on a consistent basis. In the words of Steven Covey, what might be common sense is rarely common practice. For example, leaders/prospective leaders should do the following:

- **Be courteous**: Effective leaders are active listeners who pay attention to what followers have to say.
- **Be visible**: Face-to-face contact with followers which provides tangible evidence of your interest in them as people *and* members of the organization, as well as keeping you apprised of "underground" development.
- **Proactively care and counsel your followers**: Being available to assist followers with their concerns in and out of the workplace shows a humanitarian side that people appreciate and respect.
- **Keep focused on the vision**: Management theorist Peter Drucker noted that many organizations soon lose sight of what they initially set out to accomplish. Leaders need to continually articulate and reinforce the strategic vision—through their words and behaviors.
- **Be an active listener**: Listening is an important but unfortunately overlooked link in the communication process. Effective leaders actively listen to their followers

and encourage their group or organization to embrace two-way communication. They seek and appreciate the input of all members of an organization. Unique, creative ideas are often germinated through this process, to say nothing of the inspirational uplift that followers get from knowing that their leader genuinely cares about their perspectives.

- **Use symbols**: These communication aids help reinforce the desired culture of the organization or help articulate the strategic vision for the group. They can be extremely effective for both clarity and retention purposes.
- **Celebrate success—frequently**: Effective leaders recognize and honor individuals and units for results. They let followers know that they will be held accountable, and they make others aware of the contributions of people in the group or organization.

Creating challenges for the group or organization and the people within it is the responsibility of the leader. Leaders who want dynamic, forward-thinking organizations, staffed with people who are creative and excited about realizing the predetermined goals or objectives governing the organization, would be well served taking the time to evaluate their habits in relation to these seven suggestions for challenging themselves and those they lead. An organization comprised of focused people who have high levels of commitment and seek greater levels of challenge from their own positions and the organization at large may create some challenges for the leader. However, motivation and performance will not be an issue. The leader and the empowered employee will have to negotiate other creative ways to deploy the energy and excitement of these people in concert with the needs of the organization and the other members of the group. Certainly, an organization comprised of highly motivated, focused people committed to a vision and determined to make it happen is a leader's dream—although it does not have to stay in the dream stage. It can happen.

Summary

Enthusiasm (a.k.a. passion) is an attribute that should be promoted and embraced in any group or organization. Leaders can have a significant impact on the degree to which people in an organization have a passion for their positions and the people with whom they work to pursue an agreed-upon vision. Leaders must project higher levels of enthusiasm and commitment if they expect similar motives to be evident in other members of the group. A leader's words and actions go a long way in determining how excited others will be about the organization and the task at hand. Leaders who can energize and excite others to their personal potential and channel these energies toward the fulfilment of the organizational goals will have a legacy, making similar reenergizing processes instituted by the leader much easier to implement. A community of leaders excited about the challenge and worth of fulfilling a personal and organizational mission is the natural outcome.

Successful leaders in any field will be those individuals who are able to alter the beliefs and expectations of others through inspiration and influence, not by exerting greater power or higher levels of manipulation. The true leaders of the day need to "align the resources of the organization, particularly the human ones, creating a sense of shared objectives worthy of people's support and even dedication."[209] Leader behavior outside this approach will not bring about dedicated and committed effort from people mandated to make an organizational vision a reality. Efforts invested in this type of leader will be temporary and transparent at best.

This chapter outlined the importance of creating enthusiasm within an organization. Leaders must project contagious enthusiasm if they expect others to be excited about the challenges facing them and the organization at large. Seven ways that leaders can infect others with enthusiasm were presented, along with helpful anecdotes from industry that serve to reinforce the importance of the concept and how some industry leaders effectively infected others with enthusiasm. The end results in these cases were inspired and enthusiastic people in an organization who were focused on the attainment of a clear and accepted organizational vision.

Leaders can generate enthusiasm in their groups or organizations by challenging members to attain ends that are both difficult and realistic. This method of inspiring others has been documented by many leadership writers. The ways and means that current and aspiring leaders could inspire and empower those in their realm of influence through the creation of challenges and holding people accountable for results was also documented. This process, when implemented by a respected, charismatic leader and related to the attainment of an agreed-upon and accepted goal can be very powerful and assist leaders and organizations in extracting performance beyond initial expectations. These leaders get to know their people, what makes them tick, and how they can be challenged to perform beyond what they themselves thought possible. They recognize and reward (tangibly and intangibly) those who meet the challenges and hold people accountable. These challenges serve to further guide activity and provide performance feedback to members of a group or organization.

Effective leaders create an atmosphere where people are excited about the challenges that lie ahead and have a heightened level of enthusiasm for making them a reality. In the next section, readers will be introduced to the area of organizational culture. This area holds the key to understanding how leaders can impact the deep-rooted beliefs and attitudes of people in a group or organization that ultimately guide and interpret behavior and performance.

> There is no greatness without a passion to be great, whether it's the aspiration of an athlete or an artist, a scientist, a parent, or a businessperson.
> —ANTHONY ROBBINS

C5—Culture Builder

A Reader's Guide

Upon reading this chapter, readers will understand

- the concept of organizational culture,
- that shaping and preserving a desired culture for an organization is widely recognized as the most important function of a leader,
- how leaders must be concerned with the type and strength of an organization's culture,
- how leaders can impact the type and strength of organizational culture, and
- how organizational culture relates to organizational effectiveness.

C5—Culture Builder

> Only with leadership does one get the boldness, the vision, and the energy needed to create cultural change. [210]

Arguably the most important thing that leaders do is develop and preserve a desired culture for an organization, unit, or group. This often transpires in silent, unobtrusive ways. However, leadership scholars[211] and consultants must look deeply into the intricate aspects of a leader's role to measure the indirect aspects of one's influence on organizational culture and subsequently organizational outcomes. This reality might also contribute to the notion that effective leaders operate behind the scenes, doing the less visible yet vital things that make followers and the organization effective. Changing or embedding a desired culture for an organization may be one of these things. It is difficult to see a leader doing this. Some might be doing it unconsciously.

> Leadership is a choice, not a rank.
> —SIMON SINEK

What is Organizational Culture?

> Culture is a little like dropping an Alka-Seltzer in a glass—you don't see it, but somehow it does something.
> —HANS MAGNUS ENZENSBERGER

The study of organizational culture is grounded in the parent fields of anthropology and sociology. The concept has assumed an important role in helping theorists and practitioners understand group dynamics, organizational behavior, and the critical role leaders play in shaping and embedding a desired culture for their unit or organization. Organizational culture has always existed, but it has been in relatively recent times that researchers created the term. We now know that organizational culture is the coagulating agent that holds an organization together, gives it a sense of identity, and helps shape and interpret the behavior of members of the unit or organization.

The organizational culture concept was first introduced to North American scholars by Andrew Pettigrew in his 1979 publication *On Studying Organizational Cultures.*[212] Needless to say, the interest in organizational culture has matured since this early introduction, to the point where organizational culture is now one of the most dominant areas of study in organizational-management science. However, in spite of its rising popularity as a research topic and its prevalence in the leadership and organizational-behavior literature bases, the concept remains confusing and often misunderstood. A multitude of definitions and interpretations of organizational culture bodes support for his claim.

An organization's culture is comprised of the collective beliefs or attitudes of organizational members and reflects an identity of the organization, specifically what is important for the organization, what it believes in and values, and a general code of appropriate conduct for all associated with it. Some theorists[213] referred to the concept as an organization's "values" or "shared ideals" that guide behavior within the organization. They also refer to organizational norms, defined as the formal and informal rules and codes of appropriate and inappropriate behavior within an organization. These "shared values or assumptions form the basis for consensus and integration, which encourages motivation and commitment of meaningful membership."[214] In the end, it is assumed that the culture of an organization helps bring it a sense of realism and purpose.

The most prominent organizational-culture scholars have captured similar elements in their definitions and concepts. They consistently suggest that organizational cultures are the deep-rooted values, norms, and philosophies widely held and practiced by members of an organization. These cultures help interpret organizational happenings, help shape the behavior of organizational members, and reflect an identity for the organization. The culture shapes the personality and climate of an organization, as well as impacting the behavior of employees and ultimately the success of the organization. The organizational culture outlines the dominant orientation of an organization, providing insight into the inner workings, what it stands for, and offering a frame of reference to employees relative to expected behavior codes and the reasoning behind some of the organization's activities. A sampling of the popular organizational culture definitions appears in table 5.

"Organization behaviors and decisions are almost pre-determined by the basic assumptions and values inherent in the organizational culture."[215] An organization's culture is the "social glue" for the organization, allowing members to interpret and make sense of their environment and serving as a guiding light for subsequent behaviors.

Table 5. Common Definitions of Organizational Culture

Another word for social reality ... continually created and recreated by people's ongoing interactions[216]

A set of common understandings for organizing actions and language and other symbolic vehicles for expressing common understandings[217]

Culture appears to have something to do with the way members of a collective organize their experience[218]

"A collection of beliefs, expectations and attitudes shared by the corporation's members"[219] that conveys and shapes an identity for the organization

A constellation of basic views and assumptions, expressed as beliefs and values, that is shared by the key members of an organization[220]

The shared meanings held by organizational members that form an organization's identity[221]

Edgar Schein is arguably the most prominent theorist in the organizational culture area. He proposed a three-level model of escalating depths (artifacts and creations, espoused values, and basic assumptions) to help explain the concept.[222] The first level of his model referred to the physical elements that help interpret what is important to an organization. The artifacts and creations Schein presented referred to the physical elements one sees in an organization (e.g., the clothes employees wear, the physical equipment/ supplies that exist, as well as the layout of these items, and prepared policies and procedures that govern activity for the organization). He believed that while these elements may be readily apparent to the outside eye, they become unobtrusive to those within an organization. People do not generally pay a great deal of attention to these elements, although others from outside the organization hold the objectivity to quickly see these items. However, while these elements may be easy to observe, he also suggested that these items are difficult to decipher and interpret accurately. They may have multiple meanings to different people.

The "espoused values" elements represent the second layer in his model. These aspects represent a futuristic, ideal end for the organization in the eyes of its members. These values emerge from members' experiences in their organization and help them determine what they and the organization might become. Values like synergistic teamwork, a work ethic beyond expected levels, and unchallenged dedication to the cause and raison d'etre of the organization are examples of values that would be present in an effective organization. He suggested that these values help shape and interpret human behavior for members of an organization, and if congruent with the objectives of the group or organization, assist members with articulating and upholding an agreed-upon mission for the enterprise.

The final layer in his model is labeled "basic assumptions," and this level represents the true nature of the organization's culture, the true beliefs and values that people in the group or organization hold. These beliefs are reflected in the repetitive behavior that transpires in organizational life. Activities that do not reinforce these basic assumptions are frowned upon. Consequently, the basic assumptions are rarely challenged. Behavior that runs counter to them is chastised before it is ever considered as a viable alternative. He suggested that deciphering the basic assumptions holds the key for culture researchers and consultants attempting to determine the true culture for a group or organization. He further noted that uncovering and deciphering the other two layers in his model becomes easier and clearer when one accurately interprets the third layer—the basic assumptions.

Schein's concept and model served the academy and practitioners well, but it had some critics. Mary Jo Hatch's "Cultural Dynamics Model"[223] expanded on Schein's model. While recognizing Schein's immense contributions to conceptualizing and understanding this important but slippery area of organizational culture, Hatch felt Schein's model was overly simplistic and did not adequately explain the dynamic and complex concept known as organizational culture. While she agreed that an organization's culture manifests itself in multiple ways, in her opinion Schein's model leaves too many gaps between his three layers. In response, she developed a more comprehensive organizational culture model that offered an explanation for the interplay that occurs as one moves from one level of culture (e.g., artifacts) to another (e.g., values). The arrows between the three layers in Schein's model (artifacts and creations, espoused values, and basic assumptions) are explained, in addition to the arrows linking a new area labeled "symbols." Hatch suggested that symbols differ from artifacts in that symbols refer to the meaning that members of a group or organization attach to artifacts. This refinement to the model requires the individual doing the cultural probe to interpret the artifact, moving it from an artifact to a symbol. Hatch offered that an interpretation of a symbol helps one understand the core values that members of a group or organization hold. She further noted that different contexts call for different interpretations of the artifact.

The second fundamental change that Hatch made to Schein's model was to move from a vertical, linear conceptualization to a circular, interactive model. Hatch focused her attention on the gaps that exist between the different levels of culture. She attempted to interpret the interplay that occurs as one moves from one cultural level to the next. Hatch's model does enrich and better explain the organizational culture element, and leadership enthusiasts are invited to study the model in more detail. The model helps leaders and consultants understand how the four elements of culture interact and relate to one another. It clearly delineates the four areas of organizational culture by offering an explanation for what transpires as one moves from each unit of analysis (i.e., from artifacts, symbols, assumptions, and values). Culture researchers and organizational-culture consultants can quickly and effectively analyze and interpret the four cultural elements and the processes that explain the relationship that exists among them, in their quest to uncover and interpret the culture for an organization. That said, Schein and Hatch agreed that organizational cultures differ from one another much like the cultures of nations differ one from another. Additionally, the differences that exist in an organization among behavior, commitment levels, and productivity of people cannot be fully understood without paying some attention to the culture of the organization. Culture helps to explain why behavior in one organization is similar and uniformly accepted, yet distinct, and possibly frowned upon if present in another organizational setting. Organizational culture helps to explain why actions appear to be purposeful, patterned, and relatively homogeneous in an organization. It helps to explain why conformity to the desired culture is reinforced and rewarded, while resistance or activities that counter the desired culture are discouraged and perhaps not tolerated.

> Many executives believe that strong corporate cultures create excellent performance because well-coordinated managers march energetically in the same direction. Such alignment, motivation, organization, and control can help performance, but only if the resulting actions fit the intelligent strategy for the business.[224]

There has to be a fit between the desired culture and the mission of the enterprise. In addition, individuals who do not appreciate and adhere to a shared culture for a group or organization are often ostracized and alienated from a group. They are different. They don't fit with the other members of the group or organization.

A blue-ribbon example of an individual not aligning with the desired culture of an organization rests with the example of John Z. DeLorean, a successful administrator/engineer with General Motors from 1956 to 1973.[225] In addition to being recognized as a bright, energetic administrator/engineer, DeLorean was famous for being a maverick. He detested and at times ridiculed the prevailing and desired culture of General Motors. Unfailing loyalty to the company and unquestionable subservience to one's immediate supervisor were hallmarks of the General Motors culture that DeLorean did not agree with or model. Subordinates were not to question their superiors. More accurately, they were expected to wait on them. DeLorean bucked the culture of General Motors. Unlike his colleagues, he failed to retrieve his superiors at the airport. He questioned authority when he thought they were wrong. He even opted to disobey the unspoken dress code by wearing brown suits instead of the traditional and expected blue offerings. In the end, DeLorean was fired for his value system that operated in sharp contrast to the prevailing culture of General Motors. In another industry, (one with a culture suited to individual expression and valuing unique opinions) or perhaps with General Motors in another era, DeLorean's paradigm may have aligned with the desired culture, and he may have been praised for his initiative and possibly rewarded for his approach.

Strength and Type of Culture

The organizational-culture concept has been analyzed from both the perspective of culture strength and culture type. Schein noted that both aspects are critical to the success and survival of an organization.

Many organizational culture enthusiasts turn to Peters and Waterman's *In Search of Excellence* text[226] as exhibit A when making a case that organizational-culture strength is a critical factor in determining the success of a unit or organization. Their study of successful organizations prompted them to conclude that without exception, the presence of a strong, positive organizational culture is paramount to organizational success. Successful organizations like Disney, McDonald's, and Microsoft possess strong, well- defined cultures—and not by accident. Founders and subsequent leaders of these organizations worked hard to reinforce and embed a desired culture for their organization, using some of the strategies outlined later in this chapter. Conversely, organizations with a weak culture are likely to have an ambiguous value system, an unclear focus on the organizational mission, depressed staff morale, and inconsistent decision-making.

A strong organizational culture is purported to be important at all times, but particularly in times of bringing new staff members to the organization. A strong culture assists in quickly acclimatizing these members. A strong organizational culture is most important in organizational settings employing a decentralized organizational structure. The top leadership scholars[227] concurred that an organization's culture is the most significant and influential element because employees adopt and reflect the organizational culture.

The type of culture is also an important measure of an organization's culture. Organizational-culture researchers[228] realized that they needed to focus on the practical aspects of culture that guide and underline specific activities. Culture is not the cause of action, but more accurately, the context that predisposes humans to take or not take certain actions. Some theorists noted that organizations engage in activities that are supportive and reflective of the pervading culture. Still others[229] suggested that an organization's culture could be typified to support organizational success and survival (and in alignment with Talcott Parsons's taxonomy of: (a) adapting to change, (b) achieving relevant and desired goals, (c) maintaining teamwork, and (d) creating and maintaining a customer orientation.

> The test of leadership is not what people do in your presence, but what they do in your absence.[230]

How Leaders Impact the Culture of Their Organization or Group

The culture of an organization will rise no higher than
the behavior of its leaders.
—TIM KIGHT, PERFORMANCE COACH,
OHIO STATE UNIVERSITY FOOTBALL TEAM

It is clear that an organization's culture distinguishes it from others and that it is shaped by history, tradition, leaders, and the basic values of individuals attracted to the organization. The contention that leaders can impact the formulation or modification of an organization's culture is also conventional wisdom. However, in spite of the evidence supporting its importance, many leaders do not understand how to shape or embed a desired culture for an organization. "It requires patience, reflectiveness, and a balance between focusing on results and focusing on operations while we are trying to achieve those results. So they shy away from it."[231] Some emphatically state that a leader's role in shaping and maintaining the organizational culture may be his or her most essential contribution.

> Leadership is intertwined with culture formation, evolution, transformation and destruction. Culture is created in the first instance by the actions of the leader; culture is also embedded and strengthened by leaders.[232]

Other writers weighed in on the important role leaders play in formulating and maintaining the organizational culture. "Today's leading chief executives are visionary, daring, aggressive managers who do not flinch from the hardest decisions affecting the very foundations and identities of their organizations."[233] Others noted that "excellent organizations develop cultures that have incorporated the values and practices of excellent leaders."[234]

The degree to which a leader impacts the culture of an organization has also been embraced in the literature. Some[235] theorists have led research studies that confirm that the organization's founder (e.g., Henry Ford, Walt Disney, Steve Jobs, Mark Zuckerberg, Jeff Bezos, or Elon Musk) often plays a major role in setting and embedding an organization's culture. The founder's image and words that reinforce this desired culture are often proudly displayed on plaques (e.g., McDonald's), framed posters (e.g., Wendy's) and other artifacts (e.g., founder's office under glass desk at 3M headquarters), strategically placed throughout the organization. Strong and effective leaders who follow the founders can also have a major impact on shaping and preserving the culture of the organization. "Leadership and culture management are so central to understanding organizations and making them effective that we cannot be complacent about either one."[236] Schein was one of the most prolific and convincing researchers, whose research findings supported his claim that leaders shape the culture of the organization and the culture impacts the success of the organization.

Sounds simple. However, as we know, leadership and organizational culture involve people—and their moods, emotions, thought processes, and cynicism. However, one of the most vocal supporters of the linkage between leadership and organizational culture highlighted the difficulty that leaders have in shaping the culture of an organization with his comment that "even when leadership knows where it wants to go and is open about it, it takes time and energy to get large numbers of people to hold basic assumptions about something fundamental."[237]

Now that the culture has been defined and its relative importance to organizational effectiveness presented, the following section will provide readers with an overview of how a culture can evolve and be altered by a leader. Specifically, five suggestions are presented: (a) a founder's or reference to a founder's values/vision, (b) altering the reward system, (c) specific orientation programs for employees, (d) human resources decisions, and (e) the effective use of symbols.

1. A Founder's or Reference to a Founder's Values/Vision.
The words and actions of founders are often passed down through generations, and they help shape the organization's culture. A founder often creates the culture, and it gets handed down through generations of leaders. New leaders can extend the culture, and if they are exceptionally strong and effective, change the culture of the organization. However, the culture of the organization often reflects the founder's values, priorities, and vision. Anecdotes used to reinforce the founder's values and beliefs are often passed on as a way of transmitting the desired culture through different organizational generations. As Howard Gardner noted, leaders typically reinforce founder visions through their storytelling. They often share important stories and anecdotes of company founders or heroes/heroines who made a difference in the past. These stories, eloquently shared, help shape and embed a desired culture, and subsequently an expected code of behavior for the group or organization.

An example of a founder's vision being passed down throughout a large organization is Sam Walton, late founder of the highly successful Wal-Mart department stores. Walton recognized the importance of the customer. He wanted all of his employees to be aware of the needs, wants, and desires of the customer. To highlight this customer orientation mind-set, he hired seniors to greet customers at the door and welcome them to Wal-Mart. He wanted people to smile at all times and reinforced this with his own behavior. He communicated his philosophy that the customer is the first priority. While profits were important in Walton's philosophy, he believed that they would naturally follow if customers were treated with respect and dignity.

This is not unlike the corporate culture of the Disney Corporation, where staff members work with a mission statement "to make people happy" and an overriding philosophy to make their customers "their guests." "Be Our Guest" is a song and catch phrase developed to reinforce and embed the vision of Walt Disney. Disney believed that customers deserve high-quality service. His business philosophy was that "quality will win out. Give people everything you can give them.

Keep the place as clean as you can keep it. Keep it friendly. Make it a fun place to be."[238]

> The Walt Disney Company's core values of imagination and wholesomeness stem from the founder's inner belief that imagination and wholesomeness should be nurtured for their own sake.[239]

William Hewlett, founder of Hewlett-Packard, was famous for his orientation to filling the needs of customers. He asked employees at all levels to come up with ideas that would help people at the next desk more effectively carry out their duties and then sell those ideas to every "next desk" throughout the world. This level of innovation and focus on customer needs remains a cornerstone of the culture at Hewlett-Packard. New employees are continually reminded of the "founder's vision."

IBM has a worldwide reputation for being a conservative and professional company. This philosophy continues to be reflected in the culture of the organization and can be easily traced to the vision and philosophy of founder Thomas Watson. "The symbolized dress code for IBM employees, institutionalized by Thomas J. Watson, Sr., was intended to impress customers and employees alike. The code symbolized dedication to service, uniform high-quality, and seriousness of purpose."[240] Certainly the stories and vision of Mark McCormack have been told over and over again within the offices of IMG, long after his death. His influence will remain and be evident in the actions and decisions of current and future employees. His principles will be part of employee orientation programs, and his picture will be a prominent feature in the IMG offices forever. Senior leaders will chart a course for IMG aligned with that envisioned by McCormack. His flair for working long hours, sealing a deal, and advancing the commercial aspects of sports will continue to be emulated in the behavior of staff members at IMG. His vision for the company will underlie current and future directions.

2. Altering the Reward System

An executive leader who is not the founder of the organization also has the potential to significantly modify or embed the organization's culture. What leaders pay attention to, what they react to, how they coach other organizational members, how they role model, how they allocate rewards, and how they influence the human resource functions of staff recruiting, hiring, training, and termination help to modify or embed the desired organizational culture. "Cultural norms arise and change because of what leaders tend to focus their attention on, their reactions to crises, their role modeling, and their recruitment strategies."[241] The executive leaders can alter the culture of their organization through their actions. Leaders who role model in a fashion congruent with the desired culture refer to company legends who reflect such a culture, stage company ceremonies and rituals that help reinforce this culture, are examples of leaders executing this important responsibility. However, it is important that leaders reward and emphasize things that support the desired culture, one that supports the mission and strategy of the organization or group. Leaders do not want all their people to think alike. Leaders need to emphasize and reinforce the importance of diverse opinion and alternative paradigms. The worst thing for an organization occurs when one opinion (the leader's opinion) is the only perspective that is valued. Jerry Krause, former general manager of the Chicago Bulls basketball team, summed it up best when commenting on his disagreements with his former coach Phil Jackson. Krause used to say that if two people thought the same way on every issue, then one should be fired because duplication is not needed. Leaders must ensure that what they support, encourage, and reward is not compliance with their opinion. This may be difficult for some leaders, although in the long run, this strategy will pay handsome dividends as issues will be looked at from more than one perspective. There may be times when leaders have to change their opinion. However, doing so may help reinforce the importance of diversity and suggesting alternative options. Other perspectives may lead to better decisions. Be open to the opinions of others, even those (perhaps *especially* those) that counter your perspective as the leader. Organizations that appreciate diversity and alternative opinions and strategies are those that will be successful over an extended period of time.

Some organizations reinforce their desired culture by altering their reward system. For example, the Xerox Corporation rewards employees on their performance related to servicing the customer. Wherever employees may find themselves on an organizational chart, they can relate, appreciate, and operationalize these values in their day-to-day activities. If ingrained and embedded throughout the organization, they become reflected in its culture. Another example comes from the Disney Corporation, where hiring decisions often rest on an assessment of one's personality and commitment to service. Company officials actively seek and hire people committed to helping others.

> By hiring individuals who already believe in what the organization stands for, they tap into a deeper commitment to organizational purpose and practices. Training becomes easier and morale remains strong. Employee friendliness and dedication to service have served as competitive advantages for Disney.[242]

3. Specific Orientation Programs for Employees

Leaders can ensure that the desired values and perspectives are held and practiced by members of an organization through orientation and in-service programs. The content of these sessions can be controlled, and the elements that need to be altered or embedded in the culture of the organization can be presented and reinforced. The Disney Corporation offers such an orientation program for their employees. All employees, from new full-time hires to part-time students working for Disney during a summer break, must participate in a structured, two-day orientation program called "Traditions 101." Participants in this program meet Walt Disney through a video; gain an appreciation for his vision and values; understand the underlying meaning of "be our guest"; and begin to understand the theory behind the rules, policies, and traditions surrounding employment in the Disney Corporation.

Fast-tracking McDonald's employees go through a similar process at Hamburger U, an educational program designed to orient managers to the traditions and vision of McDonald's founder Ray Kroc. Employees of the Motorola Corporation are shown a video highlighting the expected values of employees and are left with a question asking them to ponder where their values align with those at Motorola. Canon's goal of positioning the company ahead of IBM in the telecommunications industry is reinforced at all employee levels by a poster that employees walk by each day. General Electric believed in leadership development. They created a campus (Crotonville), and their CEO Jack Welch had leadership expert Noel Tichy develop and deliver leadership programs to staff members. This program reinforced a learning culture at General Electric and Welch's emphasis on leadership and personal growth. All these examples highlight the importance placed on the culture of the organization and represent higher management's efforts to develop and embed a desired culture for their respective organizations. This perspective also aligns with the insights of Marshall Goldsmith, who emphatically states that leaders must stay current and continue to learn and develop.[243]

4. Human Resource Decisions
An executive leader's influence on the selection, development, assessment, and distribution of rewards to company employees has a tremendous impact on developing and preserving a desired culture for an organization. Many leaders consciously alter or embed a desired culture for their organization through these processes. Perhaps the easiest way to alter the culture of an organization is to change the people who make up the group. Leaders should thoroughly screen applicants with respect to their personal values and philosophies and attempt to secure those candidates with perspectives that align with

the desired value set for the organization. Over my decanal career, I constantly reminded people that hiring professors and staff members was a thirty-year decision that we had to get right. I made it my practice to interview all shortlisted candidates and most staff members in advance of the appointment. I also wanted to get an assessment of attitude and fit. On a few occasions, I stopped hiring processes because I felt that the fit was not evident or some red flags were raised on my attitude assessment. We also know people are generally their best on interview day. They don't generally get better attitudes from what is on display at that time.

The reward system must also be geared to acknowledging and rewarding employees who project the values desired for the organization. These human-resource activities go a long way to altering and embedding a culture of an organization that can significantly impact the success of the enterprise. Once again, as dean, I was able to give annual salary increases to colleagues who made contributions in areas that advanced our mission and helped embed our desired culture.

5. Effective Use of Symbols

Symbols can be tangible artifacts or intangible acts. They can be powerful vehicles to communicate what organizations and leaders truly believe and what they expect from their members.

Some organizational-culture researchers[244] believe that an organizational culture can be identified in part by carefully reviewing printed materials, paying attention to the physical artifacts that present themselves in a work setting or published company document. Wendy's restaurant locations all have pictures and inspirational quotes from the founder, the late Dave Thomas. They often reflect the humble beginnings of the company and the commitment to a home atmosphere in their restaurants. Other artifacts to reinforce this culture are the linen tablecloths and Tiffany lights that are often found in these fast-food outlets. McDonald's restaurants did the same with a famous quote (power of persistence) from their founder, Ray Kroc. The photos and messages of Henry Ford are artifacts that reflect the great traditions and proud history of the Ford Motor Company.

Leaders significantly shape and reflect the culture of an organization by illustrating a model of behavior, values, and behavior norms through verbal and nonverbal communications, and in so doing, indicating what they and the organization stand for. Organizational-culture expert Edgar Schein asserted that leaders develop and maintain organizational culture through a number of behavioral activities like (a) reinforcing their personal priorities and opinions, (b) reacting to crises in certain ways that highlight these values, (c) role modeling, (d) allocating rewards in support of certain values or priorities, and (e) selecting and promoting individuals who share a similar value system and priority listing. How the leader behaves; what he or she reinforces through verbal, nonverbal, and written modes of communication; and where leaders allocate resources make strong statements about the leader's value system, as well as having the potential of impacting the culture of an organization. Even the way leaders introduce and interact with staff members helps reinforce and embed a culture for the organization. For example, if teamwork and mutual respect are a desired value for a group or organization, employees should not be referred to as subordinates. The term *associate* or *colleague* is a more appropriate and empowering title. Likewise, referring to customers as *clients* helps embed a perception of a higher value on the importance of people to an organization.

Clarifying and living a defined organizational culture may be the greatest contribution a leader can offer an organization. Leaders must reinforce and consistently act in accordance with the corporate culture or trust, stability, cohesion, and ultimately organizational performance could be in jeopardy.

The lens of history has provided leadership and organizational-culture scholars with the examples of Lee Iacocca and Ray Kroc, who thoroughly understood their own personal philosophies and the desired organizational cultures for their companies (Chrysler Corporation and McDonald's restaurants respectively). Both leaders were instrumental in the formulation and transmission of a positive organizational culture throughout all levels of their organization. Their vision for the corporation shaped the culture, which in turn attracted the organizational membership to the cause and heightened their commitment to this end. Furthermore, Iacocca shaped the inclusive culture needed at Chrysler if it was going to recover, through his personal sacrifice. He spoke about making sacrifices, starting with him. He embedded an organizational culture based on sacrifice and an enduring commitment to the cause. The company, and some say the auto industry, were saved.

The successful transmission of the culture to members of the organization can be difficult, and the organizational culture perceived by senior executives in an organization may bear minimal resemblance to the culture perceived at the middle-manager, supervisory, or worker level within the hierarchy. What is felt on the ground matters. The applicability of the culture to people at all levels of an organization is a critical factor in determining how easily people in the organization can identify with and adopt the desired culture. Connection is critical. The culture at Disney applies to everyone. Those in the CEO suite and those selling tickets can all pull in the same direction and "make people happy." Avis's slogan "We try harder" has applicability to all levels of the workforce. If all organizational members adopt this theme and indeed "try harder," the organization can be transformed to a higher-functioning unit.

Leadership theorists have clearly earmarked developing and embedding a desired organizational culture as one of the most critical roles a leader assumes. As noted above, leaders can create, change, and embed a desired culture for their group or organization. Five suggestions were offered to leaders: (a) highlighting the founder's values/vision, (b) altering the reward system, (c) delivering well-conceived orientation programs to employees, (d) the human-resources decisions they can make, and (e) effectively using symbols.

> All leadership takes place through the communication
> of ideas to the minds of others.
> — CHARLES COOLEY

The Leader's Role in Culture Change: An Epilogue

Most theorists believe that leaders can potentially alter the culture of an organization. Many comment on the leader's potential for "maintaining an organization's culture or in changing it to implement a change of direction dictated by a new vision."[245] Leaders have the unique and special opportunity to impact the culture of their organization. Edgar Schien extended the claim, noting that "the only thing of real importance that leaders do is create and manage culture"[246] and "much of what is mysterious about leadership becomes clearer if we separate leadership from management and link leadership specifically to creating and changing culture."[247]

> The top performers (leaders) create a broad shared culture, a coherent framework within which charged-up people search for appropriate adaptations. Their ability to extract extraordinary contributions from very large numbers of people turns on the ability to create a sense of highly valued purpose. [248]

Leaders shape the organizational culture by their words and actions. They help shape the culture by ensuring that there is a strong, compelling vision that members embrace and use as a touchstone to make decisions and guide activity. The leaders' behavior, their reactions to critical incidents, their human-resource decisions, their reference to company "heroes," and their influence on the physical work environment all help identify and embed an organization's culture.

Leaders must pay attention to this area. They should aspire to having members understand and adopt a culture. They need to understand the orientations, values, and beliefs of organizational members before embarking on a campaign to modify the overall culture of the organization. As noted above, leaders are essential to shaping the organizational culture, especially leaders who instill meaning and trust in followers, who in turn, are motivated beyond initial expectations and strive toward the attainment of organizational goals. They need to ensure that members are focused. The vision, developed and refined in numerous ways including consulting with organizational members, unifies the organization and has the potential of aligning organizational members toward a common purpose. The vision can and must be incorporated into the culture of the organization. It is clear that effective leadership is positively related to the development and transmission of culture within organizations. Effective leaders know what they stand for, have ensured that the overwhelming majority of members agree, and are successful in embedding this feeling into the culture of the organization. Former president and CEO of Maple Leaf Sports & Entertainment Richard Peddie[249] continually talked about the "vision and values" of the company. When he wasn't talking about them, his colleagues were. They were shared with new employees at orientation programs (and prospective candidates for positions would be well served in knowing them when interviewing for positions with Maple Leaf Sports & Entertainment). They sought to *win*—in all contexts. They sought to be champions—the best—in their sports, in the way they conducted business, and in all operations. This vision was supported by four values:

1. Excite every fan—through the performance of teams, the fan experience with parking, concessions, game presentation, and enrichments like the best video boards and in-game entertainment features.

2. Inspire our people—by engaging them, committing to their long-term learning and career development, compensation, and recognition.

3. Leaders in our community—investing in the community through charitable work, foundation spending, and engagement in community events.

4. Be dedicated to our teams—ensuring they had everything they need to be successful.

Peddie and his colleagues ensured that this vision and the four values were consistently communicated and embraced. Performance gets measured against these elements. They helped focus and guide this complex organization. The genesis of this approach came from Peter and Waterman's classic *In Search of Excellence* book and the principles that separated market leaders from their competitors. Vision and values matter—and they need to be baked into the culture of the organization, using the strategies outlined above.

> People in authority must be social architects, studying and shaping what we call the culture of work, examining the values and norms of organizations and the ways that they are transmitted to the individual, and whenever necessary, altering them.[250]

Culture and Organizational Success

> We are what we repeatedly do. Excellence, then, is not an act but a habit.
>
> —ARISTOTLE

Theorists writing and speaking on the topic of organizational culture since the release of *In Search of Excellence* generally agree that organizational culture is a phenomenon leaders need to embrace, as it impacts many things, including the bottom line. An organization's culture guides all activities by providing the framework for the organization's belief system and philosophy of operation. History tells us that organizations that are successful over time possess a strong, well-defined culture that reinforces continual learning and listening, innovation, teamwork, and a customer orientation. An "organizational culture helps to explain many organizational phenomena, that culture can aid or hinder organizational effectiveness, and that leadership is the fundamental process by which organizational cultures are formed and changed."[251] An organization's culture is an important and necessary element and consequently needs to be coaligned with the mission of the enterprise. How members of an organization structure their goals, define their objectives, serve their constituents, and promote their organization is reflected and encompassed by the organization's culture.

The presence of a positive organizational culture is linked with increased consensus around organizational strategy. The stronger the organizational culture, the more committed organizational members are to it and its strategy. "Without general agreement on acceptable behavior and value context within which we operate, the organizational members are free to follow different paths."[252] Organizations successful over time possess a strong, widely shared organizational culture that provides a clear, unambiguous, shared understanding of the organization's value system, which reflects what the organization stands for in all activities. Some researchers have linked a strong, positive organizational culture with increased employee productivity.[253] Members of organizations with a strong, positive culture have greater agreement around organizational direction, a common values system reinforcing commitment to the organization and their contribution to the organization and increased role clarity. An organization's culture is the most significant and influential element because employees adopt and reflect the organizational culture. Other researchers[254] have linked a strong, positive organizational culture with employee commitment. The stronger and more positive the culture, the greater the level of employee commitment and naturally, the organization is united and, if focused in the right direction through a vision, more effective. Some have stated that "strong cultures can make work meaningful, can galvanize employees to take action, and can generate tremendous enthusiasm."[255] Work takes on greater meaning for these employees because there is a deeply embedded value system that recognizes and appreciates effort directed toward the accomplishment of organizational goals. Strong, well-defined organizational cultures create parameters for organizational members, and these boundaries help focus members of an organization. Organizations successful over an extended period of time are more likely to possess a strong, well-defined culture.

This section has focused on the positive aspects of organizational culture and its impact on member connection, satisfaction, and performance. However, an organization's culture can cut both ways. It does not have to be positive. A negative culture that restricts innovation or adversely impacts employee recognition or satisfaction may exist and consequently impede organizational success. Organizations with weak cultures generally possess an ambiguous belief and value system, decreased continuity between staff members relative to any beliefs or values, and organizational members working in opposition because of a lack of purpose or direction. As noted by leading authorities in the area,[256] organizations with strong, positive cultures have staff members who more effectively and uniformly share: (a) a philosophy of management, (b) a greater feeling of importance and respect for the organization's mission, and (c) a tradition or corporate character that embodies a passion for excellence and continual improvement. Conversely, organizations with negative cultures include: (a) poor staff morale, (b) a short-term orientation to goals and the production of immediate results, (c) a failure to monitor and react to external factors in the marketplace, (d) inconsistent decision-making and behaviors exhibited by organizational members, and (e) frequent emotional outbursts from staff members. A summary of the important studies linking culture to various organizational outcomes is presented in table 6.

A strong organizational culture may be even more important today when staff members seek high levels of engagement and autonomy.[257] Contemporary organizations often are team-based, generally deploy a decentralized organizational structure, and usually offer employees high levels of position autonomy (because they demand it). Ensuring a strong, positive organizational culture may never be more important than it is today.

One thing that can't be lost is the need for the culture to cascade throughout the organization. There are many examples of leaders with great visions and perspectives on a desired culture that never reach members of the organization. The vision and the culture must penetrate the organization. Hopefully, the vision is something that grows organically, so members identify with it and feel that it represents them. The culture to support the vision must pervade the organization as well. The penetration of a culture throughout the various levels of an organizational hierarchy is an important indicator of the homogeneity and pervasiveness of a culture. Effective leaders ensure that the desired organizational culture penetrates deep into the organizational hierarchy.

Table 6. Impact of a Strong, Positive Organizational Culture

- increased staff alignment, resulting in enhanced organizational effectiveness

- greater consensus for the strategic direction

- heightened employee productivity

- advanced levels of employee commitment

- more uniform behavior/role clarity

While an organization's culture is generally presented in positive terms, it is possible for organizations to possess a negative culture, which could potentially contribute to decreased teamwork, reduced cohesiveness, and stunted organizational goal attainment. These negative cultures are generally based on individual accomplishment and greed.

An organization's culture can be diagnosed through a variety of methods. For example, assessing the physical appearance of the workplace, critically analyzing organizational documents and promotional literature, conducting observational techniques to monitor employee behavior, and interviewing staff members are methods of uncovering an organization's culture. Some researchers[258] have developed instruments like the Organizational Culture Assessment Questionnaire (OCAQ), a valid and reliable instrument to quantitatively measure the strength and type of an organization's culture. However, leaders not wanting to subject members of their organization to a formalized questionnaire could generate useful information[259] about the culture of their respective organization by securing answers to questions and prompts like the following:

(a) Tell me about the history of the company.

(b) What were its beginnings?

(c) Why is the company a success?

(d) What explains its growth?

(e) What kind of people work here?

(f) Who generally gets ahead in the long term?

(g) What kind of place is this to work in?

(h) What is your average day like?

(i) How do things get done?

Not all theorists are in agreement with the notion that a strong, positive, widely shared culture is critical to organizational success. A strong, coherent culture does not guarantee success, suggesting that it may be counterproductive in some situations. "Some organizational cultures will presumably be irrelevant to performance, some forms of culture will promote and some will inhibit efficient operation."[260] The type of culture must align with the mission and the goals of the organization. Researchers who concurred that culture type is important developed the Culture Building Activities (CBA) instrument to quantitatively measure four specific culture-building activities purported to align with organizational success and survival.[261] The four activities are based on the seminal work of Talcott Parsons and include: managing change, achieving goals, coordinated teamwork, and customer orientation.

The current thinking in leadership draws attention to the need for members of an organization to align with the vision of the organization and work cooperatively to attain the vision. This is measured in the coordinated teamwork scale of the CBA. This might help alleviate concerns in some quarters that leadership enthusiasts do "not give sufficient credit to teams (members of an organization) and often exaggerates the role of individual leaders."[262] The other three culture-building activities are equally important to business and volunteer organizations and consequently, leaders of these organizations should ensure that the prevailing culture sustains and promotes these activities.

The type of culture can assist or hinder the effectiveness of an organization, depending on the situational context. The culture type must parallel the mission of the organization.

Summary

It is clear that organizational culture is an area that will continue to gain popularity in future organizational studies and in management literature. Earlier research efforts that did not include an organizational culture component have been insufficient in understanding the true dynamics of organizational life and what makes organizations effective or ineffective. We needed to look deeper—and we have. The beliefs, values, and attitudes of group members have a great deal to do with understanding their commitment and contributions and consequently the goals, strategies, and outcomes of an organization. It is not easy, but it is important. Organizational culture does hold the key to interpreting meaning and activity in organizations. It is also an area that effective leaders of tomorrow will both appreciate and consciously endeavor to manage.

This chapter outlined the importance of organizational culture to the area of leadership and organizational effectiveness. The impact that leaders can have on the development, preservation, and penetration of a desired organizational culture was discussed, with practical advice to current and aspiring leaders recognizing the importance of organizational culture and seeking to embed a specific culture for their respective setting. Five specific techniques were presented.

Culture building was presented as the last "C" because it is the most difficult "C" to comprehend and put into practice. However, it also has the most dramatic effect on the organization, the people within it, and the effectiveness of the enterprise. It is a vitally important area. In the words of culture guru Edgar Schein, it is *the most important area*. The other "Cs" have to be in place first. Once embedded, the leader can focus his or her efforts on securing the desired culture for his or her organization, and in doing so, embed the desired beliefs, values, and attitudes that facilitate successful organizations over time.

Conclusion

A Reader's Guide

Upon reading this chapter, readers will understand

- the need for a new type of leader in the new millennium and beyond,
- the unique and different challenges facing the contemporary leader, and
- how the Five C model of leadership can effectively assist today's leaders in meeting and exceeding these and other challenges.

Conclusion

There is nothing more difficult to take in hand, more perilous to conduct, or more uncertain in its success, than to take the lead in the introduction of a new order of things.

—MACHIAVELLI

Jack Welch, former chief executive officer of General Electric and celebrated leader in the business world, once conveyed to Warren Bennis that the field of leadership is changing and future leaders must be cognizant of the change. He suggested that successful leaders in the new era will be those individuals who are "passionate, driven leaders—people who not only have an enormous amount of energy, but who can energize those whom they lead."[263] The need for effective leadership abounds.

Companies operating in the late 1990s were frequently in a state of downsizing, trends we continue to see in the current millennium.

This impacts the perceived level of loyalty leaders and organizations hold for employees. Competition heightens, calling forth the need for organizations to be comprised of talented, focused, and energized employees who are prepared to invest effort and energy beyond ordinary levels of expectation. Effective leaders will be able to extract these elements. Ineffective leaders will not, much to the detriment of their parent unit or organization. Finally, in times of resource scarcity, leaders will be forced to extract more from their employees, with less to offer in exchange. Employees aware of these issues yet committed to making organizational visions a reality will only appear when leaders possess and exercise the type of leadership presented earlier in this book. Leading in the current times is not easy—but it has perhaps never been so important. Management expert Peter Drucker supported this notion when he stated that leaders of the future will require special people who are willing to invest the time and energy to lead.[264] After all, leaders have to attract followers, for without them, people can't lead. He added that leaders will be results oriented, unwilling to accept the status quo, but be focused on moving the group or organization forward in obtaining a predetermined goal. They'll be in the spotlight only from the point of view as being visible. They will be watched closely, and leaders will have to ensure their credibility is maintained by "walking their talk." They will graciously and willingly accept the responsibility of leadership.

Readers of this text have been provided with an overview of the empirical research that has been undertaken in the quest to understand what constitutes effective leadership. A debt of gratitude must be extended to some of the leadership scholars whose work was highlighted throughout this book. Namely, we know more about leadership because of the intensity, intellect, and commitment of leadership scholars like those profiled in appendix D ("On the Shoulders of Giants").

Practicing leaders need to see the clear implications of the leadership research. They need to know what they can do, what they need to improve upon, and how they can precisely heighten their leadership qualities in the eyes of those they currently lead. Aspiring leaders can engage in a similar exercise from a hypothetical perspective.

The Five Cs of Leadership are founded on the writer's leadership research and practical experience. They are common sense concepts that are not common practice. Leaders can learn and improve from grasping the content in this section and engaging in the practical suggestions offered to heighten each quality. Specifically, the Five Cs of Leadership are:

> C1—Credibility: A leader perceived by followers as being trustworthy, honest, caring, and consistent
>
> C2—Compelling Vision: A leader with the ability to focus the attention of followers on a desired end and inspire them to adopt the vision as their own
>
> C3—Charismatic Communicator: A leader with the ability to effectively communicate with followers in a fashion that is perceived as both uplifting and inspiring
>
> C4—Contagious Enthusiasm: A leader who excites and inspires others to go above and beyond the call of duty through his or her own words and actions and by creating challenges for people
>
> C5—Culture Builder: A leader who can interpret the dominant beliefs and values of followers and modify them in a fashion that is consistent with the aims of the organization

As noted in the preface, the Five Cs might be best presented as a leadership house. Credibility (C1) serves as the bedrock or the foundation upon which the other leadership practices are built. The leader must be a credible source of information and be honest and trustworthy or authentic leadership has no chance. Vision (C2), communication (C3), and enthusiasm/passion (C4) are represented by the rooms in the house. They are the components of leadership that followers see and experience. The best leaders develop and embed a desired culture for their organizations through their words and actions. This is presented by the roof/enclosure (C5). Effective leaders are great roof builders. They shape and embed the beliefs, values, and attitudes of colleagues in ways that support and sustain excellence. Finally, relentless discipline is required to ensure leaders and their teams remain honest and trustworthy, focused, progressive, and passionate. This is represented in the model by the mortar holding the bricks together. Discipline is the fuel that drives and holds the model (and the house) together. This model is revisited in figure 2.

The Five C leadership practices align with those of Alan Mulally, who led the transformation of the automobile industry following the market crash of 2009. He wanted colleagues to come to work each day inspired to build a cathedral, not simply earn a paycheck. His simplistic but effective leadership philosophy aligned perfectly with the Five C concept (be clear and honest, ensure everyone knows the plan and the status of the plan, value people, celebrate achievement, and enjoy the journey together). He has been described as one of the best leaders in the modern era.

Mortar Holding Bricks Together
Relentless Discipline

<u>Roof/Enclosure</u>
    C5 – Culture Builder

<u>Rooms</u>
    C4 – Contagious
         Enthusiasm
    C3 – Charismatic
         Communication
    C2 – Compelling Vision

<u>Foundation</u>
    C1- Credibility

Figure 2. The Five C House (Revisited)

Readers have also been presented with an instrument to measure Five C Leadership. The "self" and "other" versions of this instrument, as well as the Interpretive Guide, appear in appendixes A and B respectively.

The study of leadership is a journey, at times long and arduous. Finding specific, precise concepts that describe and defend the concept of leadership in every circumstance is akin to finding the proverbial needle in a haystack. As times change, leaders must change. However, the Five Cs of Leadership are universal concepts that do not have to be compromised in changing times. The specific components like C5—Culture Building have some flexible elements that can be modified as times and circumstances change. Other aspects like credibility, vision, charismatic communication skill sets, and enthusiasm will be as important one hundred years from now as they are today.

Truly effective leaders in the years ahead will have personas determined by strong values and belief in the capacity of individuals to grow. They will also have an image of society in which they would like their organizations and themselves to live. They will be visionary, they will believe strongly that they can and should be shaping the future, and they will act on those beliefs through their personal behavior.[265]

I sincerely hope you find this work valuable and that it serves to guide your future involvement in your field. Leadership is not easy, but it has the potential to be one of the most rewarding and challenging components in human interaction. I wish you well in your quest to experience and deliver Five C Leadership. It will be something worth which to strive.

> I'd rather have an army of rabbits led by a lion than an army of lions led by a rabbit.
>
> —NAPOLEON[266]

> Let us be the leader we wish we had.
>
> —SIMON SINEK

Appendix A

Five C Leadership Assessment
Questionnaire "Self" Version

Further Information:
Dr. W. James Weese
Faculty of Health Sciences
The University of Western Ontario
London, Ontario, Canada
N6A 5B9
Office Phone: 519-661-2111 ext. 84239
Home Phone: 519-660-4392
Office Fax: 519-850-2347
email: jweese1@uwo.ca
2018

Five C Leadership Assessment Questionnaire—Self

Instructions:

This instrument was developed by Dr. Jim Weese at the University of Western Ontario in London, Ontario, Canada. It is designed to measure leadership at the executive level in a group or organization. For each of the following questions, please assess yourself relative to how frequently you display the behavior. Please use the following response key:

PLEASE CIRCLE THE APPROPRIATE RESPONSE:

ALMOST ALWAYS	OFTEN	SOMETIMES	RARELY	NEVER
A	B	C	D	E

Items:

Your information will be held in strict confidence. Thank you

I, (leader's name) _____.

1. can be trusted to follow through on tasks I agree to undertake .. ..   **A B C D E**

2. have a clear idea of where the group/organization can be in the future.. ... ...   **A B C D E**

3. leave little doubt as to what others expect from me....   **A B C D E**

4. exhibit a genuine passion for my job ... ...   **A B C D E**

5. relay success stories from this or other organizations   **A B C D E**

6. take clear positions on issues.. ... ... A B C D E

7. have a clear idea of what it will take to achieve the
    desired end for the group/organization ... . A B C D E

8. have an advanced command of the language ... ... A B C D E

9. exhibit enthusiasm for my employees .. .. A B C D E

10. encourage teamwork among staff members . ... A B C D E

11. act in a manner consistent with my stated values/
    positions ... ... A B C D E

12. take a long-term perspective on most issues. ... ... A B C D E

13. capture the attention of people in the organization... A B C D E

14. exhibit a genuine passion for the group/organization A B C D E

15. remind people of their role in the organization .. ... A B C D E

16. behave consistently .. .. A B C D E

17. see beyond the day-to-day activities ... ... A B C D E

18. believe that "when I talk, people listen". ... ... A B C D E

19. energize others.. ... ... A B C D E

20. behave in a fashion that supports "what is important
    around here" ... ... A B C D E

21. am perceived as being an honest person ... ... A B C D E

22. bring clarity to most issues ... ... A B C D E

23. am an attentive listener .. .. A B C D E

24. am as interested in the activities of others as my own A B C D E

25. keep staff members apprised of changes in the
    industry/field ... ... A B C D E

26. know how to get things done in this organization ... A B C D E

27. know how to draw others into a vision for the future A B C D E

28. am a captivating speaker . ... A B C D E

29. make work fun.. ... ... A B C D E

30. let people know the expected codes of behavior.. ... A B C D E

31. am perceived as a reliable resource person .. .. A B C D E

32. consult others in the group or organization
regarding their views of the future. ... ... A B C D E

33. am persuasive... ... ... A B C D E

34. empower others to be the best they can be .. .. A B C D E

35. challenge others who behave in a fashion that
violates an expected code of conduct... ... ... A B C D E

36. am perceived to be highly ethical.. ... ... A B C D E

37. expand the vision/organizational goal to include
most members of the group or organization. ... ... A B C D E

38. believe my words help clarify issues ... ... .A B C D E

39. make others more confident in their abilities ... ... .A B C D E

40. visibly recognize outstanding contributions of staff
members... ... ... .A B C D E

41. do the right thing when in doubt.. ... ... .A B C D E

42. have the ability to translate vision for the future into
activity ... ... .A B C D E

43. have a magnetic personality .. .. .A B C D E

44. involve people in decisions that affect them. ... ... .A B C D E

45. act in accordance with the desired organizational values. . ... .A B C D E

46. understand our products or services well... ... ... .A B C D E

47. reinforce the vision through my words and actions . . .A B C D E

48. am self-confident ... ... .A B C D E

49. disburse credit to others when appropriate . ... .A B C D E

50. reinforce the importance of pursuing excellence. ... .A B C D E

Appendix B

Five C Leadership Assessment Questionnaire "Other" Version

Further Information:
Dr. W. James Weese
Faculty of Health Sciences
The University of Western Ontario
London, Ontario, Canada
N6A 5B9
Office Phone: 519-661-2111 ext. 84239
Home Phone: 519-660-4392
Office Fax: 519-850-2347
email: jweese1@uwo.ca
2018

Five C Leadership Assessment Questionnaire—Other

Instructions:

This instrument was developed by Dr. Jim Weese at the University of Western Ontario, London, Ontario, Canada. It is designed to measure leadership at the executive level in a group or organization. For each of the following questions please assess your leader relative to how frequently he or she displays the behavior. Please use the following response key:

PLEASE CIRCLE THE APPROPRIATE RESPONSE:

ALMOST ALWAYS	OFTEN	SOMETIMES	RARELY	NEVER
A	B	C	D	E

Items:

Your information will be held in strict confidence. Thank you

(Leader's name) _____,

1. can be trusted to follow through on tasks he or she agrees to undertake.. ... ... **A B C D E**

2. has a clear idea of where the group/organization can be in the future . ... **A B C D E**

3. leaves little doubt as to what others expect from him or her.. ... ... **A B C D E**

4. exhibits a genuine passion for his or her job . ... **A B C D E**

5. relays success stories from this or other organizations **A B C D E**

6. takes clear positions on issues. ... ... A B C D E

7. has a clear idea of what it will take to achieve the desired end for the group/organization . ... A B C D E

8. has an advanced command of the language . ... A B C D E

9. exhibits enthusiasm for his or her employees ... ... A B C D E

10. encourages teamwork among staff members ... ... A B C D E

11. acts in a manner consistent with his or her stated values/positions . ... A B C D E

12. takes a long-term perspective on most issues ... ... A B C D E

13. can capture the attention of people in the organization A B C D E

14. exhibits a genuine passion for the group/organization A B C D E

15. reminds people of their role in the organization . ... A B C D E

16. behaves consistently . ... A B C D E

17. sees beyond the day-to-day activities ... ... A B C D E

18. believes that "when he or she talks, people listen" ... A B C D E

19. has the ability to energize others... ... ... A B C D E

20. behaves in a fashion that supports "what is important around here" .. .. A B C D E

21. is perceived as being an honest person.. ... ... A B C D E

22. brings clarity to most issues... ... ... A B C D E

23. is an attentive listener ... ... A B C D E

24. is as interested in the activities of others as his or her own ... ... A B C D E

25. keeps staff members apprised of changes in the industry/field ... ... A B C D E

26. knows how to get things done in this organization ... **A B C D E**

27. knows how to draw others into a vision for the future **A B C D E**

28. is a captivating speaker... ... ... **A B C D E**

29. makes work fun . ... **A B C D E**

30. lets people know the expected codes of behavior . ... **A B C D E**

31. is perceived as a reliable resource person ... ... **A B C D E**

32. consults others in the group or organization
    regarding their views of the future . ... **A B C D E**

33. is persuasive ... ... **A B C D E**

34. empowers others to be the best they can be . ... **A B C D E**

35. challenges others who behave in a fashion that
    violates an expected code of conduct ... ... **A B C D E**

36. is perceived to be highly ethical ... ... **A B C D E**

37. expands a vision/organizational goal to include most
    members of the group or organization . ... **A B C D E**

38. offers words to help clarify issues .. .. **A B C D E**

39. makes others more confident in their abilities ... ... **A B C D E**

40. visibly recognizes outstanding contributions of staff
    members ... ... **A B C D E**

41. does the right thing when in doubt ... ... **A B C D E**

42. translates vision for the future into activity . ... **A B C D E**

43. has a magnetic personality ... ... **A B C D E**

44. involves people in decisions that affect them ... ... **A B C D E**

45. acts in accordance with the desired organizational
    values.. ... ... **A B C D E**

46. understands our products or services well .. .. **A B C D E**

47. reinforces the vision through his or her words and actions. ... ... **A B C D E**

48. is self-confident . ... **A B C D E**

49. disburses credit to others when appropriate . ... **A B C D E**

50. reinforces the importance of pursuing excellence ... **A B C D E**

Appendix C

The Five C Leadership Assessment Questionnaire Interpretive Guide

The Five C Leadership Assessment Questionnaire is a quantitative instrument that measures the perceptions of executive leadership over five scales, one for each of the Five Cs of Leadership. Each scale is comprised of ten items that are measured on a five-point Likert scale.

The instrument is designed to be used by leaders exclusively (Self form), or in concert with other members (Other form) of a group or organization. It is recommended that scores from as many people who work with a leader also be collected using the "Other" form and averaged into an aggregate score. The leader's self-perceptions alone are generally not the most valid indicator of a leadership situation and therefore should be considered with the "Other" scores.

Scoring: Scores can be analyzed one of two ways. For example:

1. **Congruence Score:** Add the leader's scores and compare them with those collected from subordinates. Leaders who find their scores to be considerably higher or lower than those of other members of the organization may take efforts to determine why the perceptual disparity exists. Leaders may be undervaluing or overvaluing the quality of leadership they are delivering.

2. **Average Score:** Add the leader's score and all "Other" scores and divide by the total number of respondents to attain an average Five C score. The leader will be given a total averaged score (ranging from 50

to 250). Using the interpretative guide below, leaders can determine where they fit in the scale at present.

From a diagnostic perspective, leaders can uncover their scores for each of the five scales (use average scores). These scores will range from a low of 10 to a high of 50. Each scale will provide insight on the specific area(s) or strength(s) and those that need improvement.

C1—Credibility Score: (All C1 scores/N) =
(Items: 1, 6, 11, 16, 21, 26, 31, 36, 41, 46)

C2—Compelling Vision Score: (All C2 scores/N) =
(Items: 2, 7, 12, 17, 22, 27, 32, 37, 42, 47)

C3—Charismatic Communicator Score: (All C3 scores/N) =
(Items: 3, 8, 13, 18, 23, 28, 33, 38, 43, 48)

C4—Contagious Enthusiasm Score: (All C4 scores/N) =
(Items: 4, 9, 14, 19, 24, 29, 34, 39, 44, 49)

C5—Culture Builder Score: (All C5 scores/N) =
(Items: 5, 10, 15, 20, 25, 30, 35, 40, 45, 50)

Scale Score Meaning:

Very High—225–250
High—200–224.99
Moderately High—175–199.99
Low—150–174.99
Very Low—149 or less

Scales Descriptions:

C1—Credibility: (Items: 1, 6, 11, 16, 21, 26, 31, 36, 41, 46)
Much has been made in recent times of both the importance of credibility to leadership and the collapse of credibility in leaders. Effective leaders must be credible sources of information for others in the group or organization, and they must be trusted to be ethical and follow through on their claims. This scale measures the degree to which people believe that a leader is both trustworthy and competent.

C2—Compelling Vision: (Items: 2, 7, 12, 17, 22, 27, 32, 37, 42, 47)
One of the consistent themes in the leadership literature is the need for leaders to have a plan that is perceived as a better situation for those affected by the plan. Often termed a vision, this plan has to be widely shared and adopted by those charged with its implementation. This scale measures a leader's visioning abilities, coupled with his or her success in transmitting the vision throughout the group or organization.

C3—Charismatic Communicator: (Items: 3, 8, 13, 18, 23, 28, 33, 38, 43, 48)
The area of charisma has long been purported to be an important ingredient to leadership, dating back to the early writings of Max Weber. Charisma refers to the magnetic appeal an individual has that positions him or her to influence others. This is usually reflected in one's communication (e.g., linguistic abilities; ability to speak clearly, coherently, and passionately). This scale measures charisma as reflected in the leader's communication skills.

C4—Contagious Enthusiasm: (Items: 4, 9, 14, 19, 24, 29, 34, 39, 44, 49)
Ralph Waldo Emerson once noted that "Nothing great has ever been achieved without enthusiasm." Enthusiasm is the lifeblood of an organization or group. Leaders who exhibit a passion for what they do and the people with whom they do it are energizers. This enthusiasm

can be contagious and spread to other areas of the organization. This scale measures the degree to which the leader exhibits enthusiasm and energizes his or her staff members.

C5—Culture Builder: (Items: 5, 10, 15, 20, 25, 30, 35, 40, 45, 50)
The area of organizational culture has garnered considerable attention in the organizational science literature. Organizational culture refers to the beliefs, values, and attitudes of members of a group or organization. Many leadership and organizational-culture experts agree that leaders have tremendous opportunity to shape and embed a culture for their respective group or organization. Organizational-culture expert Edgar Schein noted that this function was the most important duty a leader can carry out. This scale measures the leader's attention to developing and embedding a desired culture for the group or organizational culture, with specific emphasis on the culture-building activities (attaining goals, managing change, coordinating teamwork, and customer orientation) that Talcott Parsons and Marshall Sashkin both agreed contribute to organizational success and survival.

Appendix D

On the Shoulders of Giants

The Five Cs of leadership are a compilation of my research, teaching, and consulting experiences. I also acknowledge the intellectual contributions of a number of leadership theorists like those noted below. I recognize the strength of their shoulders on which I stand and the foundation they have provided for my work. I honor and applaud their contributions that are summarized below.

Seminal Work of Bernard Bass

It is my opinion that fellow Ohio State alumnus, the late Bernard Bass, stands alone as the leading researcher in the field of leadership. I had the pleasure of spending a few days with Dr. Bass and published an article based on our deep conversation.[267] He has earned an international reputation as the foremost authority on the topic. His immense publication record dwarfs all others in a field that has many top producers, especially those highlighted in this section of the book. His leadership research has earned its way into the top journals that publish leadership research. His books, like *Leadership and Performance Beyond Expectations* (1985) and *Handbook of Leadership* (1990), are highly acclaimed titles and must be read by anyone who hopes to study or practice leadership.

Bass's most influential work, his cognitive theories of leadership, include his transactional and transformational leadership work. In concert with his colleagues from the Center for Leadership Studies at SUNY-Binghamton, Bass spearheaded numerous research studies set in a variety of diverse settings. On the basis of research emerging from his Center, Bass concluded that effective transformational leaders routinely display four distinct characteristics. He labeled these the "Four I's of Leadership," and each is discussed below.

Individualized consideration refers to a characteristic of leaders who are not scripted in the bureaucratic method. They do not go "by the letter of the law or the printed word." They realize the varied and unique circumstances that exist in situations. Consequently, they make case-by-case decisions. All people are not treated the same way, since their situations usually differ as well.

These leaders get to know their people on a personal basis. They try to get to know their personal situations that might warrant special or unique consideration. Because they get to know their people, they are accurately perceived as being "individually considerate." They show appropriate and genuine concern for their people. They follow the lead of people like Herb Kelleher, founder and chairman of Southwest Airlines. Kelleher's claim to fame is that he truly appreciates and respects his staff members. He tries to get to know as many of them by name as he can (and Southwest Airlines employs seven thousand people). His "walk" and "talk" align. He can be seen visiting with the baggage handlers, chatting with the ticket-takers, or helping the inflight staff prepare refreshments for the passengers. His staff members feel special. He is not above doing anything that they do as part of their regular duties.

The late president of the University of Windsor, Dr. Ron Ianni, had similar habits. He'd walk through campus, often agreeing to an invitation from students to join them for a coffee in the campus cafeteria or dropping by a floor party later in the evening to honor a commitment to "drop by if you are in the area." Some of the testimonials shared at his funeral carried similar themes of his willingness to be human—to never consider himself above others who make up the campus community.

These leaders also get to know their people. They have a solid understanding of their personal and professional goals. They try to uncover their respective strengths and weaknesses, and together with the individual, help to establish professional development goals and programs of activity to maximize their personal potential. They are "individually considerate" of the developmental needs of specific people, their current situations, and their future aspirations. They work closely with their staffs and genuinely try to help them overcome their shortcomings. The individually considerate leader is concerned about the total development of his or her staff members.

Individually considerate leaders also stand behind their people. They will do all they can to secure the essential resources so staff members can fulfill their responsibilities. They also act quickly to eliminate any unnecessary delays or roadblocks that might impede a follower's progress towards contributing to the attainment of the organization's vision.

Intellectual stimulation has been an overlooked characteristic by leadership scholars. An "intellectually stimulating" leader asks people to break their normal paradigm and think about challenges in new and different ways. These leaders arouse the intellectual curiosities of those in their realm of influence. They seek input from people, asking for the constituents' insights and perspectives on situations and possible decision alternatives. They encourage their people to be creative problem-solvers. They believe in the concept of lifelong learning, and consistent with that approach, they are not threatened by the possibility of learning from followers. Everyone benefits from this type of leader. An energized, creative workforce emerges to make the organization vibrant and alive with people committed to the ideals of excellence and the program of activity designed to realize this state.

Today's followers seek fulfilment in their positions. The "intellectually stimulating" leader recognizes this fact and is quick to integrate this facet into his or her leadership style. He or she challenges followers on an intellectual basis and lets them know their intellectual contributions are expected and appreciated. He or she knows that followers who are meaningfully involved gain a greater feeling of importance.

Followers of this type of leader are not punished for presenting ideas that go against the grain of current or traditional thinking.

They know that their leader believes that a new approach will be valued, given full consideration, and possibly implemented. They feel appreciated, personally challenged, and inspired by these leaders. "As a consequence of being intellectually stimulated by their leaders, followers develop their own capabilities to recognize, understand, and eventually solve future problems."[268] In essence, what emerges is a community of leaders all focused on a similar vision for their organization.

Followers come to appreciate that how they feel and what they say is important. They begin to see that their thoughts and perspectives will be taken seriously and that the leader genuinely cares for their contributions. This feeling is energizing for followers seeking fulfillment from their experience with the leader and the organization, and consequently, their loyalty and personal expectations exceed previous benchmarks.

Inspirational motivation is the third "I" in Bass's framework and refers to the charismatic qualities a leader employs. This type of leader inspires followers to believe in him or her as a leader and to have faith and a personal stake in the vision of the organization or unit. These leaders have the ability to charismatically communicate a plan of action to followers in a manner that they identify with the plan and adopt a sense of ownership for making it happen. They arouse followers to the vision of the organization and to the prospects of being associated with this type of leader.

The charismatic aspects of this concept have been difficult for researchers to grasp and accept as legitimate. Some theorists have documented the problems that researchers had with the charisma concept and suggested that a major contributor to the high degree of uncertainty rested with the notion held by many that charisma was a gift. Certainly, the work of Bass and his associates at the Center for Leadership Studies should alleviate any concerns that charismatic behavior is not a learnable concept.

Bass and his colleagues were quick to illustrate that inspirational motivation is not the sole province of the person in the executive leadership position, although these individuals do carry a higher profile and often are attributed with higher levels of charisma. Conversely, these scholars noted that inspirational leadership could and should filter down throughout the organizational hierarchy. Certainly, leaders who engage in the other three "I's" make followers feel meaningfully involved, and as such, will be attributed with some degree of charisma. A leader's command of language in conjunction with the ability to deliver speeches and rally the forces will also contribute to the level of charisma attributed to him or her. One's charisma is frequently linked to his or her communication skills. This area forms the basis of the third C (C3—Charismatic Communicator) of the Five C Model.

Idealized influence is the fourth "I" conceptualized by Bass. This area refers to transformational leaders displaying genuine concern and respect for followers. This is evidenced many ways, but most of all by engaging in the other three "I's." Followers of leaders exhibiting idealized influence are moved by them. They typically possess heightened levels of confidence in both the leader and his or her vision. Consequently, they are willing to invest their interest, energy, and confidence in this individual to make a difference as to whether the group or organization will be successful.

Followers build trust in leaders who are successful time and time again. Minor successes build confidence in the leader and an emotional bond toward the individual. They believe that the leader can engineer results, and they want to be associated with a "winner." Followers will strive harder for this leader. They too want to be part of a successful enterprise, as long as they believe that they have a meaningful involvement with the group. The leader employing idealized influence leads by example. His or her work habits and mannerisms are often shadowed and emulated by followers who also want to be recognized as a winner.

> Setting an example is not the main means of influencing others, it is the only means.
>
> —ALBERT EINSTEIN

The idealized influence characteristic also relates quite closely with the charisma concept noted in the inspirational motivation characteristic. Other writers agree that charisma is a major component of contemporary leadership thought. However, charisma cannot stand alone. It must be linked to the vision of the organization or group and held by a leader of strong principles and credible character. Charismatic leaders must also be concerned with the development and intellectual stimulation of followers, otherwise a feeling of cynicism may emerge with followers who do not feel meaningfully involved in the activities of the group or organization. As a result, charisma must be considered an important element of the new thinking in leadership, but only to the degree that it embodies the Four I's of Leadership.

Contemporary leaders need to instill confidence and commitment in their followers, who consequently validate a charismatic presence in the leader with their emotional bonds and heightened personal expectations. Once charisma spreads throughout an organization that is focused on an accepted vision or mission, immense possibilities begin to unfold. An air of excitement within the organization emerges. A community of leaders begins to focus on the vision of the organization and creatively inspires each other to go above and beyond the call of duty. A culture of excellence is unveiled. Charisma has unfortunately been viewed as a mystical gift that people have or don't have, although research has empirically proved that charismatic behavior can be learned.

Bass and Avolio's Multifactor Leadership Questionnaire (MLQ)
Bass and his colleagues at the Center for Leadership Studies at the State University of New York (Binghamton) have been very successful in uncovering the antecedents to leadership emergence, the precursors to leadership effectiveness, and uncovered an empirically valid method of training and developing leaders. To do this, Bass and Avolio developed the Multifactor Leadership Questionnaire (MLQ) instrument to quantitatively measure the degree to which

an individual engages in transactional, transformational, or laissez-faire leadership. The content for the instrument is based on their extensive research in the leadership area, in concert with the theoretical advances made by other theorists. Most important to both the leadership researcher and practitioner, this valid and reliable instrument can be used for research, selection, training, and development of current and future leaders. It integrates the most recent thinking in leadership, specifically the charismatic and inspirational aspects of the concept. It has been used in a variety of domestic and international settings to identify and develop leaders (e.g., military, government, education, high-technology, religious, correctional, health care, manufacturing, and volunteer organizations). The instrument has also been utilized as a diagnostic tool to help individuals assess their current level of functioning and possibly maximize their transformational leadership potential in the future. Scholars and practitioners alike have embraced the instrument. It takes twenty minutes to complete and it is purported to be suitable for use "at all levels of organizations and across different types of profit, nonprofit, and military organizations."[269] The MLQ Ranking Form is an alteration of the MLQ instrument and is designed exclusively for research purposes. It is comprised of eighty-five questions that measure the degree to which the subject in question engages in leadership behaviors linked to personal and organizational effectiveness, along with five questions that produce demographic data on the respondent. Consistent with most of the top leadership instruments, the MLQ was designed to quantitatively measure a leader's tendencies from his or her perspective (MLQ-self version) as well as from the perspective of others who work with the leader (MLQ-rater version). It has been updated and modified five times to its current state (Form 5X). The instrument produces four scales that include transactional leadership, transformational leadership, nonleadership (laissez-faire), and outcome measures (i.e., satisfaction with the leader, individual and group effectiveness, and extra effort by followers).

Seminal Work of Warren Bennis

The late Warren Bennis was a prolific writer on the topic of leadership for over fifty years. I had the cherished opportunity to spend time with him at one of his leadership-development workshops. What a treat! Arguably his best work was his study of ninety successful leaders from a variety of different settings.[270] His personal leadership experiences (researcher, teacher, and for a short time a university president) have also shaped his thinking and enriched his understanding of leadership. He was a remarkable and prolific writer in the field of leadership.

Bennis preferred the use of the term "visionary leadership" to describe the type of leadership Bass might call "transformational." The *visionary* label draws attention to a major component of this type of leadership—vision. An accepted vision guides personal and organizational decision-making. While there are other elements to this type of leadership (e.g., charismatically inspiring followers to invest in the vision and expend exceptional effort to making it a reality), the notion that a "vision" plays a major part in this theory of leadership is an undisputable fact.

Bennis's study of ninety effective leaders uncovered a number of interesting elements. For example, he noted that:

> the median age was 56. Most were white men, with six black men and six women in the group. The only surprising finding was that all the Chief Executive Officers (CEOs) were not only married to their first spouse, but also seemed enthusiastic about the institution of marriage.[271]

Bennis also determined that these leaders consistently engaged in activities that could be partitioned into four general themes. These themes were: (a) management of attention, (b) management of meaning, (c) management of trust, and (d) management of self. A discussion of the four activities is presented below.

Bennis's Four Managements

Management of Attention. Bennis cited the ability of the manager to draw others into his or her vision by presenting a supreme focus as an essential skill of a visionary leader. This individual knows exactly what is necessary, and employees have unbridled faith in the leader to lead them in the correct direction without undue delay or effort. These leaders have an agenda. Their intentions are always clearly evident, and followers know that their own time and energy will be focused on the critical aspects of the task, not extraneous factors.

Management of Meaning. Bennis described the "management of meaning" as the ability of the leader to communicate meaning to followers, and in so doing, align them to work in harmony. Words take on meaning for this leader, and the followers have faith in the leader's ideas. The leader is consistent in all aspects of the communication and behavior, leaving no doubt as to his or her beliefs and orientations. These leaders provide the essential direction to the organization and its members. If the leader is unsure of his or her agenda or cannot communicate it in a compelling fashion, the organization runs the risk of carrying out activities that in actuality may be operating at cross purposes.

Management of Trust. This competency is described by Bennis as the ability to convey a feeling of integrity to the followers. They understand what the leader believes in and come to trust the leader to listen and consider the opinions of others, even if their opinions run counter. These leaders were labeled by their followers as being both predictable and reliable.

Management of Self. The final visionary component of Bennis's four managements is the management of self. Leaders carrying out these behaviors typically understand and accept their personal limitations. They are comfortable knowing that they have specific strengths and weaknesses. They know that mistakes will be made at times; however, their reaction to mistakes makes the distinction between them and others pretending to lead. These genuine leaders view mistakes as learning opportunities that everyone can learn from and not repeat. Visionary leaders are willing to accept risks and view mistakes as learning opportunities. This type of management requires an individual who is confident in his or her abilities and accepting of his or her limitations. "The task, then, of the leader is to lead. To lead others, he must first of all know himself."[272] These leaders set an admirable example for all organizational members to observe and emulate.

Seminal Work of Marshall Sashkin

Marshall Sashkin served as a personal mentor to me. His guidance to me as I completed my doctoral studies was invaluable. I also had the pleasure of hosting him at the University of Windsor, where he delivered a lecture on leadership that people continue to talk about, some twenty years later.

Sashkin believed that the great leaders from the fields of business, politics, and social causes share special characteristics and engage in unique behaviors not fully investigated by or explained by earlier leadership theorists. He purported that effective leaders (a) have a mental image of both the current and possible future status of their unit or organization, (b) understand the critical components that need to be completed to attain a desired end, and (c) have the charismatic abilities to communicate this focus to followers so that they assume ownership for both the vision and making it transpire. *Vision* is also a major component of Sashkin's conceptualization; he also subscribes to the "visionary leadership" label.

Sashkin offered that visionary leaders reflect the components outlined in the three earlier approaches to leadership. He noted that the great leaders of the day share a menu of characteristics that distinguish them from those not considered to be leaders. They know what behaviors are critical to be effective in the leadership role, and they consistently engage in these activities.

They understand the importance of the situational factors, and as such, know which leadership approach is most effective given the circumstances. Each of these aspects is discussed below under the respective heading. Later, an overview of an instrument (Leadership

Behavior Questionnaire, LBQ) is provided. This instrument was developed to quantitatively measure the visionary leadership tendencies of individuals. It is theoretically based on the characteristics, behavioral, and situational aspects of Sashkin's theory of visionary leadership.

Sashkin's Characteristics of Leaders

On the basis of Sashkin's synthesis of Bennis's research on effective leaders, in concert with his own research, he suggested that effective visionary leaders consistently display five characteristics that distinguish them from others not considered visionary leaders. Specifically, he noted that visionary leaders: (a) provide a focus for followers, the group, or the organization; (b) possess advanced communication skills to get their messages across without equivocation; (c) are trustworthy; (d) are genuinely respectful of people who make up the organization; and (e) have an openness to taking calculated risks and inspire or challenge followers to assume them as their own. Some of these characteristics overlap to the degree that one is strengthened by possessing another. (For example, the focus characteristic is strengthened by a leader's heightened communication skills and his or her ability to get the messages across.)

The first characteristic of visionary leaders is that they *focus* the members of the group. These leaders have the ability to inspire members of a group or organization to zero in on the important and relevant issues. These leaders focus on the details in a clear and concise fashion. There is no room for personal interpretation, as these leaders clearly call attention to the most important aspects facing the group or organization. Followers of this type of leader appreciate the clarity and direction this leader brings to the organization. Uncertainty becomes a thing of the past. This component of Sashkin's theory aligns with Bennis's "Management of Meaning" factor.

Sashkin noted that visionary leaders possessed heightened communication skills. These leaders have a great command of the language as well as the necessary interpersonal skills to get their message across in a clear and effective way. They are effective orators. At times they might even employ some unorthodox method of effectively reinforcing and transmitting their message. However, in the final analysis, these leaders have the ability to effectively communicate with their people. This element is also consistent with Bennis's "Management of Attention" scale. Sashkin furthered Bennis's classification by noting that the silent side of communication—listening—is also an important characteristic of visionary leaders. Effective leaders are also active listeners. They seek the opinions of followers with a view to fully understand their perspective. Followers recognize and respect this characteristic in their leader. They also appreciate the opportunity to be heard and considered as a valuable contributor to the group or organization.

The leader's trust factor is the third consistent characteristic, according to Sashkin. Visionary leaders have strong convictions or stick to their guns unless they are convinced that an alternative course of action is best. They are not inclined to alter their position to make a colleague or follower feel more comfortable. Their followers respect this quality, even if the leader holds a contrary position. These leaders can be counted on. Their followers always know the leader's perspectives on issues. They are perceived as being trustworthy.

Visionary leaders have extremely high levels of personal integrity. This characteristic is fundamental to gaining and maintaining the trust of followers and inspiring them to invest their hearts, brains, and energy to the leader and the vision of the organization. The fourth characteristic that Sashkin offered as being critical to his theoretical conception of visionary leadership was titled "respectful leadership." This characteristic directly aligns with Bennis's "Management of Self" factor. Visionary leaders hold genuine affection for their followers and treat them as people. These leaders appreciate the feelings that people have and attempt, where possible, to let followers know that they are valued as individuals and people. The visionary leader treats people with respect simply because they are people. The leader may disapprove of, even punish, certain behaviors, but that does not change the leaders positive attitude toward the individual as a person.[273]

The fifth and final characteristic that Sashkin suggested separated visionary leaders from their counterparts is best described as "risk leadership." Visionary leaders have tremendous confidence in both what they are engaged in and the followers who are involved in the organization's activities. They are willing to take calculated risks and invest the necessary time and energy to make them pay off, for both the organization and the people who make up the group. This factor represents more than high levels of personal confidence. More accurately, this characteristic includes a measure of the leaders' confidence in others and their abilities to reach attainable and meaningful personal and organizational goals, even if there is an element of risk involved in the undertaking. This factor also aligns with Bennis's "Management of Self" factor.

While Sashkin's work assimilated that of Bennis and his collaborators, he extended their "Four Managements of Leadership" to include leadership behavior and situational/cultural elements. This material is presented in the following sections.

Sashkin's Behavior of Leaders

Sashkin's five characteristics distinguishing leaders from others were outlined. He also offered that visionary leaders engage in behaviors that distinguish them from their colleagues. Specifically, he noted that visionary leaders behave in a fashion that reinforces their belief that they (a) impact the bottom-line consequences of the group, (b) empower their followers, and (c) frame issues in a long-term perspective. Sashkin believed that visionary leaders have a high degree of self-efficacy. They truly believe they can make a difference in the outcomes of the organization, and this confidence is generally transferred to other members who come under the influence of this leader.

Minor successes contribute to this perception in the minds of both the leader and followers. A self-fulfilling prophecy begins to unfold. These leaders believe that they make a difference, and often they do. Their staff members are more likely to place their faith and invest their efforts in a proven winner—someone with a plan, someone who will lead them in the correct direction, and someone who won't waste their time or energy doing extraneous things that do not relate to the overall vision of the group or organization.

The second behavioral dimension that Sashkin believed all visionary leaders engaged in is entitled "empowered leadership." These leaders recognize that the realities of organizational life (e.g., the need to make decisions, delegate responsibility, etc.) necessitate power. In order to be effective, leaders must have power. Visionary leaders seek power as well; however, they strive to attain power so it can be later transferred to followers, so that they might be empowered to carry out their respective assignments.

Visionary leaders want to provide followers with whole assignments and they recognize that these people also need power to get things accomplished. The followers of this type of leader appreciate the faith the leader shows in them and, consequently, feel even more committed to the leader and to the established vision of the organization.

The final behavioral dimension that Sashkin linked to visionary leadership is related to how the leader behaves with respect to a time orientation. This area was labeled "long- term leadership" and was designed to measure the length of time leaders extend their vision for their respective group or organization. Visionary leaders are not day-to-day thinkers. Their frame of reference is far more expansive. According to Sashkin, these leaders think in ten- to twenty-year time frames. They also understand the key steps that need to be undertaken to move their organization forward to this long-term position.

Sashkin's Situational Considerations for Leaders

The final two components of Sashkin's theory of visionary leadership deal with the situational contexts within which visionary leaders operate. However, unlike the situational leadership models of the past (Fiedler's LPC or Hersey & Blanchard's SLT) where leaders are "victims of their situation," the visionary leader consciously shapes the situation. As Bennis suggested, these leaders take action. They shape their situations—a process they referred to as being a "social architect." However, leaders must recognize the developmental levels of their followers and lead them in a manner consistent with their needs. Unlike Hersey and Blanchard's SLT model, where all subordinates in a specific developmental quadrant are led in a similar fashion, Bass suggested that leaders have to be "individually considerate" of each unique situation and lead accordingly. All employees cannot be treated the same, as they all have different situations and scenarios. Bass's view aligned with those of both Sashkin and Bennis.

> Success doesn't come to you ... you go to it.
> —MAURA COLLINS

The situational content that Sashkin refers to in his theory of visionary leadership extends beyond the notions of time, place, and circumstance. He suggested that visionary leaders are the "culture builders" of their organization and consciously set out to engineer a desired culture for their respective unit or organization. Sashkin presented this in two forms in his concept of visionary leadership: organizational leadership and cultural leadership.

"Organizational leadership" refers to the leader developing and embedding a culture that supports the four tried-and-true functions that contribute to organizational success and survival. Sashkin believed visionary leaders must be concerned with the four Parsonian functions of managing change (being aware of market forces, new trends, potential avenues of entrepreneurial advantage); attaining goals (being focused on predetermined and regularly monitored organizational goals); coordinated teamwork (harmoniously integrating the efforts of many people in a systematic, designed pattern); and customer orientation (being aware of and responsive to customer wants, needs, and desires). These elements can be ingrained into the culture of the organization (see C5—Culture Building) through a number of leader-initiated activities and orientations. Sashkin argued that "to the degree that visionary leaders can do these things, they can improve the organizational functioning and construct elements of their organizational visions."[274]

Cultural leadership is a term Sashkin uses to measure the leader's impact on developing, modifying, and preserving the desired beliefs, values, and attitudes of organizational members deep into the organization. Sashkin noted that effective leaders have the ability to influence people to accept and appreciate a desired culture. This measure is an indication of how widely the culture is shared, in both vertical and horizontal directions. Edgar Schein and Marshall Sashkin both offered that leaders have a tremendous influence on the development and preservation of the culture, which subsequently impacts organizational functioning. This advance is central to the current thinking in visionary or transformational leadership. Schein also argued that embedding a desired culture of an organization is the leaders most important responsibility. Readers are directed to the C5 (Culture Builder) chapter of this book for more precise information on the importance of culture to the area of leadership and the leaders role on the development and preservation of the organization's culture.

The desired culture of an organization impacts an organization in a positive fashion, and Sashkin noted that visionary leaders positively impact the desired culture of their organization. Sashkin described this function as a leader's most basic, yet most difficult task.

Sashkin's Leadership Behavior Questionnaire (LBQ)

Sashkin developed the Leadership Behavior Questionnaire (LBQ) as a way of quantitatively measuring people's visionary leadership tendencies. The first edition of the LBQ was prepared in 1984, and it has undergone a number of improvements to increase the scale reliabilities of each of the ten indices that make up the instrument. The 1988 edition of the instrument is a reflection of

Sashkin's efforts to improve the wording and consequently the scale reliabilities, and it stands today as a valid and reliable measure of visionary leadership. Sashkin (1988) said that the LBQ has been used in the study of over twenty thousand managers throughout North America and is recognized as "one of the most widely used measures of organizational leadership."[275]

The instrument is comprised of fifty questions that are grouped into ten separate indices, each representing the current thinking in the area of leadership. The ten scales can be further grouped into three categories or clusters that include (a) visionary leadership behaviors, (b) visionary leadership characteristics, and (c) visionary culture-building scores. The first cluster is based primarily on Bennis's study of exceptional leaders. The second cluster taps the leader's confidence level, desire for empowerment, and extended visioning powers, while the third cluster measures the degree to which the leader impacts the internal functioning of the organization. An overview of the three clusters and the ten scales within the instrument is presented in table 7.

Table 7. Sashkin's Leadership Behavior Questionnaire (LBQ)

Cluster A: Visionary Leadership Behavior Score:

1. Focused Leadership: Ability of leader to focus his or her own attention and that of the group on the key aspects of the vision.

2. Communication Leadership: Measure of the leader's interpersonal communication and listening skills.

3. Trust Leadership: A measure of the leader's consistency, reliability, and trustworthiness.

4. Respectful Leadership: The degree to which leaders hold positive feelings for the followers as people. Degree that leaders are concerned for group members and their well-being.

5. Risk Leadership: Degree to which leaders are willing to take calculated risks and challenge followers in assuming and overcoming the risk.

Cluster B: Visionary Leadership Characteristics Score:

6. Bottom-Line Leadership: A measure of the leader's self-efficacy, that they can and will make a difference.

7. Empowered Leadership: Degree to which the leader acquires and distributes power throughout the organization.

8. Long-Term Leadership: Degree to which leader thinks long term (at least a few years in duration). Visionary leaders have an overall plan that generally extends into the long-range future.

Cluster C: Visionary Culture-Building Score:

9. Organizational Leadership: A measure of the degree that leaders impact four critical factors (managing change, coordinating teamwork, attaining goals, and customer orientation).

10. Cultural Leadership: Degree to which the leader helps develop and/or embed the desired culture for the organization.

The instrument takes approximately fifteen minutes to complete and is designed to be completed by both the leader (LBQ-self) and the followers (LBQ-other). The form has utility as a diagnostic tool for organizations, to guide training and development programs for current and aspiring leaders, or as a research instrument for leadership studies. Although data sets are still being generated in an effort to provide concrete evidence on the overall validity and reliability of the LBQ, the research and subsequent analyses provided by this author prompts a conclusion that it is a valid and reliable instrument. This is important given the fact that Sashkin argued that leaders scoring higher in visionary leadership measures as measured by the LBQ lead (a) more productive organizations, (b) employees with greater perceptions of job satisfaction, and (c) organizations with cultures that reflect and sustain excellence.

Seminal Work of James Kouzes and Barry Posner

Kouzes and Posner are revered for two major theoretical contributions to the developments in the leadership area, namely their Leadership Practices Inventory work and their extensive survey of leaders and followers that underscored the importance of credibility to developing relationships with followers and consequently being in a position to inspire and influence them. Their work broke with tradition where leadership scholars focus on leader behavior and subsequently organizational outcomes. Some researchers[276] have suggested that these approaches pay insufficient attention to what people and organizations desire from leaders—a paradigm adopted successfully by Kouzes and Posner.

Kouzes and Posner's early research was focused on uncovering through survey methods the "personal best leadership experiences" of both leaders and followers and attempting to extract the desired and consistent themes into a comprehensive and progressive theory of leadership. Their second contribution, and by far the most valuable contribution they make, emerges from their review of four hundred case studies and survey of fifteen thousand managers. Based on the findings of this research, Kouzes and Posner suggested that "credibility" was the most important leadership quality. Furthermore, establishing and nurturing relationships with others is the essence of leadership, and relationship-building is founded and maintained on one's credibility quotient.

In their earlier work, Kouzes and Posner developed research instruments designed to produce information on the nature of "ideal" leadership. Their first instrument, the Personal Best Questionnaire, was employed by the researchers to tap a leader's "best leadership experience." The leaders were subsequently interviewed to produce enriched qualitative data relative to the experience.

Based on this research, they developed their second instrument, the Leadership Practices Inventory (LPI). This thirty-item instrument was designed to measure the degree to which leaders engage in the five critical activities or "practices" essential to leading: challenging the process, inspiring a shared vision, enabling others to act, modeling the way, and encouraging the heart. The five practices forwarded by Kouzes and Posner are presented in table 8.

Table 8. Kouzes and Posner's Leadership Practices Inventory (LPI) Scales

1. Challenging the Process
   A measure of the leader's willingness to investigate new opportunities or market the leader's receptivity to new ideas or approaches to current problems or situations.

2. Inspiring a Shared Vision
   A measure of the leader's ability to focus the organization through a shared vision, providing meaning and clarity to the direction that the organization is headed. The leader's ability to charismatically communicate this message to followers is also captured in this scale.

3. Enabling Others to Act
   A measure of the leader's willingness to empower followers by giving them important tasks to carry out that relate to the vision. This scale also measures the leader's tendencies to share praise and rewards as a result of organizational successes. Finally, the leader's previous success in removing unnecessary impediments to follower success is captured in this scale.

4. Modeling the Way

   This scale measures the degree to which leaders' behavior is consistent with the stated/desired values and vision of the organization. This scale also measures the leader's perceived trustworthiness.

5. Encouraging the Heart

   This scale measures the degree to which leaders inspire their followers through their words and actions. A leader's ability and tendencies to challenge followers and recognize and influence them to offer even higher levels of commitment and contribution is captured in this scale.

The LPI is an instrument similar to both the MLQ and the LBQ, in that it was designed to uncover leader perceptions (self-assessment) as well as those of followers (other assessments).

In 1993, Kouzes and Posner authored a leadership book entitled *Credibility*. They offered readers some interesting insights into what followers appreciate, if not expect, from leaders. Their results may not be what one might initially expect. For example, those who believe that effective leaders must work hard, invest extensive numbers of hours, and display unparalleled levels of commitment and dedication to the organization or unit might be surprised by their findings. They uncovered that this quality is not as important today as it was when they did their initial study on leader expectations six years earlier. They found that people are not as impressed today by the ambitious, self-serving leader. They are impressed, however, with the supportive leader who carries his or her fair share of responsibility, shares credit with others, and challenges people to higher levels of accomplishment. They found that the most important component of leadership today is exactly the same as it was in the 1987 study. Notably, leaders who are honest and trustworthy are respected and viewed as more credible in all cultures and situations. Credibility is also central to the leadership themes forwarded by Sashkin, Bennis, Covey, and Bass. People want leaders they can trust, who know what they stand for on issues, and who will not flip-flop their stance, even in the face of adversity.

The second element that Kouzes and Posner uncovered in their survey research was that followers want their leaders to be forward thinking, a theme that is consistent with the notions forwarded by other leadership theorists like Bass, Bennis, and Sashkin. They too believed that leaders must have a vision for where the group or organization currently is, as well as what it could become in the future. They are not concerned with where they've been; they are more concerned with where they are going. According to famous college football coach Lou Holtz, "This is why God put our eyes in the front of our heads." These leaders are not overly concerned with the crisis of the moment. They are more concerned with the long-term direction of the unit or organization. Followers need to know that their efforts matter. They need assurance, offered by a clear and compelling vision, that their efforts are contributing to a purposeful plan that moves the organization progressively forward. (Readers are directed to the C2—Compelling Vision chapter for additional insights on the importance of vision to the new thinking in leadership.)

The third component that Kouzes and Posner uncovered as being central to leadership was the area of inspiration. Followers want leaders who are inspiring, dynamic people who possess the ability, through their words and actions, to excite others around a particular challenge. This component cuts across two of the Five Cs of Effective Leadership (C3—Charismatic Communicator and C4—Contagious Enthusiasm). According to Kouzes and Posner, followers admire and respect leaders who can charismatically excite others. These leaders are positive people, always looking at the bright side of issues and encouraging others to follow suit. They are enthusiastic about the group, the people who make up the group, and the challenges that lie ahead.

If you have a problem, hang a lantern on it.
—ROBERT F. KENNEDY

Kouzes and Posner had a significant impact on furthering our understanding of the essential components of leadership. Their methodology, while heavily scripted in the descriptive area, offered new insights into survey techniques and qualitative research paradigms. They also helped us understand what makes a leader effective, based on what followers want from their leaders. Their suggestion that leadership distills into the social process of forming relationships with others, and the key ingredient to this relationship-building process is credibility forms the basis of their theoretical contribution. While it is admittedly simplistic, leaders must realize that without credibility, they cannot inspire and challenge followers to go above and beyond the call to attain a desired vision.

Credibility takes a lifetime to build and only a moment to destroy. As I tell participants in my leadership workshop, you build credibility one step at a time—but it is the fire pole down if you slip up. One wrong move and one's credibility can be destroyed. The credibility quotient that a leader assembled may come tumbling down with the one act that undermines the trust followers have built up in a leader. Leaders are always on call—always under the microscope and must constantly be on the alert for acts and words that might irreparably damage their credibility balance.

Related Work of Noel Tichy and Mary Devanna

Noel Tichy and Mary Devanna also made significant contributions to leadership theory and helped inform the Five C concept. I had the pleasure of introducing Noel at a leadership workshop hosted by my university. I consider his *The Leadership Engine*[277] one of my favorite leadership books. Is this classic book, Tichy makes the case that leadership matters and effective leaders can be developed. He suggests that the best companies invest in leadership development. His more recent texts deal with the critical leadership function of decision-making and exercising good judgment.[278]

Tichy and Devanna based their leadership theory on information gleaned from an extensive study of fourteen chief executive officers from large corporations. The researchers conducted in-depth interviews with thirteen of the fourteen CEOs and used secondhand sources for the other individual (Lee Iacocca). These leaders were selected because each was considered an outstanding leader, and each had a track record for transforming his or her own organization into a higher-functioning unit in an environment categorized by uncertainty, change, and global competition. While the researchers focused on leadership at the top of the organizational hierarchy, Tichy and Devanna were quick to point out that aspiring leaders and middle managers can benefit from an understanding and application of their theory.

On the basis of their extensive probing with these individuals, Tichy and Devanna were able to uncover seven distinguishing characteristics that set these transformational leaders apart from their counterparts. Specifically, Tichy and Devanna offered that these people consistently:

1. **Identify themselves as change agents:** They have high levels of self-efficacy and project an image and confidence that they can and will make a positive difference. Peter Drucker once noted that the effective leaders of today and in the future will get results. They are not concerned with whether they are loved or admired, but more concerned with whether the group or organization is making progress toward predetermined goals. They concern themselves with whether their members are making personal and professional progress and when given the opportunity, do the right thing.

2. **Are courageous:** They are prudent risk-takers who will take positions on issues that serve the best interests of the organization, even if they suffer ridicule in the process. Winston Churchill suggested that courage was the most important component of

leadership. He was credited with the statement that courage was the quality which guarantees all others." One can't lead without the courage to make decisions or take calculated risks for the good of the group, unit, organization, or country.

> You are stronger than you imagine, braver than you know, and more cared for than words can say.
> —INSPIRATIONAL NOTE KATHLEEN TURNER
> OFTEN REFERS TO (FROM HER MOTHER)

3. **Believe in people:** They have strong and positive feelings about the capacity and potential of people. Consequently, they empower people at all levels of the organization. What develops is a reciprocal respect.

> Though everyone knows at some level that all leader-follower relations will end, no one is ever quite ready for the exact moment or circumstances.[279]

4. **Are value-driven:** They have a clear vision of their personal and organizational values and have the ability to clearly articulate these values with their words and behaviors. While changing conditions may call for different strategies, leaders recognize that their personal values and those of the organization are not negotiable. "Companies that enjoy enduring success have core values and a purpose that remain fixed while their business strategies and practices endlessly adapt to a changing world."[280]

5. **Are lifelong learners:** They view mistakes as opportunities for growth and learning. They are enthusiastic readers and learners in a variety of divergent fields. They are excited about learning and professional development—both their own and that of their staff members.

6. **Have the ability to deal with complexity, ambiguity, and uncertainty:** They are able to cope with high degrees of uncertainty by framing and interpreting uncertainty more effectively than their colleagues. They articulate current realities and possible futures effectively.

7. **Are visionaries:** They are forward-thinking people who can see and articulate a desired future for members of an organization. In the words of Stephen Covey, they "begin with an end in mind." Vision provides direction to decision-making, reinforces the core values that must be preserved, and stimulates and guides action to achieve desired outcomes.

Tichy and Devanna also categorized the process of a leader transforming an organization in three steps that they metaphorically linked to the staging of a play. In act one, leaders must recognize the need for revitalization. Slumping productivity, decreased competitiveness, or a stagnant workforce may serve as indicators of an organization in need of revitalization. Tichy and Devanna suggested that a challenge for the leader may rest in alerting members of the environmental threats and the need to recharge and revitalize to remain competitive.

"Creating the vision" refers to the second act in the transformational process. Here the leader is concerned with focusing the attention of organizational members on a bright and prosperous future. This vision provides the spark that ignites members of the organization to strive toward the attainment of a desired end that is known and accepted by the organizational workforce. This process of visioning, although described in a slightly different manner, is consistent with the necessary phase outlined by Bennis and Sashkin.

The third and final act outlined by Tichy and Devanna involves the institution of the vision. It is during this step that the leader attempts to solidify his or her vision with the members of the organization. It is believed that the long-term adoption of the vision is comforting to the leader, as it assists in stabilizing his or her leadership position.

Seminal Work of Robert House

Bob House and his associates have also been successful in influencing advancements in the area of leadership. Although House has been credited with a number of theoretical developments in the area of leadership (e.g., path-goal theory of leadership), his contributions in the charismatic leadership area offer the most significant contribution to current leadership theory. House has influenced a number of leadership writers who have followed his lead in outlining the importance of charisma to the leadership process.

House believed that this type of leadership is most effective in situations where leaders do not have personal relationships with every follower, such as in situations where people lead corporations, social movements, or nations. Because these leaders do not have the opportunity to individually inspire people, they must rely on a more global inspirational process that comes with being a charismatic leader. Specifically, these leaders must transform the needs, values, preferences, and aspirations of followers. These leaders motivate followers to make significant personal sacrifices in the interest of some mission and to perform above and beyond the call of duty. Followers become less motivated by self-interest and more motivated to serve the interests of the larger collective.[281]

House's earlier charismatic leadership theory considered the personality and behavioral dimensions of leadership. He found charismatic leaders to be dominant, confident in their abilities, possessing strong feelings for their convictions, and having a strong need to influence others. These characteristics were not found to the same degree in noncharismatic leaders. House also noted that charismatic leaders were more successful than noncharismatic leaders in focusing followers on the goals of the organization. These leaders presented an appealing vision to followers in a compelling and charismatic way. They excited followers to this vision, inspiring them toward it and influencing followers to adopt the vision as their own. They emotionally engaged their followers, arousing in them their higher-order needs, such as the need for affiliation, the need for achievement, and the need to become self-actualized. As a result, followers transform their expectations to a higher level when associated with this type of leader. They can be presented with higher expectations, and leaders can be confident that these followers will follow through at the advanced performance level.

House and his associates have studied the concept of charisma within United States presidents. Using archival data to measure charisma, as well as content analyses of biographies and presidential speeches of those who concluded their terms, these researchers found charismatic presidents to be more effective than their counterparts. They empirically demonstrated that "personality and charisma do make a difference."[282]

Seminal Work of Jay Conger

Jay Conger emerged as a strong researcher and theorist based on his work on charismatic leadership and leadership development. Educated and influenced by many of his professors at the Harvard Business School, Conger sought to understand what sets leaders apart from their contemporaries. He also set out to uncover how charisma is utilized by leaders. He wanted to investigate why these leaders were effective in moving large groups of people to higher standards of performance and conviction.

Conger studied the leadership literature and conducted an in-depth qualitative study of people considered to be effective charismatic leaders and those not considered effective or charismatic. His research results prompted him to conclude that leaders focus others. Specifically, he noted that leaders have visions that help lead a group to a desired end. They have the ability to focus others around an agenda. Secondly, he uncovered that effective leaders possess the ability to clearly articulate their thoughts and feelings. They used charismatic methods to capture the attention of many people and impart a sense of meaning and purpose to their current and future activities. Thirdly, he found that these leaders empower their follow-ers. They meaningfully engage the hearts and minds of their followers in activities designed to move the group or organization toward goal attainment. Finally, Conger discovered that effective leaders engage in risk-taking activities. They willingly and enthusiastically assume positions and pursue directions that have an element of risk. They are enthused about the challenges of realizing a difficult or arduous task and usually inspire others to adopt a similar level of enthusiasm and excitement around the challenge. Throughout the text, he cites examples of leaders like Lee Iacocca (Chrysler), Steven Jobs (Apple Computer), Mary Kay Ash (Mary Kay Cosmetics), Archie McGill (AT&T), Donald Burr (People Express Airlines), Jack Welch (General Electric), Jan Carlzon (Scandinavian Airlines System), and Ross Perot (Electronic Data Systems). These real-life examples and the accompa-nying anecdotes serve to reinforce and embed Conger's viewpoints and theory. His views of future leaders include the need for leaders to become strategic opportunists, globally aware and sensitive to the changes that take place on an international stage, and willing to lead decentralized organizations.

> In times of great transition, leadership becomes criti-cally important.[283]

The final chapter in Conger's *The Charismatic Leader* is entitled "Developing Exceptional Leadership in Organizations." In this chap-ter, Conger questions the merits and long-term benefits of current leadership-development seminars, workshops, and training programs. He outlines some of the popular programs in light of these criticisms. This chapter serves to foreshadow his next text, which systematically and thoroughly evaluates leadership programs on the basis of their merits, transfer, and permanence. There are many myths and fallacies that Conger introduces, and in his later book, explores relative to the development of leaders.

Conger authored a book a few years later entitled *Learning to Lead:*

The Art of Transforming Managers into Leaders, and in it he offers readers a critique of five of the most popular leadership-training programs that aspiring leaders often take to heighten their leadership potential and transform themselves from manager to leader. Corporations, desperately hoping to develop better leaders, spend millions of dollars sending their executives to these sessions. Conger went undercover in these programs and participated fully in them, with a view to providing an objective, firsthand evaluation of each program and the anticipated results. He fully participated in vision-development sessions, classroom seminars devoted to exploring and understanding leadership, and outward-bound experiences. He later interviewed participants about their perceptions of what worked and what didn't. He also provided an objective and thorough critique of each of the five programs. Given the tremendous resources that industry invests in leadership-development programs (running the gamut from purchasing a thirty-dollar leadership book to having leadership scholars and practitioners paying upward of $150,000 for a one-hour speech from Bill Clinton), Conger's effort offers very valuable information about the cost-benefit factor that must be considered prior to enrolling in and subscribing to a leadership-development program. The problem with many of these programs is the lack of long-term transfer from the training site to the host organization. Consequently, training programs done on-site and involving more members of an organization may have greater transfer and longevity and consequently might be more effective.

He concluded, quite rightly, that "the art of leadership development is still in its infancy"[284] and that leadership-development programs must be changed to reflect the future needs of leaders (e.g., international focus, diversified and higher-educated workforce, rapidly changing marketplace, etc.). Conger offered that "future leaders will have to think far more strategically for the long-term, carefully targeting limited resources and resist the short-term mind-set leadership."[285]

About the Author

Dr. Jim Weese is an authority on leadership, a gifted speaker, and a community leader. He teaches and conducts research at one of Canada's top universities, where he also excelled in senior leadership roles. He has also consulted with some of the most admired companies in the world.

Weese is a professor of leadership and the former dean of the faculty of health sciences (2004–2015) at The University of Western Ontario in London, Ontario, Canada. He has also served as the special advisor to the provost and later as the acting associate vice-president (international) at Western. He was the dean of the faculty of human kinetics (1999–2004) at the University of Windsor prior to moving to Western in 2004. He is a transformational leader who has garnered impressive results in a variety of senior leadership positions throughout his distinguished career. He has engaged and informed audiences across many sectors on the merits of a team approach to leadership. His Five C Concept of Leadership serves as the foundation to his approach to leadership.

He is heralded as a transformational academic leader whose research papers appear in the top journals in his field. He is a dynamic speaker who has delivered a number of scholarly and keynote addresses to national and international audiences, as well as to practitioners who find his content and delivery style to be highly relevant and scalable. He has served as a leadership consultant with both non-profit organizations and multinational companies, and he specializes in delivering workshops to academic leaders.

Those who have been influenced by his writing or presentations or experienced his leadership firsthand understand the importance and utility of his Five C concept, credibility, compelling vision, charismatic communication, contagious enthusiasm, and culture building, to facilitating leadership success and survival. Weese places specific emphasis on the importance of team leadership and leading from an emotional intelligence perspective. Through his words and actions, he teaches others how to effectively engage colleagues so they feel valued, engaged, and respected. It is not lost on him that others are writing and speaking about the merits of a team approach to leadership. It has made sense to him throughout his thorough training and his distinguished career.

He has served in a number of senior leadership positions during his career, including serving as the president of the North American Society for Sport Management and president of the National Deans Councils for both Kinesiology (CCUPEKA) and Health Sciences Deans (CAHSD). He is currently a member of a number of volunteer boards, including the YMCA of Western Ontario and the Sunningdale Golf and Country Club.

He has earned a number of academic and leadership awards throughout his distinguished career, including the top research and leadership awards from his profession, the Queen's Jubilee Medal by the government of Canada in 2002 for his academic leadership and, ten years later, the Queen's Diamond Jubilee Medal in recognition for his leadership and advocacy for exercise and physical activity. In 2014, his alma mater, the University of Windsor, inducted him into its Sports Hall of Fame.

Dr. Weese lives in London, Ontario, with his wife, Sherri; son, Zach; and daughter, Haylee. His passions include golf, hockey, guitar, and gardening.

Notes

Preface

1   Direct quote from Bennis, W. (1996, p. 154) from his article entitled "The leader as storyteller" that is published in *Harvard Business Review, 74*, 1, 154-157

2   Peters, T. J., and Waterman, R. H. (1982). *In search of excellence.* New York: Harper and Row.

3   Collins, J. (2001). *Good to great.* New York. Harper and Collins.

4   Collins, J., and Hansen, M. T. (2011). *Great by choice: Uncertainty, chaos, and luck – why some thrive despite them all.* New York: Harper and Collins.

5   Bennis, W. (2007). The challenges of leadership in the modern world: Introduction to the special issue. *American Psychologist, 62*, 2-5.

6   Support for this statement can be taken from many sources including the definitive works of Bernard Bass and his 1,182 page book (Bass, B. M. (1981). *Stogdill's handbook of leadership: A survey of theory and research.* New York: Free Press). This book contains over 7,500 citations and is testament to the incredible attention that this topic has garnered since the turn of the century. Warren Bennis and his colleague Patricia Biederman provide a similar and equally exhaustive syntheses and arrive at the same conclusion in their two books. Readers are directed to: Bennis, W. and Ward Biederman, P. (2009). *The essential Bennis. Essays on Leadership.* San Francisco: Jossey-Bass and Bennis, W. and Ward Biederman, P. (2010). *Still surprized: A memoir of a life in leadership.* San Francisco: Jossey-Bass. They all conclude, without qualification or reservation that **leadership makes a difference!!!**

7   Weese, W. J. (1983). *Peer Rating and Observable Leadership Behavior: Determinants of Leadership Emergence Within High School Baseball Teams.* Unpublished Masters thesis. University of Windsor.

8   Readers are referred to Covey, S. R. (1991). *Principled-Centered Leadership.* New York: Summit.

9   Support garnered from Bennis, W. G. (1989). *Why leaders can't lead: The unconscious conspiracy continues.* San Francisco: Jossey-Bass; Bennis and Ward Biederman (2009; 2010); Collins, J., and Hansen, M. T. (2011); Lencioni, P. (2002). *The five dysfunctions of a team.* San Francisco, CA: Jossey-Bass, and; Lencioni, P. (2016). *The ideal team player: How to recognize*

and cultivate the three essential virtues. Hoeboken, NJ: Jossey-Bass. They all arrived at the same disheartening conclusion – that many groups and organizations suffer from ineffective leadership.

10 Readers are encouraged to read the insightful writings of James Kouzes and Barry Posner. They explicitly highlight the critical importance of honesty and trustworthiness in their 1993 text entitled: *Credibility: How leaders gain it and lose it, why people demand it.* San Francisco: Jossey-Bass.

11 Readers would learn a great deal about effective leadership by reviewing Michael Reagan's (2010) book on his father entitled *The New Reagan Revolution: How Ronald Reagan's Principles can restore America's Greatness.* New York. St. Martin's Press.

12 Readers are encouraged to review Bert Nanus' 1989 text entitled: *The leader's edge: The seven keys to leadership in a turbulent world.* Chicago: Contemporary Books.

Acknowledgments

13 Readers are directed to McChesney, C., Covey, S., and Huling, J. (2012). *The four disciplines of execution: Achieving your wildly important goals.* New York: Free Press. McChesney and his coauthors offer some helpful insights on the importance of discipline to success in any endeavor.

A Leadership Primer

14 Support for this claim comes from Patrick Lencioni, *The Advantage: Why Organizational Health Trumps Everything Else in Business* (San Francisco: Jossey-Bass, 2012). Lencioni provides compelling evidence that leadership is far more than looking after the business at hand. Trusted leaders support and inspire followers (what some write about in the servant leadership and emotional intelligence areas) and in doing so, make for stronger and committed groups and organizations.

15 Alan Bryman, *Charisma and Leadership in Organizations* (London: Sage, 1992), ix.

16 Warren Bennis and Ward Biederman (2009; 2010) have also focused on the dark side of leadership, as have Barbara Kellerman, *Bad Leadership: What It Is, How It Happens, Why It Happens*, (Boston: Harvard Business School Press, 2004), and Jean Lipman-Blument, *The Allure of Toxic Leaders: Why We Follow Destructive Bosses and Corrupt Politicians—and How We Can Survive Them* (New York: Oxford University Press, 2006). They highlight that the process of leadership works equally well for those with dark motives.

17 Bruce J. Avolio and Jane M. Howell, "Charismatic Leadership: Submission or Liberation," *Business Quarterly* 60, no. 1 (1995): 63.

18 Readers would be well served in reading and sharing Stewart Friedman, *Total Leadership: Be a Better Leader, Have a Richer Life* (Boston, MA: Harvard Business School Press, 2008). He convincingly drives home the point that leaders need balance and perspective in their lives and that they would be well served if they did their best to overlap roles in leading themselves, their families, their workplaces, and their communities as much as possible. Every reader can identify with some or all of aspects that Friedman covers.

19 Bass (1981, 7) noted that "there are almost as many definitions of leadership as there are persons who have attempted to define the concept." Bennis and Nanus (1985), in their seminal book entitled *Leaders* noted that there are over 350 definitions of the term leadership; see Warren Bennis and Burt Nanus, *Leaders* (New York: Harper and Row, 1985). The multitude of definitions, coupled with the immense number of leadership studies carried out, leads one to appropriately conclude that leadership has been one of society's most studied yet least understood terms. Nanus (1989, 45) once noted that countless philosophers, scholars, and poets have consumed oceans of ink and forests of paper on the subject. When I used this quote in a manuscript, my dear friend and colleague the late Trevor Slack offered a refinement by suggesting that the ink and paper have been *wasted* in efforts to define leadership. I loved debating the merits of leadership with my good friend Trevor.

20 Bennis and Nanus, *Leadership*, 5.

21 Warren Bennis, *Why Leaders Can't Lead: The Unconscious Conspiracy Continues* (San Francisco: Jossey-Bass, 1989).

22 Filley, A. R., House, R., and Kerr, S, *Managerial Process and Organizational Behaviour*, 2nd ed. (Glenview, IL: Scott, Foresman and Co, 1976), 211.

23 Gary A. Yukl, *Leadership in Organizations* (Englewood Cliffs, NJ: Prentice-Hall, 1989a), 204.

24 Bryman, *Charisma and Leadership in Organizations*, 2.

25 Howard Gardner, *Leading Minds: An Anatomy of Leadership* (New York: Basic Books, 1995), 6.

26 Readers should consult the seminal work of Filley, House, and Kerr (1976) and Gary A. Yukl, "Managerial Leadership: A Review of Theory and Research," *Journal of Management* 15, no. 2: 251–89. These thinkers were instrumental in forwarding the notion that leadership is synonymous with influence.

27 Readers are directed to the insightful research findings of Richard Boyatzis and colleagues in the emotional intelligence and leadership area. Excellent

sources include Goleman, D., Boyatzis, R., and McKee, A. (2002) *Primal Leadership: Realizing the power of emotional intelligence*. Boston: Harvard Business School Press and Nadler, R.S. (2010). *Leading with emotional intelligence: Hands-on strategies for building confident and collaborative star performers*. New York: McGraw-Hill.

28 Quote from Patterson, K., Grenny, J., McMillian, R., and A. Switzler. (1996). *The balancing act: Mastering the competing demands of leadership*. Cincinnati, OH: Thompson Executive Press. (p. viii).

29 Bennis, W. (1996). The leader as storyteller. *Harvard Business Review, 74*, 1, 154-157. (p. 154).

30 Bennis, W. B. (1984). Good managers and good leaders. *Across The Board, 21*, (10), 7-11. Bennis (1984) stated that "leaders are people who do the right thing; managers are people who do things right" (p. 8). He elaborated by stating that people in high administrative positions often do things well, but they are not doing the things that align with leading a group or organization. "It is obvious that a person can be a leader without being a manager, and a person can be a manager without leading" (Yukl, 1989, p. 253). Nanus (1989) offered that there are plenty of excellent managers; but few leaders. Bryman (1992, p. 113) offered that the term "Leadership has been reserved for an individual who "... exhibits vision, empowers others, inspires, challenges the status quo, and adopts a proactive stance. Such actions are seen as highly motivating and as greatly enhancing people's commitment and performance."

31 Adapted from Westfall, B. (1992). Leaders care for the spirit. *Executive Excellence, 9*, (9) 11-12. (p. 11).

32 The concept of transactional and transformational leadership was first advanced by Burns in his seminal book: Burns, J. (1978). *Leadership*. New York: Harper and Row. He noted that transactional leaders "approach followers with an eye to exchanging one thing for another: jobs for votes, or subsidies for campaign contributions" (Burns, 1978, p. 3) or the two-way exchange of valued ends. The ability to execute the task (follower control) or deliver the reward (leader control) must be within the perceived capabilities of the person wishing to participate in the exchange process. In addition, followers must clearly see the linkage between their actions and the securing of the desired reward. Although extensive research has illustrated that this form of leadership is effective in maintaining or attaining standards of performance, this type of leadership has its limits. Bass, in his classic text (Bass, B. M. (1985). *Leadership and performance: Beyond expectations*. New York: Free Press) suggested that transactional leadership may be most effective in situations where marginal improvement or the maintenance of

the organization's status quo are sought. Burns (1978) suggested that these leaders "bargain" their way to success and consequently, do not extend people of the organization beyond the status quo state. This type of leadership, identified and labelled by Burns (1978), is founded on a two-way, *quid pro quo* exchange process. These leaders ". . . encourage maintenance of the status quo". An excellent source is: Nahavandi, A. (1993). Integrating leadership and strategic management in organizational theory. *Canadian Journal of Administrative Sciences, 10,* 297-307. (p. 300)

33 Gardiner, 1995, p. x.

34 Bryman, 1992, p. ix.

35 Blanchard, K. and, Ruhe, D. (1992). Total quality leadership. <u>Executive Excellence, 9,</u> (9) (p. 20).

36 Locke E. (1989). *The essence of leadership: The four keys to leading successfully.* Lanham, MD: Lexington Books.

37 Readers are encouraged to review the works of the following who offer a balanced approach to whether leadership makes a difference. Locke, E. (1989); Hannan, M. T., and Freeman, J. (1989). *Organizational ecology.* Cambridge, MA: Harvard University Press, or; O'Reilly, C.A., Caldwell, D. F., Chatman, J. A, Lapiz, M., and Self, W. (2010). How leadership matters: The effects of leaders' alignment on strategy implementation. *The Leadership Quarterly, 21,* 104-113.

38 Fiedler, F. E., and Garcia, J. E. (1987). *New approaches to effective leadership: Cognitive resources and organizational performance.* New York: John Wiley.

39 Locke (1989).

40 Hersey, P., and Blanchard, K. H. (1988). *Management of Organizational Behaviour.* (5th edition). Englewood Cliffs: Prentice-Hall. (p. 85).

41 Sashkin, M. (1987). A new vision of leadership. *The Journal of Management Development, 6,* (4), 19-28. (p. 23).

42 Avolio, B. J., Waldman, D. A., and Einstein, W. O. (1988). Transformational leadership in a management game simulation. *Group and Organizational Studies, 13,* 59-80.

43 Bennis and Nanus (1985, p. 90-91).

44 Source of support: Bass and his colleagues like Avolio, B. J., and Bass, B. M. (1988). Transformational leadership, charisma, and beyond. In J. G. Hunt, B. R. Baliga, H. P. Dachler, and C. A. Schriesheim (Eds.) *Emerging leadership vistas* (pp. 29-50). Lexington, MA: Lexington as well as Avolio, Waldman and Einstein, (1988); Bass (1990), and Hater, J. J., and Bass, B. M. (1988). Superior's evaluations and subordinate's perceptions of transformational and transactional leadership. *Journal of Applied Psychology, 73,* 695-702.

45 Bass, B. M., Avolio, B. J., and Goodheim, L. (1987). Quantitative description of world class industrial, political and military leaders. *Journal of Management, 13,* 7-19 (p. 7).

46 Howell, J. M., and Frost, P. J. (1989). A laboratory study of charismatic leadership. *Organizational Behaviour and Human Decision Processes, 43,* 243-269.

47 Edgar Schein is a world authority on the topic of organizational culture and leadership. His groundbreaking research served as the foundation for my 5C – Culture Building concept. His work is best summarized in Schein, E. H. (1990). *Organizational culture and leadership.* San Francisco: Jossey-Bass Publishers. Hatch's research extends the Schein model and can be accessed at: Hatch, M. J. (1993). The Dynamics of organizational culture. *The Academy of Management Review, 18,* 657-693.

48 Schein, 1990, p. 24.

49 Bennis, W. B. (1984). Good managers and good leaders. *Across The Board, 21,* (10), 7-11.

50 Bennis and Nanus (1985, p.7).

51 Tichy, N. M., and Devanna, M. (1990). *The transformational leader.* (2nd ed.). New York: John Wiley and Sons.

52 Collins, J. (2001). *Good to Great.* New York. Harper and Collins.

53 Kelly, R. E. (1988). In praise of followers. *Harvard Business Review, 66,* (6), 142-148. p. 142.

54 Sources for this claim include: Pfeffer, J. (1977). The ambiguity of leadership. *Academy of Management Review, 2,* 104-112 and Pettigrew, A. M. (1987). Context and action in the transformation of the firm. *Journal of Management, 24,* 649-670.

55 Brown, M. C. (1982). Administrative succession and organizational performance: The succession effect. *Administrative Science Quarterly, 27,* 1-16. p.1

56 Bryman (1986, p. 17).

57 Bennis (1989, p. 12).

58 Fairholm, G. W. (1991). *Values leadership: Toward a philosophy of leadership.* New York: Praeger. p. 47

C1 - Credibility

59 David Brooks (2015) chronicles the critical role that character plays in the lives and personal/professional success of people profiled in his acclaimed 2015 publication entitled *"The Road to Character.* New York: Random House. Stephen Covey's 1991 (Principled-Centered Leadership) and Kouzes and Posner's (1993) *Credibility: How leaders gain it and lose it, why people*

demand it also lend testimony to the long-standing fact that honesty, trust-worthiness as well as knowledge, and experience are essential elements to effective leadership.

60 Augustine, N. R. (1994). The cost of being ethical. <u>Executive Excellence, 11,</u> (2), 5-6. p.5

61 Readers are referred to Seijts G. (2014) *Good leaders learn: lessons from lifetimes of leadership.* New York: Routledge. Seijts breaks character down into three component parts – virtues (i.e., behavioral habits), values (i.e., core beliefs relative to what is important), and traits (i.e., habitual patterns of behavior). Authentic leaders align all three of these component parts.

62 Kouzes and Posner (1993).

63 Gardiner (1995, p. 10).

64 Kouzes and Posner (1993, p. 286).

65 Many scholars have written on the connection between ethics and leadership, but no one has been more convincing that Kim Cameron and Rosabeth Moss Kantor. Readers are encouraged to read Cameron, K. (2012). *Positive leadership.* San Francisco: Berrett-Koehler and Kantor, R.M. (2009). *SuperCorp: How vanguard companies create innovation, profits, growth and social good.* New York: Random House.

66 Brooks (2015)

67 Kouzes and Posner (1993, p. 109).

68 Covey (1991, p. 58).

69 Schmalz, J. (June 14, 1992). Word's on Bush's lips in '88 now stick in voters' craw. *New York Times*, p. 16.

70 Kouzes and Posner (1993, p. xvii).

71 Researchers like Bowden, A. C. (1926). A study of the personality of student leaders in the United States. *Journal of Abnormal and Social Psychology, 21,* 149-160 and Bernard, L. L. (1926). *An introduction to social psychology.* New York: Holt first documented the connection between personal traits and leadership emergence/effectiveness.

72 Brooks (2015), Covey, (1992), Kouzes and Posner (1993).

73 Kouzes and Posner (1993).

74 Ibid (p. 111).

75 Ibid (p. 111)

76 Readers are encouraged to review the works of Patrick Lencioni (2002; 2016).

77 Schein (1990).

78 Inclusion is a key component of team leadership, but readers are cautioned to complete their leadership teams in a way that respects and celebrates diversity. Readers would be well served in reading and deploying the helpful

advice offered in Susan Cain's (2012) book entitled *Quiet: The power of introverts in a world that can't stop talking*. New York: Random House.

79   Bryman (1992, pp. 175-176).

80   Carstedt, G. (1993). A culture of virtuous learning. *Executive Excellence, 10*, (2), 6-7. p. 6.

81   Covey (1991, pps. 153-154).

82   Loeb, M. (1994). Where leaders come from. *Fortune, 130*, 6, 241-242. p. 241.

C2- Compelling Vision

83   Bennis, 1989; Bennis and Nanus, 1985, Sashkin, 1986 have all written extensively on the importance of vision. In fact, and in support of the centrality of vision to leadership they have all of labelled their concepts visionary leadership.

84   Bryman (1992, p. 175).

85   Nanus, (1989, p. 105).

86   Burton, B. J. (1994). Leadership. *Recreation Canada, 52*, 2, 6-9. p. 8.

87   Katz, R. L. (2009). *Skills of an effective administrator*. Cambridge: MA: Harvard Business Review Classics.

88   Readers who need further convincing that vision and clarity of focus are important (or work with leaders who have problems with this area) are advised to read/recommend this book - Keller, G.W. and Papasan, J. (2013). *The one thing: the surprisingly simple truth behind extraordinary results*. Austin, TX: Bard Press.

89   Collins, J. and Hansen, M. T. (2011).

90   Buzzotta, V. 1997) Achieving high performance. *Executive Excellence, 14*, 11, 19. p. 19.

91   Bennis and Nanus, (1985, p. 30).

92   Swift, E. M. (1990, May 21). The most powerful man in sports. Sports Illustrated,72, p. 98-120. p. 120.

93   John Kotter is a recognized expert in the leadership and change area. His seminal book - Kotter, J. P. (1996). *Leading change*. Cambridge: Harvard Business School Press – is a must read for leaders preparing to embark in a change process (which many leaders find exciting and challenging).

94   Conger, J. A. (1989). *The charismatic leader: Behind the mystique of exceptional leadership*. San Francisco: Jossey-Bass. p. 30.

95   Marshall Sashkin (1986) and his colleagues have been prolific writers in the leadership field. They have constantly, and effectively highlighted the centrality of vision to the leadership process. He noted that reinforced the notion that process of "visioning" is an essential function of visionary

leadership although majority of people create visions for shorter terms (i.e., one to two years), rather than the 10 - 20 year time frame that truly distinguishes them as visionary or transformational leaders.

96 Huey, J. (1994). The new post-heroic leadership. *Fortune, 129*, 42-50.

97 Bennis and Nanus, (1985, p. 109).

98 Sashkin, (1986).

99 Nanus (1989).

100 Sashkin (1986).

101 The classic work of Talcott Parsons that can be found at Parsons, T. (1960). *Structure and process in modern societies.* New York: The Free Press.

102 Sashkin (1986) was a prolific leadership author in the mid to late 1980's. His work was theoretically informed by the work of Talcott Parsons, and later by the insights offered in the highly acclaimed text of Peters, T. J., and Waterman, R. H. (1982).

103 Sashkin (1986).

104 Hesselbein, F. (1994). Strategic leadership. *Executive Excellence, 11*, (8), 13-14. p. 13

105 Conger, (1989).

106 Collins, J. C., and Porras, J. I. (1996). Building your company's vision. *Harvard Business Review, 74*, 5, 65-77. p. 69

107 Bennis, W. (1997). Managing people is like herding cats. *Executive Excellence, 14*, 11, 20, p. 20.

108 Sashkin (1986).

109 Readers are directed to Cockerell, L. (2008). *Creating magic: 10 common sense leadership strategies from a life at Disney.* New York: Doubleday. Cockerell shares 10 of the leadership principles deployed to make the Disney mission of "making people happy" a reality. These principles could and should be part of any leader's arsenal and include common sense practices like: everyone is important, make people your brand, recognize and reward achievement that advances the mission, give people purpose, not a job. These leadership principles are supported by core values like quality, character, courage, enthusiasm, and integrity.

110 Peddie shares his insights and leadership experiences in his highly readable book - Peddie, R. (2015). *21 leadership lessons: Successes, failures, and discoveries from a life in business and sports.* Georgetown, ON: Georgetown Publications.

C3 – Charismatic Communicator

111 Conger (1989, p. xiv).

112 Bass (1990).

113 Howard Gardner (1995) notes that highly effective leaders share messages and embed a desired organizational culture through the stories they tell and translate through their actions. Their words signal their values and priorities but that actions underscore and reinforce their words (if aligned. Courageous leaders behave in a brave fashion. Committed leaders demonstrate their commitment their actions. Generous leaders act generously as well. Gardner believes that the best leaders communicate via storytelling.

114 A scan of the literature confirms that pioneer leadership scholars were focused on the linguistic abilities of leaders. Early researchers like Malloy, H. (1936). Study of some factors underlying the establishment of successful social contacts at the college level. *Journal of Social Psychology, 7*, 205-228; and Burks, F. W. (1938) noted that linguistic ability was a critical ingredient to leadership emergence and success. Others followed this line of reasoning. Scholars like Baldwin, L. E. (1942) a study of the factors usually associated with high school male leadership. Unpublished master's thesis. The Ohio State University. Columbus, OH. Baldwin reinforced the understanding that a leader's speaking ability (i.e., articulate, effectively using voice inflections and intonations) was important to leadership emergence and success. Thurstone, L.L. (1944) *A factorial study of perception*. Chicago: University of Chicago Press arrived at a similar conclusion when he found that significant differences existed between the linguistic abilities of leaders compared to non-leaders. Fifty years after this pioneering work linking linguistic ability and leadership, Bass (1990), perhaps the top scholar in the leadership area confirmed that one's ability to persuade others is a skill quintessential to the leadership act. These pioneers were clearly on to something (i.e., the fact that that leaders must have advanced communication skills to tell and relate stories to those they lead).

115 Readers are invited to read more about Amy Cuddy's practical advice on assume the role of leader in her book Cuddy, A. (2015). *Presence: Bring your boldest self to your biggest challenge*. Little, Brown and Company.

116 Gardner, H. (1995, p. 62).

117 Bass (1990) Conger, (1989), House (1977), and Howell and Frost (1989) are only a few who have written on the connection between charisma and leadership. Some have labelled their concepts Charismatic Leadership to underscore that connection between the two concepts.

118 Bass, B. M., and Avolio, B. J. (1993). Transformational leadership: A response to critics. In Bass, B. M., and Avolio, B. J. (Eds.), *Leadership theory and research perspectives and directions*, (pp. 49-80). San Diego: Academy Press. p. 62).

119 Conger (1989).

120 Ibid.

121 Ibid, *p. 17.*

122 Bryman (1992).

123 Waldman, D. A., Bass, B. M., and Yammarino, F. J. (1990). Adding to contingent-reward behaviour: The augmenting effect of charismatic leadership. *Group and Organizational Studies, 15*, 381-394.

124 Bass (1990, p. 199).

125 Ibid (1990, p. 184).

126 Conger, J. A., and Kanungo, R. N. (1987). Toward a behavioural theory of charismatic leadership in organizational settings. *Academy of Management Review, 12*, 4, 637-647.

127 House, R. J., and Howell, J. M. (1992). Personality and charismatic leadership. *The Leadership Quarterly, 3*, 2, 81-108.

128 Hossack, R. (1993). A new style of leadership. *Canadian Business Review, 20*, 3, 30-33. p. 32.

129 Turner, S. (1993). Charisma and obedience: A risk cognition approach. *The Leadership Quarterly, 4*, 3, 235-256. p. 250.

130 Farquhar, K. (1994). The myth of the forever leader: Organizational recovery from broken leadership. *Business Horizons, 37*, 5, 42-49. p. 45.

131 Peters, T. J. and Austin, N. K. (1985). *A passion for excellence: The leadership difference.* New York: Random House.

132 Blanchard (1994, p. 5).

133 Goleman, Boyatzis, and McKee (2002).

134 In 2015 the Harvard business School Publishing Company released a seminal book entitled *On emotional intelligence.* The book contains ten of the definitive emotional intelligence articles published in the *Harvard Business Review.* It is a must read for leadership scholars, practitioners, and enthusiasts.

135 Boyatzis, R., and McKee, A. (2005). *Resonant leader*ship. Boston, MA: Harvard Business School Press. p. 4.

136 Conger and Kanungo (1987).

137 Waldman, Bass, and Yammarino, (1990).

138 Howell and Higgins, (1990, p. 321).

139 Bass (1990, p. 189).

140 House, R. J. (1977). A 1976 theory of charismatic leadership. In J. G. Hunt and L. L . Larson (Eds.), *Leadership: The cutting edge* (pp. 189-207). Carbondale: Southern Illinois University Press.

141 Hunt, J. G. (1991). *Leadership: A new synthesis.* Newbury Park, CA: Sage. p. 1987.

142 Kouzes and Posner (1993, p. 172).

143 Lindholm, C. (1990). <u>Charisma</u>. Oxford: Basil Blackwell and Willner, A. R. (1984). *The spellbinders: Charismatic political leadership*. New Haven: Yale University Press both make this claim.

144 Conger (1989).

145 Bryman (1992, p. 61).

146 Yammarino, F. J., and Bass, B. M. (1990). Transformational leadership and multiple levels of analysis. *Human Relations, 43*, 975-995.

147 Bass (1990).

148 Bryman (1992).

149 Kouzes and Posner (1993, p. 97)

150 Ibid (p. 192).

151 Townsend, P.L., and Gebhardt, J. E. (1997). *Executive Excellence, 14*, 4, 10. p. 10.

152 Readers are encouraged to read and implement the helpful advice offered in Lencioni, P. (2002).

153 Kouzes and Posner (1993, p. 93).

154 See Cuddy (2015) and Gardner (1995)

155 Bradley, B. (1996). *Time present, time past: A memoir.* New York: Knopf..

156 Ibid (p. 362).

157 Bennis (1991, p. xiv).

158 Lebow, R. (1994). Transformation at warp speed. *Executive Excellence, 11*, (3), 11-12. p. 11.

159 Loeb, M. (1994). Where leaders come from. *Fortune, 130*, 6, 241-242. p. 241.

160 Readers are especially encouraged to review Lencioni, P. (2002) and Lencioni, P. (2016). *The ideal team player: How to recognize and cultivate the three essential virtues.* Hoeboken, NJ: Jossey-Bass.

161 Bryman (1992), Conger (1989), and House (1977) all labelled their concept of leadership Charismatic Leadership, underscoring the centrality of charisma to the topic of leadership.

162 Bass (1985;1990), Bass and Avolio (1993), and Yukl (1989) all wrote about charisma and weaved the concept into their models of leadership

163 Bennis and Nanus (1985), Covey (1991), and Sashkin (1989) have elements that some would label "charisma" in their leadership models although they do not explicitly use the term.

164 K Katz, D., and Kahn, R. L. (1978). *The social psychology of organizations.* New York: Wiley.

165 Bass (1990).

166 Quinn, R. E., and Cameron, K. (1983). Organizational life cycles and shifting criteria of effectiveness: Some preliminary evidence. *Management Science, 29*, 33-51.

167 Nanus (1989, p. 107).

168 House, R. J., Spangler, W. D. and Woycke, J. (1991). Personality and charisma in the U.S. presidency: A psychological theory of leader effectiveness. *Administrative Science Quarterly, 36*, 364.396., p. 365.

169 Avolio, B. J., and Gibbons, T. C. (1988). Developing transformational leaders: A life span approach. In J. A. Conger and R. N. Kanungo (Eds.). *Charismatic leadership: The elusive factor in organizational effectiveness.* San Francisco: Jossey-Bass and Gardner (1995).

170 Gardner (1995, p. 33).

171 Bryman (1992).

C4 - Contagious Enthusiasm

172 Bass, 1990; Bryman, 1992; Covey, 1991, all speak to the importance of enthusiasm and passion (for the industry, for people and for leadership. Tichy, N. and Cohen, E. (2002). *The leadership engine: How winning companies build leaders at every level.* New York: HarperCollins write about a similar concept which they refer to as "edge". Other writers like Sinek, S. (2014*). Leaders eat last: Why some teams pull together and others don't.* New York: Penguin Books writes extensively in a similar vein, referring it leaders who are inspiring and builders of excitement and emotional attachment. The author captures this phenomenon under the C4 - Contagious Enthusiasm.

173 Covey (1991, p. 221).

174 Leadership enthusiasts would be well served in reading Cain, S. (2012). Quiet: the power of introverts. Cain highlights the passion and competence of introverts who often get overlooked (or drowned out by extroverts) when assessing the leadership potential in people. Cain encourages us to look deeper. She believes that that is prudent – and look for passion.

175 Kouzes and Posner (1993, p. 225).

176 Hightower, D. (1993). Creativity is our business. Executive Excellence, 10, (9), 5-6. p.5.

177 Labak, A. S. (1973). The study of charismatic college teachers. *Dissertations Abstracts International, 34*, 1258B.

178 Bass (1990, p. 199).

179 Bennis (1989); Kouzes and Posner (1991).

180 Bennis (1991).

181 Fairholm, G. W. (1991). *Values leadership: Toward a philosophy of leadership.* New York: Praeger.

182 Kouzes and Posner (1993, p. 101).

183 Ibid.

184 Bass and Avolio (1990, p. 16).

185 Bryman (1992, p. 97).

186 Ibid (p. 4).

187 Bennis and Nanus (1985, p. 93).

188 Sashkin (1987, p. 13).

189 Covey (1991, p. 179).

190 Burns (1978), Bass, Waldman and Avolio (1987), and Peters and Waterman (1982) are only an example of researchers who have suggested that strong and effective leaders build the self confidence in those they lead.

191 Nader, D. A., and Tushman, M. L. (1990). Beyond the charismatic leader: Leadership and organizational change. *California Management Review, 32,* 77-97. p. 53.

192 Bradley, B. (1996). *Time present, time past: A memoir.* New York: Knopf. pp. 22-23).

193 Kouzes and Posner (1993, p. 31).

194 Avolio (et al., 1991, p. 8).

195 Patterson (et al., 1996, p. 82).

196 Kouzes and Posner (1993).

197 Nader and Tushman (1990, p. 83).

198 Bass, (1990).

199 Fairholm, 1991, p. 118.

200 Bass (1990).

201 Bennis and Nanus, 1984.

202 Kouzes and Posner (1993).

203 Bennis, W., and O'Toole, J. (1993). Large vs. small. *Executive Excellence, 10,* (6), 3-5.

204 Lord, R. G., and Hall, R. J. (1992). Contemporary views of leadership and individual differences. *The Leadership Quarterly, 3*(2), 137-157. p. 139.

205 Barnes, B. K. (1993). Intelligent risk-taking. *Executive Excellence, 10,* (9), 11-12. p. 11.

206 Kouzes and Posner (1993, p. 110).

207 House, Spangler, and Woycke. (1991). p. 364.

208 Fairholm (1991).

209 Bennis (1992, p. xii).

C5- Culture Builder

210 Kotter (1993, p. 13).

211 A number of theorists have written about the area of organizational culture but it could be argued that Edgar Schein has made the most significant

contributions. Readers are well advised to review his classic text (Schein, E. H. (1990). *Organizational culture and leadership*. San Francisco: Jossey-Bass) for an overview of the concept and the need to see themselves as culture builders. Mary Jo Hatch's (1993) Cultural Dynamics Model" presented in her exceptional (1993) article entitled: The Dynamics of organizational culture. *The Academy of Management Review, 18,* 657-693) extended the model of Schein (1990). Hatch recognized the theoretical contributions of Schein but suggest that his model was over-simplistic and did not adequately explain the dynamic and complex concept.

212 Hofstede, G., Neuijen, B., Daval Ohayv, D., and Sanders, G. (1990). Measuring organizational cultures: A qualitative and quantitative study across twenty cases. *Administrative Science Quarterly, 35,* 286-316.

213 Connor, P. E., and Lake, L. K. (1988). *Managing organizational change.* New York: Praeger Publishers.

214 Hunt, J. G. (1991). *Leadership: A new synthesis.* Newbury Park, CA: Sage. p. 217.

215 Ott, J. S. (1989). *The organizational culture perspective.* Pacific Grove, Cal.: Brooks/Cole. p. 2.

216 Jelinek, Smircich, and Hirsch, 1983, p. 331.

217 Louis, M. R. (1980). Surprise and sense-making: What newcomers experience in entering unfamiliar organizational settings. *Administrative Science Quarterly, 25,* 226-251. p. 227.

218 Barley, S. R. (1983). Semiotics and the study of occupational and organizational culture. *Administrative Science Quarterly, 28,* 3, 393-413. p.393.

219 Wheelen, T. L., and Hunger, J. D. (1986). *Strategic management and business policy.* Reading Mass: Addison-Wesley Publishing Co. p. 113.

220 Miller, D. (1993). The architecture of simplicity. *Academy of Management Review, 18,* 1, 116-138. p. 122.

221 Schein, 1990.

222 Ibid, 1990

223 Hatch (1993).

224 Kotter, J. P. (1993). Culture impacts the bottom line. *Executive Excellence, 10,* (10), 12-13. p. 12.

225 Wright, J. P. (1979). *On a clear day you can see General Motors.* Avon: New York.

226 Peters and Waterman (1982).

227 Bass (1990); Bennis and Ward Biederman (2009; 2010).

228 Deal, T. E., and Kennedy, A. (1982). *Corporate cultures: The rites and rituals of corporate life.* Reading, MA: Addison-Wesley Publishing Co.; Feldman, S. P. (1986). Management in context: An essay on the relevance of culture

to the understanding of organizational change. *Journal of Management Studies, 23*, 6, 587-607; Golden, K. (1992). The individual and organizational culture: Strategies for action in highly-ordered context. *Journal of Management Studies, 29*, 1, 1-21.

229 Glaser, R., and Sashkin, M. (1989). *Corporate culture survey.* King of Prussia, PA: Organizational Design and Development.

230 Patterson, et.al., 1996, p. 23.

231 Senge, P.M. (1997), Sharing knowledge. *Executive Excellence, 14,* 17-18 (p. 18)

232 Schein, (1990, p. 316-317)

233 Potts and Behr (1987, p.210).

234 Fairholm (1991, p. 144).

235 Denison, D. R. (1984). Bringing corporate culture to the bottom line. *Organizational Dynamics,* 5-22; Hofstede, Neuijen, Ohayv, and Sanders (1990), and; Golden, K. (1992). The individual and organizational culture: Strategies for action in highly-ordered context. *Journal of Management Studies, 29*, 1, 1-21. all made major contributions in the organizational culture area and specifically on the role that the founders can have on shaping and embedding a culture for their organization.

236 Schein, (1990, p. 327).

237 Ibid (1990 p. 291).

238 Brinkoetter, T. (1993). Service, Disney style. *Executive Excellence, 10,* (8) 3-5. p. 3).

239 Collins and Porras (1996, p. 66).

240 Bass (1990, p. 209).

241 Ibid (p. 588).

242 Blanchard (1994, p. 11).

243 Readers are encouraged to read and heed the advice of Marshall Goldsmith who believes, strongly, that leaders must remain current and continually learn and develop. These and other insights can be found in Goldsmith, M. (2007). *What got you here won't get you there.* New York, NY: Hyperion Books Inc.

244 Hatch, 1993; Schein, 1990.

245 Bryman, 1992, p.175.

246 Schein (1990, p. 2).

247 Ibid (p. ix).

248 Peters and Waterman (1982, pp. 293 - 294).

249 Peddie, R. (2013). *Dream Job:* Toronto: HarperCollins Publishers.

250 Bennis (1989, p. 155).

251 Schein (1985, p. ix).

252 Fairholm (1991, p. 141).

253 Deal and Kennedy (1982), Denison (1990).

254 Meyerson, D., and Martin, J. (1987). Cultural change: An integration of the different reviews. *Journal of Management Studies, 24,* 6, 623-647 and Smircich, L. (1985). Is the concept of culture a paradigm for understanding organizations and ourselves? In P. J. Frost, L. F. Moore, M. R. Louis, C. C. Lundberg, and J. Martin (Eds.), *Organizational Culture* (pp. 55-72). Beverly Hills, CA: Sage.

255 Miller (1993, p. 122).

256 Deal, T. E., and Kennedy, A. (1982). *Corporate cultures: The rites and rituals of corporate life.* Reading, MA: Addison-Wesley Publishing Co.

257 Simon Sinek talks of contemporary organizations where employees seek engagement, empowerment and autonomy. This may place a higher premium on the need for a clear and strong organizational culture. Readers are encouraged to read Sinek, S. (2009). *Start with why: How great leaders inspire everyone to take action.* New York: Penguin Books. In this book Sinek highlights the special role that leaders play in developing a culture that arouses the curiosity of colleagues, inspiring them – and their organizations (e.g., Microsoft, American Express, Hollywood) to greater levels of achievement. A later title reinforces the role that leaders play in shaping and imbedding a culture of sacrifice and emotional attachment. Readers are also encouraged to read Sinek, S. (2014). *Leaders eat last: Why some teams pull together and others don't.* New York: Penguin Books. Sinek provides compelling evidence that leaders who sacrifice for their members generate incredible loyalty and commitment that when coupled with a strong vision, can translates to heightened effectiveness.

258 Sashkin (1990).

259 Deal and Kennedy (1982, p. 132-133).

260 Wilkins, A. L., and Ouchi, W. G. (1983). Efficient cultures: Exploring the relationship between culture and organizational performance. *Administrative Science Quarterly, 28,* 3, 468-481. p. 478).

261 Glaser and Sashkin (1989).

262 Bryman (1992, p. 76).

Conclusion

263 Bennis, (1992, p. xi).

264 Drucker, P.F. (1996). Forward. In Hesselbein, F., Goldsmith, M. and R. Beckhard (Eds.), *The leader of future: New visions, strategies and practices for the new era* (pp. xi--xvii). San Francisco: Jossey-Bass.

265 Beckhard, R. (1996). On future leaders. In Hesselbein, F., Goldsmith, M. and R. Beckhard (Eds.), *The leader of future: New visions, strategies and practices for the new era* (pp. 125-129). San Francisco: Jossey-Bass. p.129).

266 As cited in Bass (1990, p. 7).

On the Shoulders of Giants

267 Weese, W. J. (1994). A leadership discussion with Dr. Bernard Bass. *Journal of Sport Management, 8.* 179-189.

268 Avolio, et al. (1991, p. 6).

269 Bass and Avolio (1990, p. 2).

270 Bennis (1984).

271 Ibid (p. 8).

272 Bennis (1976, p. 140).

273 Sashkin (1986, p. 9).

274 Ibid (p. 13).

275 Sashkin, (1988, p. 1).

276 Bryman (1992).

277 Tichy, N. M., (1997). *The leadership engine: How winning companies build leaders at every level.* New York: Harper Collins.

278 Tichy, N. M. and Bennis, W. G. (2007). *Judgement: How wining leaders make great calls.* New York: Penguin, and; DeRose, C. and Tichy, N. M. (2012). *Judgement on the front line: How smart companies win by trusting their people.* New York: Penguin.

279 Farquhar (1994, p. 44).

280 Collins and Porras (1996, p. 65).

281 House, Spangler and Woycke (1991, p. 364).

282 Ibid (p. 364).

283 Conger (1993, p. 33).

284 Ibid,(p. 57).

285 Ibid (p. 50).

Suggested Reading

Bass, B. M. (1985). *Leadership and performance: Beyond expectations.* New York: Free Press.

Bass, B. M. (1990). *Bass and Stogdill's handbook of leadership: Theory, research and managerial applications.* New York: Free Press.

Bennis, W. G. (1989). *Why leaders can't lead: The unconscious conspiracy continues.* San Francisco: Jossey-Bass.

Bennis, W. G., and Thomas, R. J. (2007). *Leading for a lifetime.* Boston, MA: Harvard Business School Publishing.

Bennis, W., and Nanus, B. (1985). *Leaders. New York: Harper and Row.*

Bennis, W., and Ward Biederman, P. (2009). *The essential Bennis. Essays on Leader*ship. San Francisco: Jossey-Bass.

Bennis, W., and Ward Biederman, P. (2010). *Still surprized: A memoir of a life in leadership.* San Francisco: Jossey-Bass.

Boyatzis, R., and McKee, A. (2005). *Resonant leader*ship. Boston, MA: Harvard Business School Press.

Brooks, D. (2015). *The Road to Character.* New York: Random House.

Bryman, A. (1992). *Charisma and leadership in organizations.* London: Sage.

Cain, S. (2012). *Quiet: The power of introverts in a world that can't stop talking.* New York: Random House.

Cockerell, L. (2008). *Creating magic: 10 common sense leadership strategies from a life at Disney.* New York: Doubleday

Cohn, J., and Moran, J. (2011). *Why are we so bad at picking good leaders? A better way to evaluate leadership potential.* San Francisco: Jossey-Bass.

Collins, J. (2001). *Good to G*reat. New York. Harper and Collins.

Collins, J., and Hansen, M. T. (2011). *Great by choice: Uncertainty, chaos, and luck – why some thrive despite them all.* New York: Harper and Collins.

Conger, J. A. (1989). *The charismatic leader: Behind the mystique of exceptional leadership.* San Francisco: Jossey-Bass.

Covey, S. R. (1991). *Principled-centered leadership.* New York: Summit.

Cuddy, A. (2015). *Presence: Bring your boldest self to your biggest challenge.* Little, Brown and Company

Friedman, S. (2008). *Total leadership: Be a better leader, have a richer life.* Boston, MA: Harvard Business School Press.

Gardner, H. (1995). *Leading minds: An anatomy of leadership.* New York: Basic Books. Gardner, J. (1990). *On leadership.* New York, NY: Free Press.

George, B. (2009). *7 lessons for leading in a* crisis. San Francisco, CA: Jossey-Bass.

Goldsmith, M. (2007). *What got you here won't get you the*re. New York, NY: Hyperion Books Inc.

Goleman, D., Boyatzis, R., and McKee, A. (2002). *Primal leadership: Realizing the power of emotional intelligence.* Boston, MA: Harvard Business School Press.

Kellerman, B. (2004). *Bad leadership: What it is, how it happens, why it happens.* Boston: Harvard Business School Press.

Kotter, J. P. (1996). *Leading change.* Boston, MA: Harvard Business Press.

Kouzes, J. M., and Posner, B. Z. (1993). *Credibility: How leaders gain it and lose it, why people demand it.* San Francisco: Jossey-Bass.

Lencioni, P. (2002). *The five dysfunctions of a team.* San Francisco, CA: Jossey-Bass. Lencioni, P. (2016). *The ideal team player: How to recognize and cultivate the three essential virtues.* Hoeboken, NJ: Jossey-Bass.

Lipman-Blument, J. (2006). *The allure of toxic leaders: Why we follow destructive bosses and corrupt politicians – and how we can survive them*. New York: Oxford University Press.

McChesney, C., Covey, S., and Huling, J. (2012). *The four disciplines of execution: Achieving your wildly important goals*. New York: Free Press.

Mintzberg, H. (1989). *Mintzberg on management: Inside our strange world of organizations*. New York, NY: The Free Press.

Nadler, R.S. (2010). *Leading with emotional intelligence: Hands-on strategies for building confident and collaborative star performers*. New York: McGraw-Hill.

Northouse, P.G. (2015). *Introduction to leadership: Concepts and practice*. Thousand Oaks, CA: Sage.

On emotional intelligence. (2015). Boston: Harvard Business School Publishing. Parks. S. D. (2005). *Leadership can be taught*. Boston, MA: Harvard Business School Press.

Peddie, R. (2015). *21 leadership lessons: Successes, failures, and discoveries from a life in business and sports*. Georgetown, ON: Georgetown Publications.

Peters, T. J., and Waterman, R. H. (1982). *In search of excellence*. New York: Harper and Collins.

Schein, E. H. (1990). *Organizational culture and leadership*. San Francisco: Jossey- Bass Publishers.

Seijts, G. (2014). *Good leaders learn: Lessons from lifetimes of leadership*. New York: Routledge.

Scott, D. (2014). *Contemporary leadership in sport organizations*. Champaign: IL: Human Kinetics.

Sinek, S. (2009). *Start with why: How great leaders inspire everyone to take action*. New York: Penguin Books.

Sinek, S. (2014). *Leaders eat last: Why some teams pull together and others don't*. New York: Penguin Books.

Tichy, N. M., and Cohen, E. (2002). *The leadership engine: How wining companies build leaders at every level.* New York: Harper Collins.

Welty Peachey, J., Damon, J., Zhou, Y., and Burton, L. J. (2015). Forty years of leadership research in sport management; A review, synthesis, and conceptual framework. *Journal of Sport Management, 29,* 570-578.

Yukl, G. A. (1989). *Leadership in organizations.* Englewood Cliffs, NJ: Prentice-Hall.